I0709760

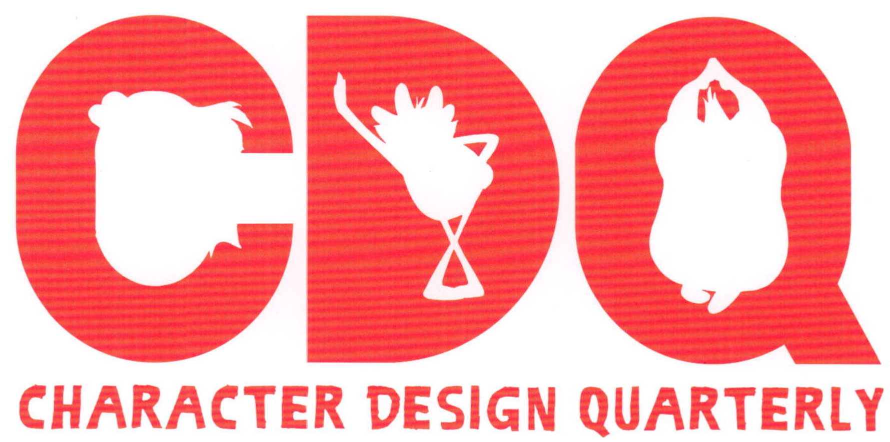

CONTENTS

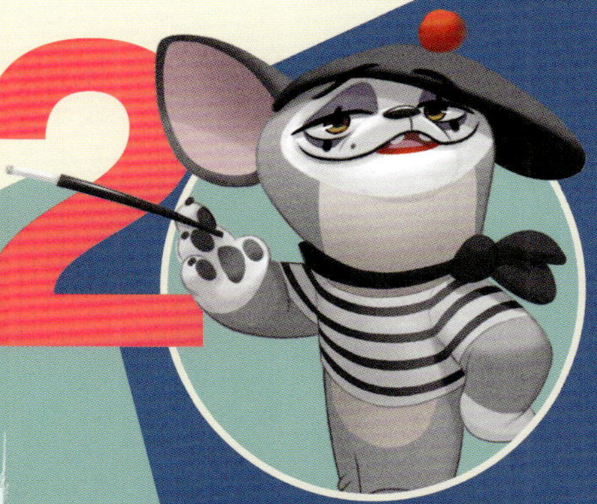

52

FRENCH FANCY
Brian Weisz shows us how he creates a new character from scratch

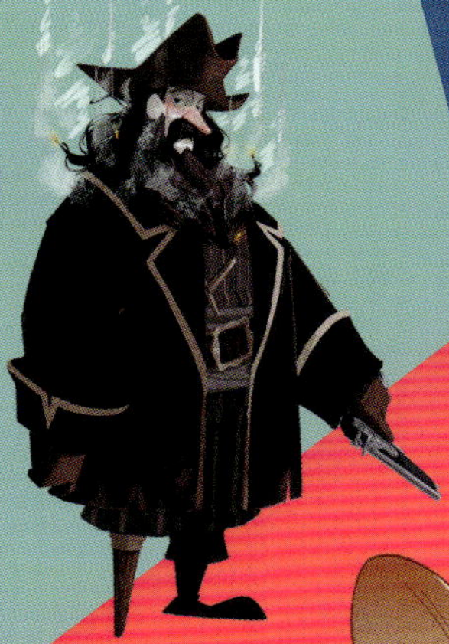

54

DEVELOPMENT GALLERY
Agathe Molin breaks down how three unique characters were made

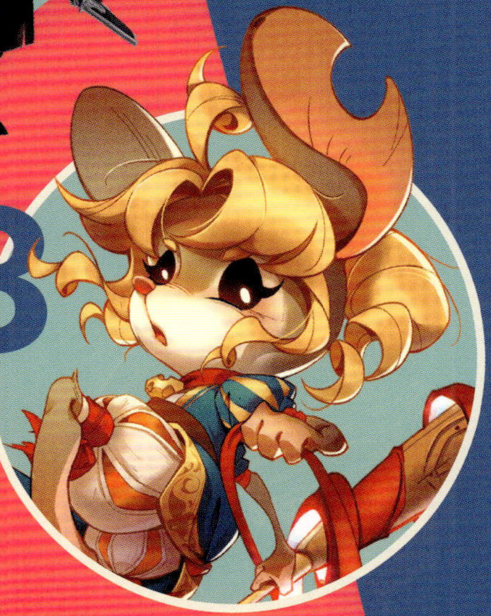

58

THE MIGHTY MOUSEKETEER
Sabrina Sentoso creates a 'rat princess' in this in-depth tutorial

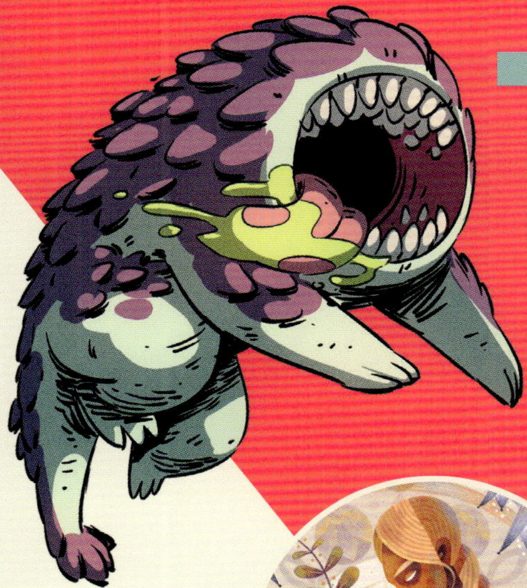

70

MEET THE ARTIST
Derek Laufman talks with us about his long and varied career in the industry

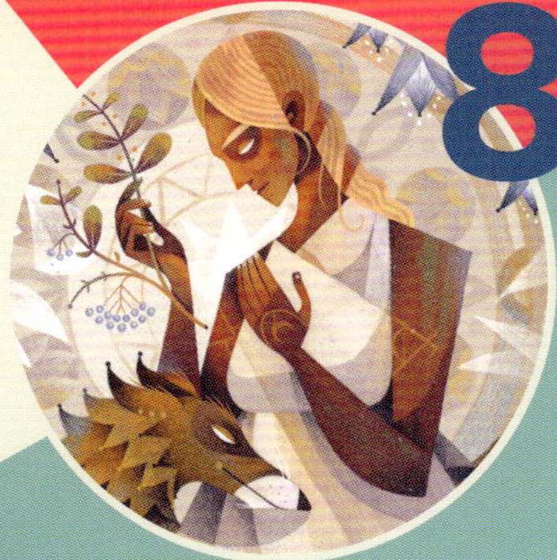

82

HOW I STYLIZE
Dan Gartman shares how he creates his distinct, angular characters

86

UP IN THE CLOUDS
Meike Schneider reimagines the Germanic fairy-tale character, Mother Hulda

WELCOME TO *CHARACTER DESIGN QUARTERLY 33*

This issue of *CDQ* is a fantastic showcase for just how varied the world of character design can be. Gretel Lusky's stylish cover art leads the charge with a design unlike anything we've featured before. Find out how the illustration came together in an in-depth tutorial, and learn more about Gretel's art journey in our exclusive interview.

There are a diverse set of creatures explored, too. From Brian Weisz' French poodle, to Sabrina Sentoso's swashbuckling rat, and Tessa Nelissen's detailed look at how to draw cats, the animal kingdom is well represented throughout.

And of course there are also tutorials for more human-shaped characters. Meike Schneider brings the fairy-tale Mother Hulda to life, Lulu Chen shows us how she created the characters for her award-winning film *The Market*, and Athena dela Victoria designs a medieval warrior princess.

No matter the species or style of character you're thinking of making, there's bound to be something in this issue to inspire you. Think of your favourite animal or person and get drawing.

SAM DRAPER
EDITOR

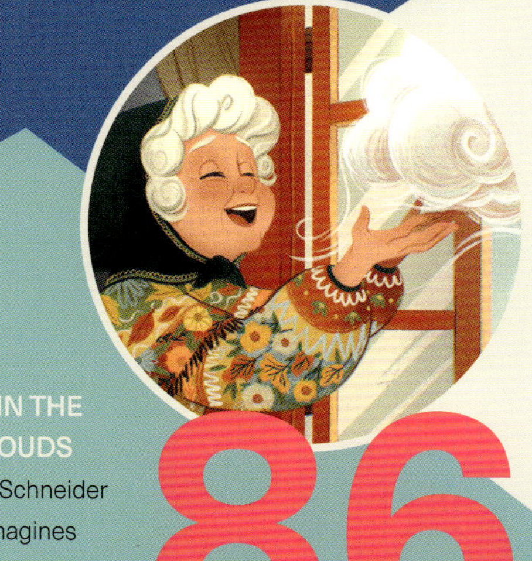

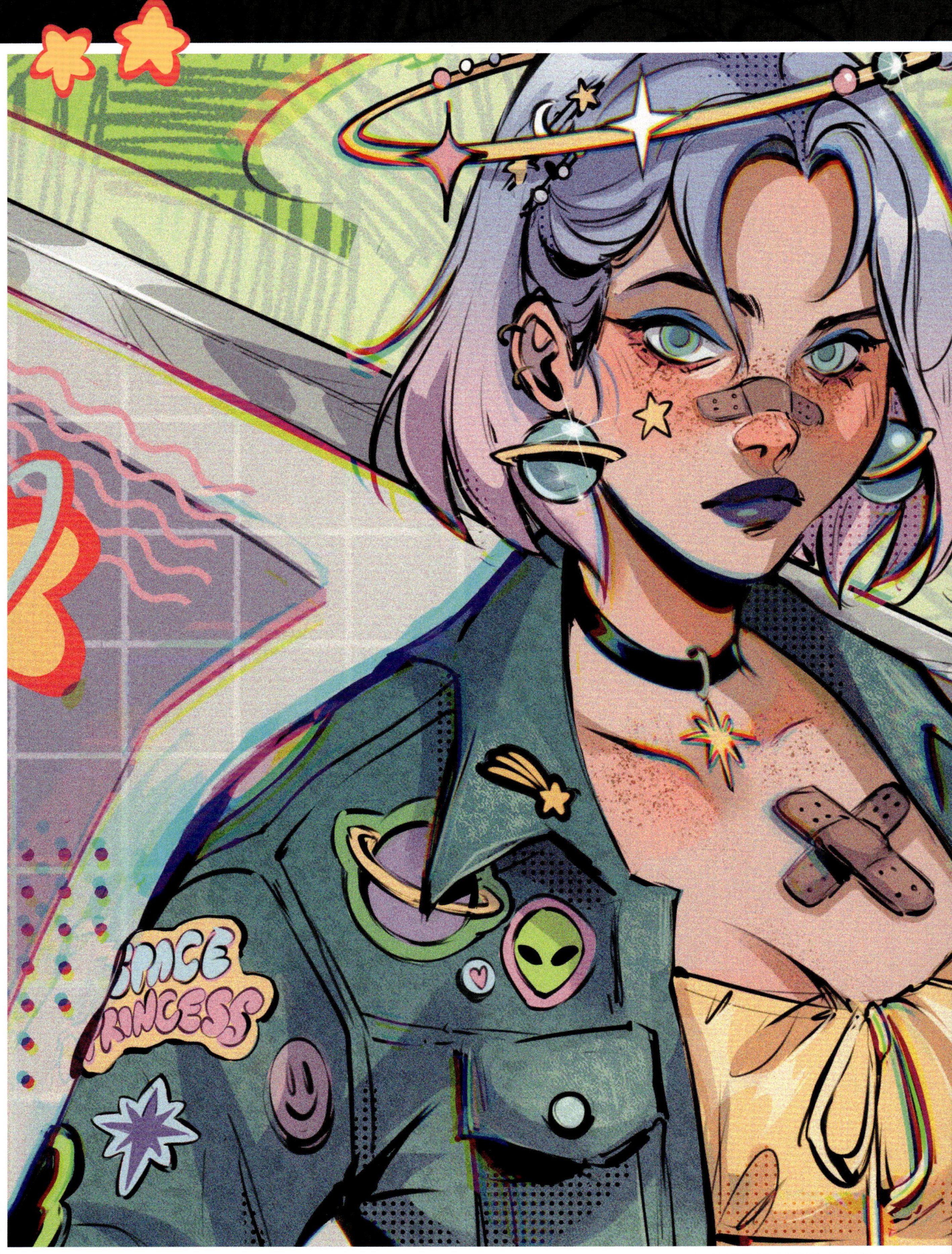

SPACE PRINCESS

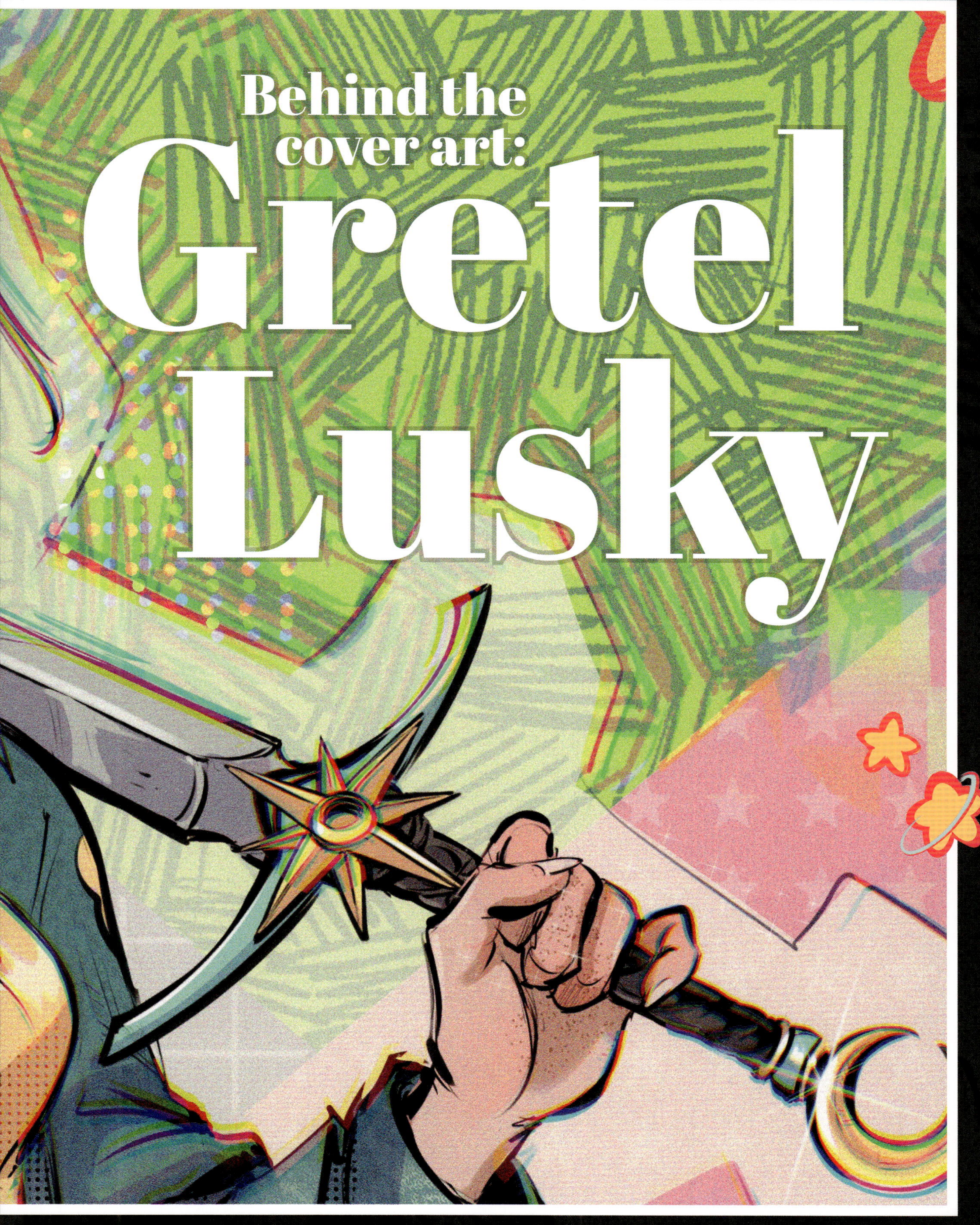

All images © Gretel Lusky

Hi Gretel, welcome to *CDQ*! Could you start by telling our readers a little about your art journey so far?

Hi, thank you so much for having me! For the readers who might not know me, I'm a freelance illustrator and comic artist from Argentina. I've enjoyed drawing for as long as I can remember, but I think more specifically my journey started at the age of twelve, when my mom bought me the *W.I.T.C.H.* comics and, simultaneously, I started watching cartoons more regularly. I would obsessively try to capture and recreate what I saw, and that's how I discovered a passion for drawing that changed me forever.

After finishing high school, I really had no idea what I wanted to do; I just knew I liked to draw. I decided to study Visual Arts and see where that path could take me. A few years later, someone I met in college put me in contact with an animation studio and I ended up getting hired as a character designer. My years in animation were truly eye-opening and made me grow so much as an artist. In 2019, DC Comics reached out to me with a project and that pretty much launched me into my journey as a freelance artist.

In tandem with client work, I've always made time for my own personal art and projects whenever it's possible. This allowed me to grow an audience on social media over the years and eventually find other ways to be more independent, such as opening an online shop and a Patreon.

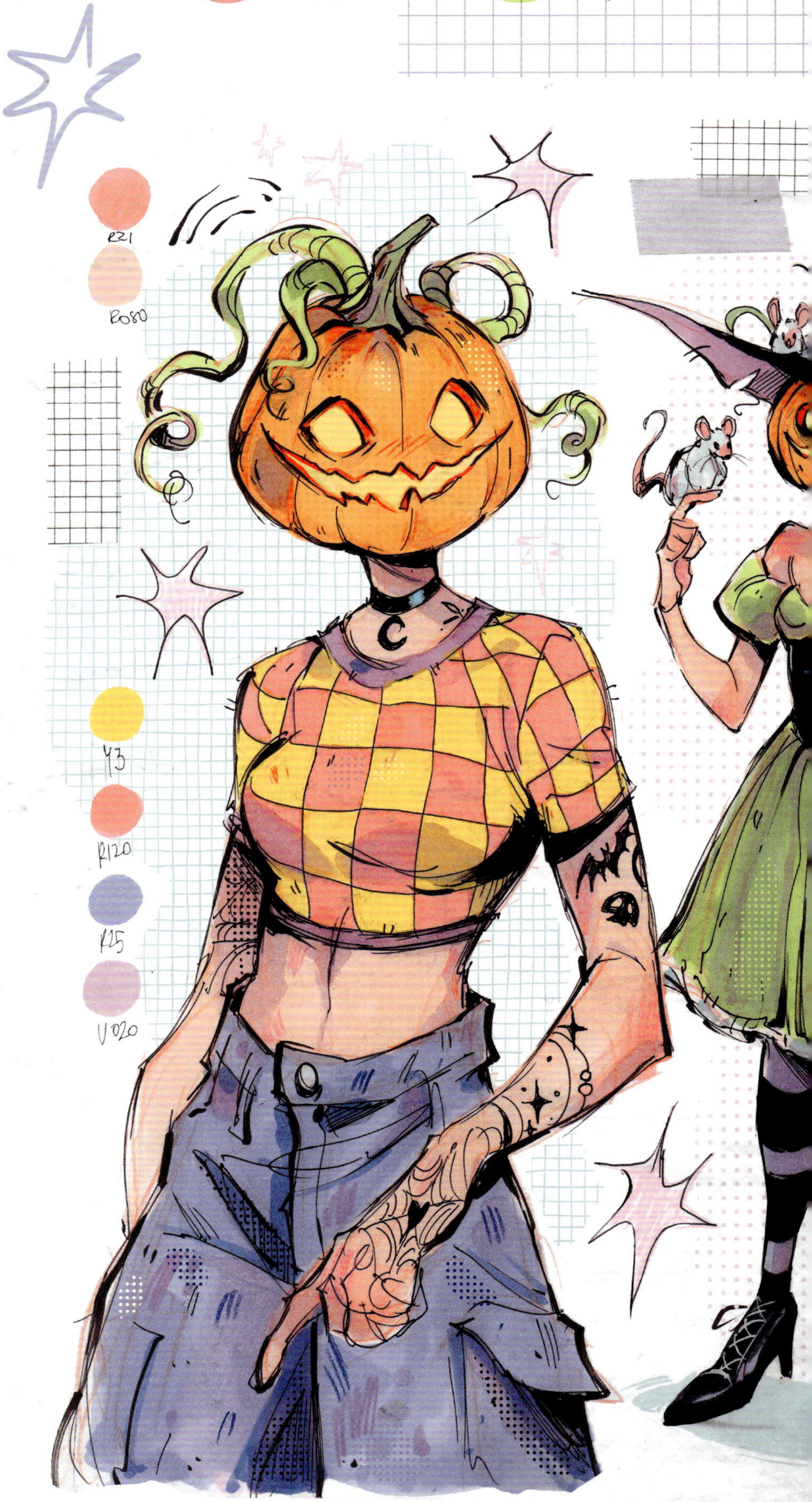

Pumpkin girls – Drawing these pumpkin characters is great for when I feel like practising anatomy or having fun with clothes, colours, and patterns – when I don't feel like wasting too much energy drawing faces

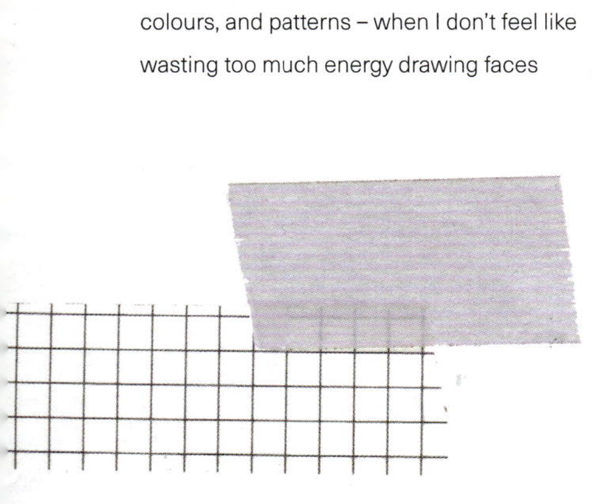

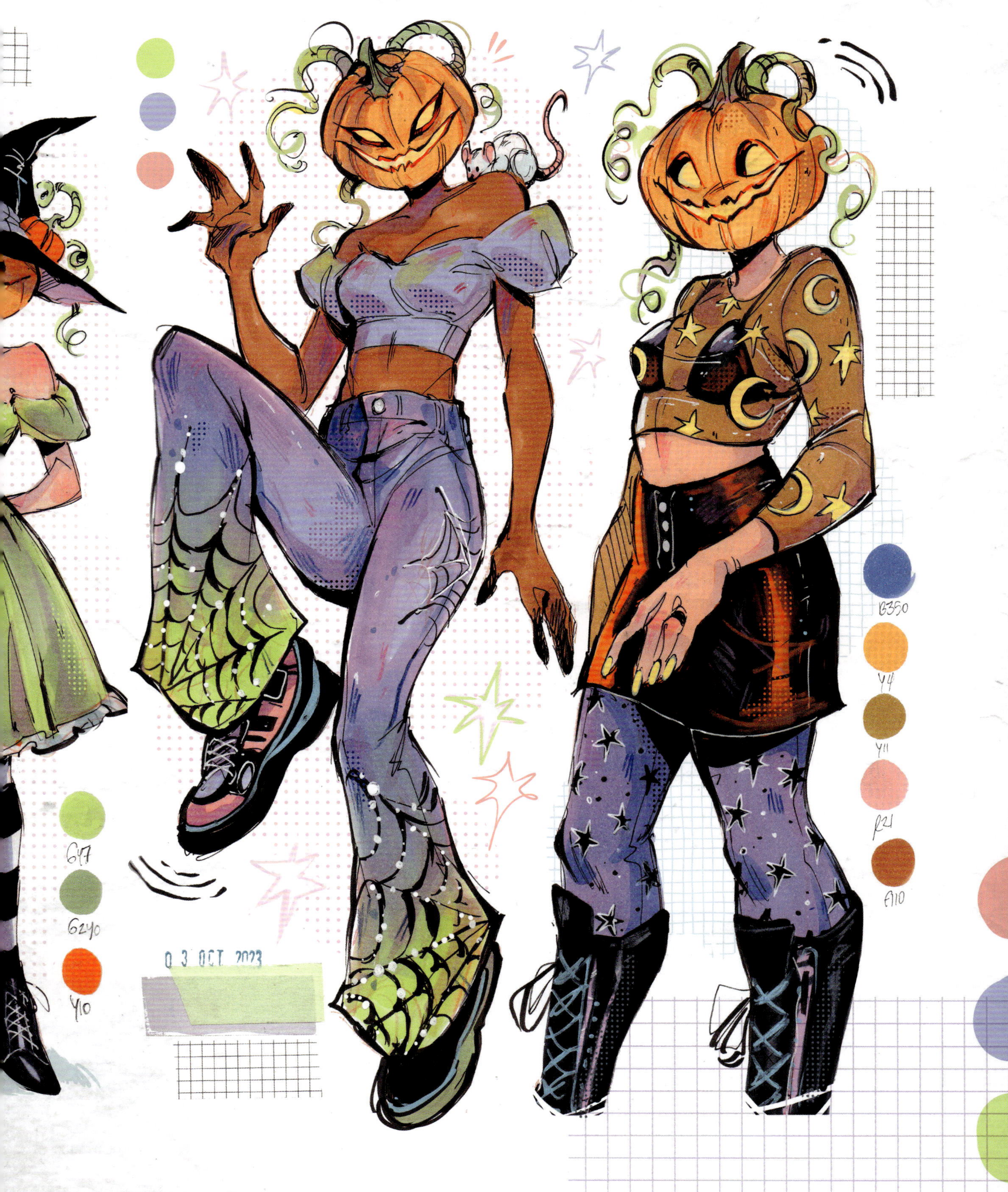
647
62Y0
Y10
03 OCT 2023
B350
Y4
Y11
R21
E10

Your use of colour is exceptional – I feel like you manage to find subtlety amongst bright neon colours in a really unique way. What does your process for working with colour and choosing your palettes look like?

My process of choosing colours is very experimental. I don't have a formula that I strictly follow and most of the time I go back and forth trying to find what works and what doesn't. I think with time you start to learn that certain colours seem to vibrate when they are together, while others can evoke particular emotions, and you start to incorporate those elements into your work. Sometimes I'll use certain colour combinations simply because I find them appealing and they make my heart happy; these days I'm all in on pastel and soft combinations. My use of colour has changed quite a lot throughout the years and I'm sure it will continue to evolve and change many times over, as it's directly related to my current artistic preferences.

Experimenting with limited colour palettes in my sketchbooks is one of my favourite ways of playing around with colour and discovering new exciting combinations. I always make sure to observe my surroundings and take inspiration from real life, photography, and art I find online.

Enchanted waters – For this illustration, I had this idea of a whimsical toad that has the ability to grant three wishes to anyone who finds it

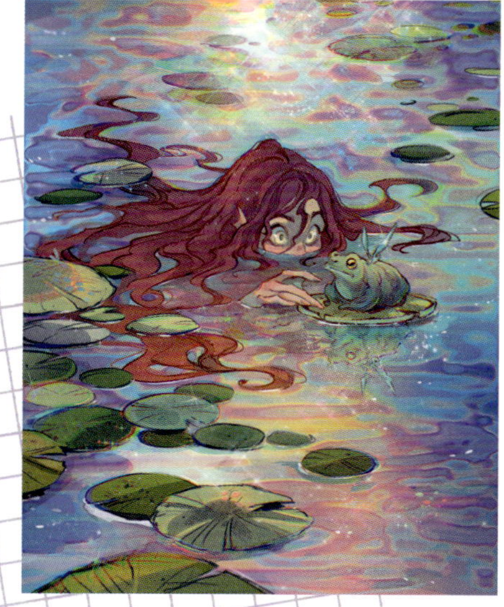

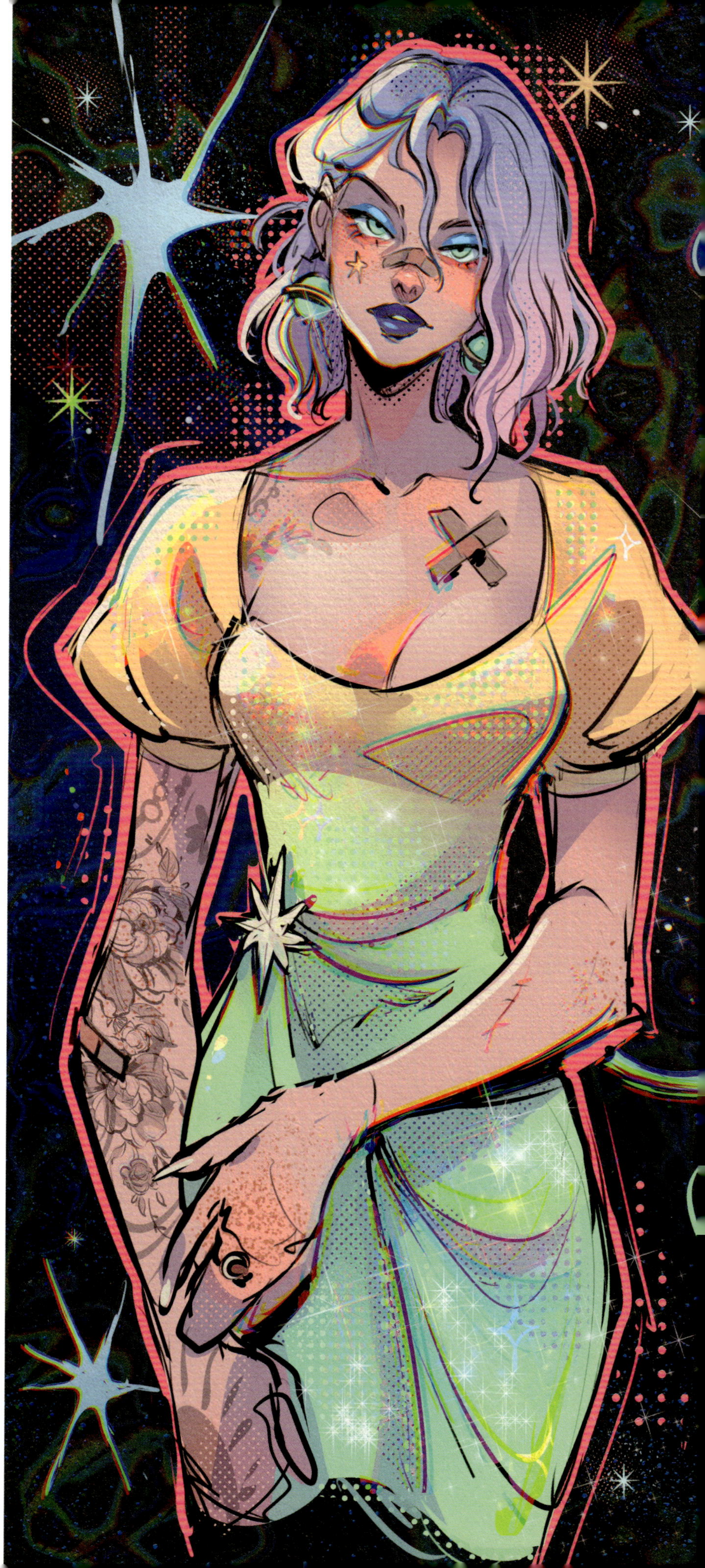

Polaris – Exploring a range of different expressions and emotions helps me to understand who a character is, but also how to draw them from different angles

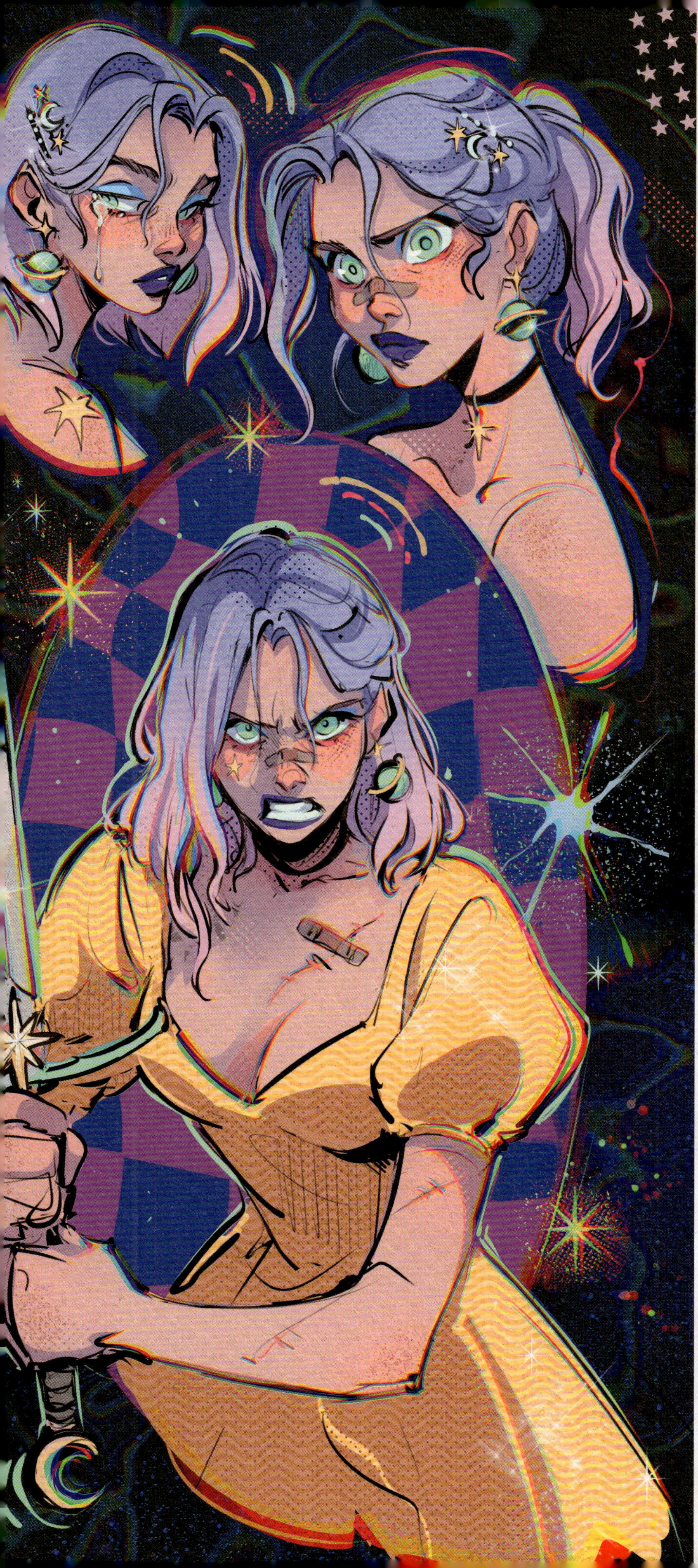

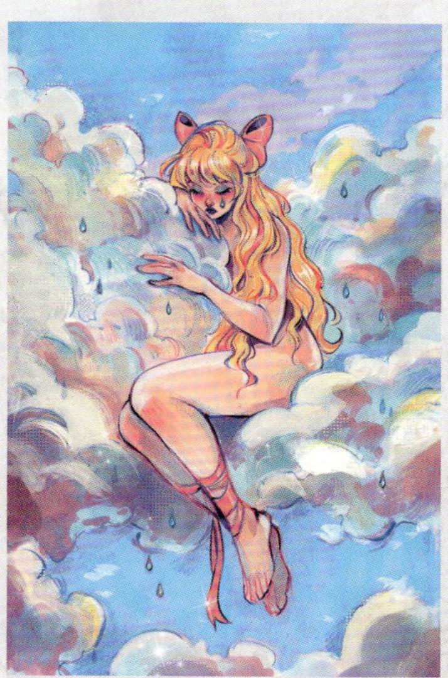

Your characters will often mix fantasy and reality seamlessly – what were the inspirations behind this unique style, and how long did it take for your signature 'look' to take shape?

That's a tricky question, because for a long time drawing was something I did purely for fun. I never really thought about whether or not I had a distinctive look – it took someone telling me that they liked my style for me to realize I had one to begin with! I learned to draw by copying a lot of the shows I loved when I was a kid – there's no doubt that cartoons such as *Teen Titans* and *Winx Club* shaped my art style in a way that is still clearly visible to this day. As years passed, I started to discover many new artists online, particularly on DeviantArt, which was not only a huge influence on my art style but also opened my mind to the possibility that drawing could be more than just a hobby, but a career as well. I also started to take inspiration from real life, my own experiences, and feelings. All those additional elements made my initial 'style' a lot more nuanced over time, although the fantasy theme apparently stuck with me forever. Finding a signature look can definitely be a lengthy process, but I think not obsessing too much over it made it easier for me. I'm excited to keep learning and improving and seeing my art style become whatever it wants to become!

Bottle of Mermaid –
A character's setting will sometimes contribute a lot to the narrative

Let's talk a little about your work on *Primer* – how did the opportunity to work with DC come about, and what were the specific challenges of designing characters for comics?

DC reached out to me with this new potential job and ask me to do a few character designs to see if I was a good fit for the project. Very often for these projects, you get a short brief of the story and the characters' personalities, but not a lot about their physical appearance, so I remember I had a lot of creative freedom when I tackled the characters, which I appreciated. That being said, when designing for comics you have to keep in mind you'll be drawing those characters a million times to a very tight deadline, so you have to be mindful of how complicated you want the designs to be. In the particular case of *Primer* considering representation was a huge part of the project, given the target market was middle grade. I had to be careful not to fall back on common superhero tropes and draw more inclusive, less hegemonic bodies. Overall, working with the writers and editor's feedback made the process very smooth and enjoyable.

Valentine's day – A drawing I did for Valentine's Day. I find maritime imagery fascinating and I love the look of old diving helmets, so I'm always trying to incorporate them into my work

A sketchbook spread that reminds me sometimes a black pen is all you need

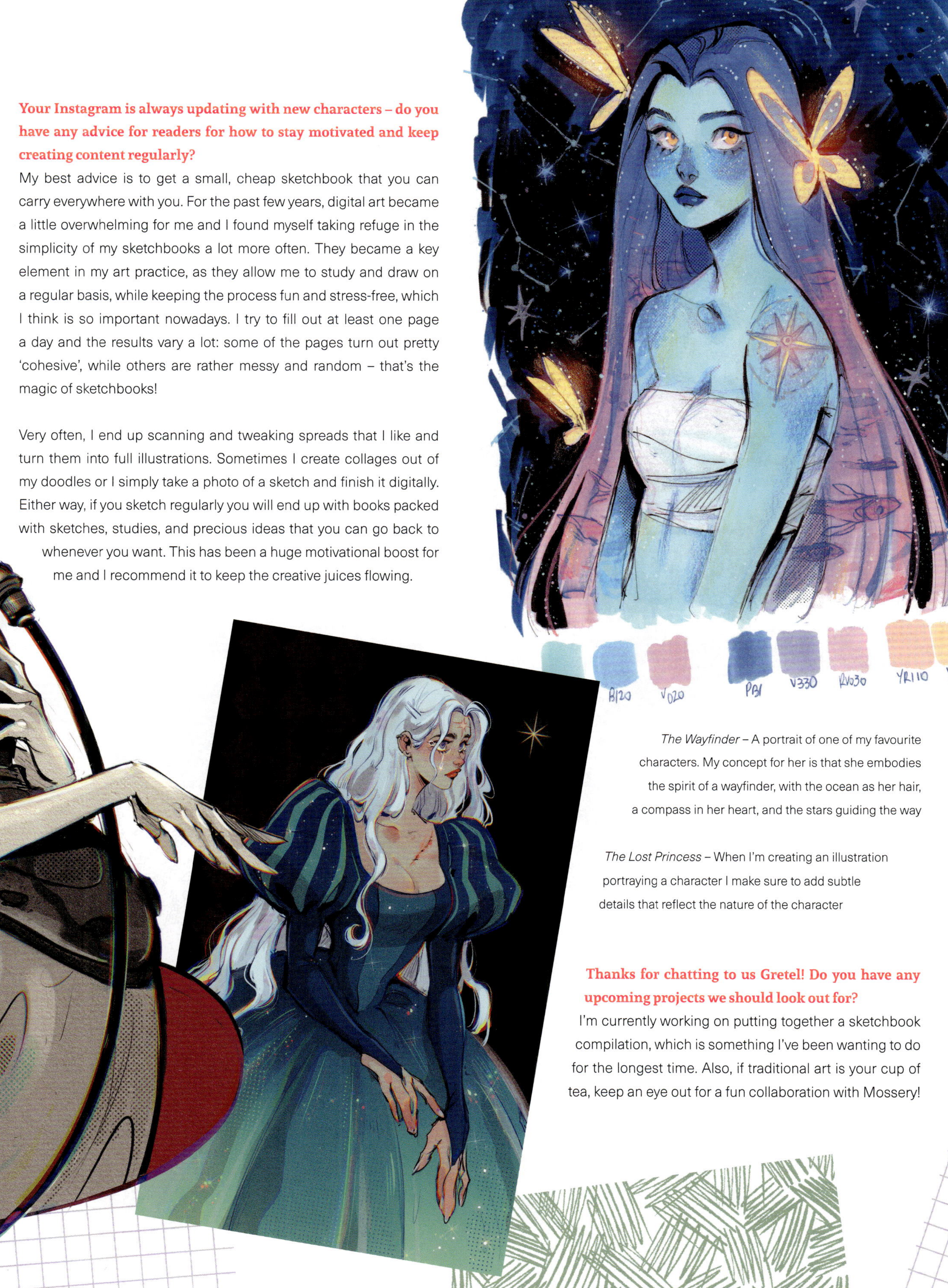

Your Instagram is always updating with new characters – do you have any advice for readers for how to stay motivated and keep creating content regularly?

My best advice is to get a small, cheap sketchbook that you can carry everywhere with you. For the past few years, digital art became a little overwhelming for me and I found myself taking refuge in the simplicity of my sketchbooks a lot more often. They became a key element in my art practice, as they allow me to study and draw on a regular basis, while keeping the process fun and stress-free, which I think is so important nowadays. I try to fill out at least one page a day and the results vary a lot: some of the pages turn out pretty 'cohesive', while others are rather messy and random – that's the magic of sketchbooks!

Very often, I end up scanning and tweaking spreads that I like and turn them into full illustrations. Sometimes I create collages out of my doodles or I simply take a photo of a sketch and finish it digitally. Either way, if you sketch regularly you will end up with books packed with sketches, studies, and precious ideas that you can go back to whenever you want. This has been a huge motivational boost for me and I recommend it to keep the creative juices flowing.

The Wayfinder – A portrait of one of my favourite characters. My concept for her is that she embodies the spirit of a wayfinder, with the ocean as her hair, a compass in her heart, and the stars guiding the way

The Lost Princess – When I'm creating an illustration portraying a character I make sure to add subtle details that reflect the nature of the character

Thanks for chatting to us Gretel! Do you have any upcoming projects we should look out for?

I'm currently working on putting together a sketchbook compilation, which is something I've been wanting to do for the longest time. Also, if traditional art is your cup of tea, keep an eye out for a fun collaboration with Mossery!

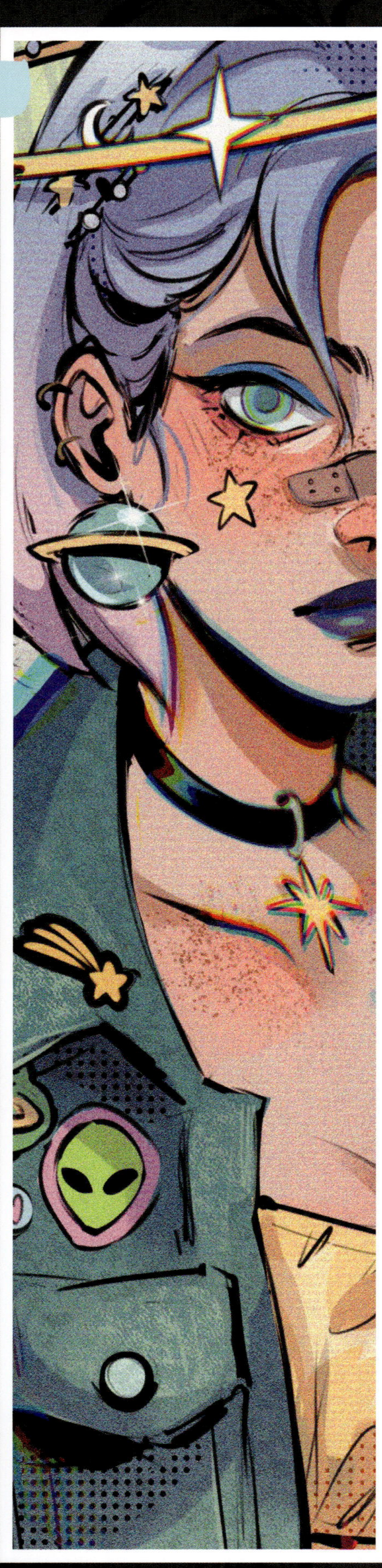

In this tutorial, I'll break down the steps I went through to create the cover artwork, walking you through the creative decisions I took along the way: from exploration and brainstorming in my sketchbook, to how I approach colouring, shading, and rendering with digital tools. I'll be using a Wacom Cintiq and Adobe Photoshop, but most steps can easily translate to Procreate or any other software. I hope you find this little glimpse into my creative process helpful!

All my ideas usually start in my sketchbook. I like to take my time to doodle whatever comes to mind, always guided by the themes and subjects that make my heart beat. For this particular illustration, I know I want to portray a character in a way that feels cool enough for the cover of a magazine, perhaps with a striking colour palette, or some sort of retro aesthetic. Naturally, I think there's nothing cooler than a girl with a sword, so I decide to further explore a character of mine that I enjoy drawing a lot: a space princess.

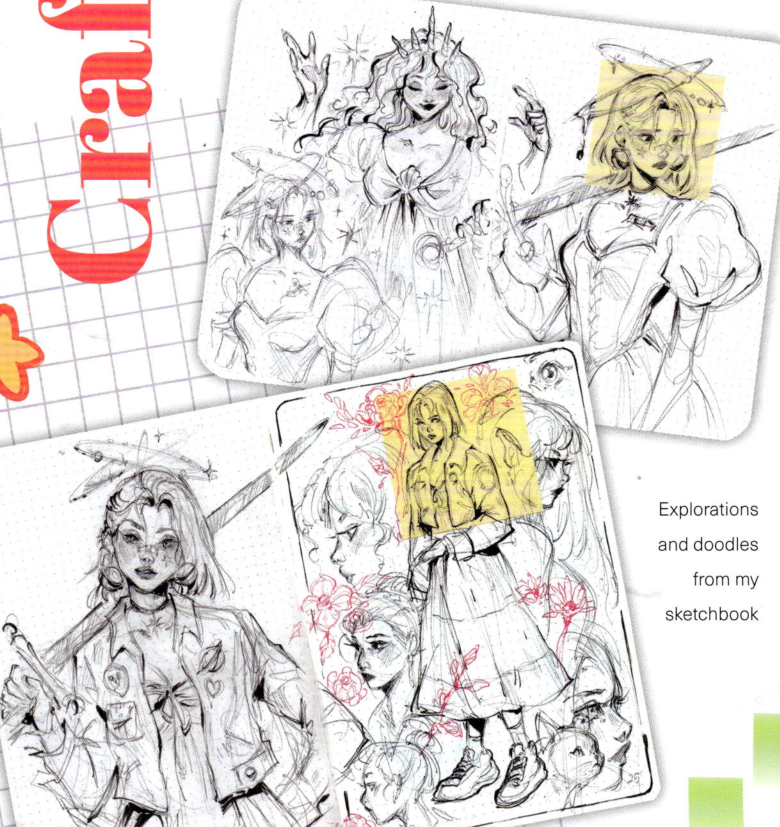

Explorations and doodles from my sketchbook

Once I have a general idea of what I want to draw, I move to my digital tablet and start sketching potential compositions. I try different poses and play around with basic shapes, thinking how to fill the negative space around the character in a balanced way. The rectangles remind me of little comic panels – I like the idea of incorporating graphic novel elements into the cover. I decide to add a couple of drawings that reinforce the retro space theme. This step is always a little bit puzzling, as most of the time I'm never completely sure where a drawing is going. Regardless, I try to enjoy the process and see where it takes me, as I know all the pieces will fall into place eventually.

Explorations of different layouts and poses for the character

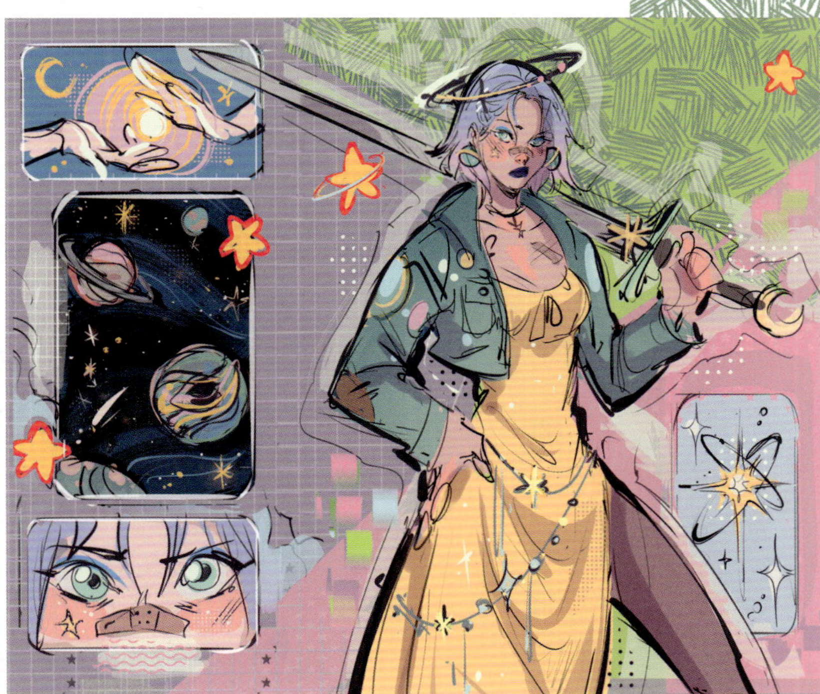

The chosen sketch, with a quick layer of colour to set the mood

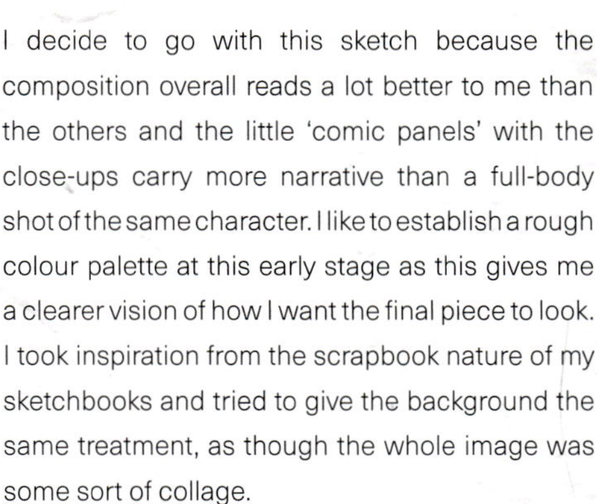

I decide to go with this sketch because the composition overall reads a lot better to me than the others and the little 'comic panels' with the close-ups carry more narrative than a full-body shot of the same character. I like to establish a rough colour palette at this early stage as this gives me a clearer vision of how I want the final piece to look. I took inspiration from the scrapbook nature of my sketchbooks and tried to give the background the same treatment, as though the whole image was some sort of collage.

Line work is one step of the process that I never skip. This is a crucial aspect of my style and I tend to spend a lot of time polishing my sketchy lines to make them look more clean, legible, and expressive. This step can become tedious really fast, so I try to only focus on the parts that have more information and need more detail, such as the character's face and clothes. Defining all the important lines at this stage will make the process of colouring and rendering much quicker.

A clean pass, tracing over the sketch with a hard round brush

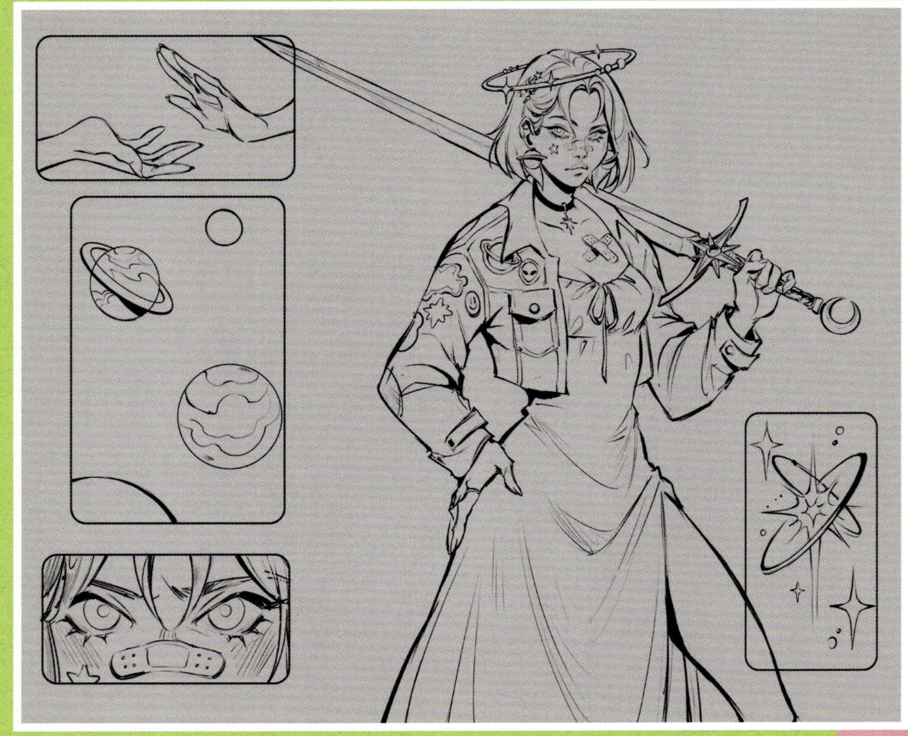

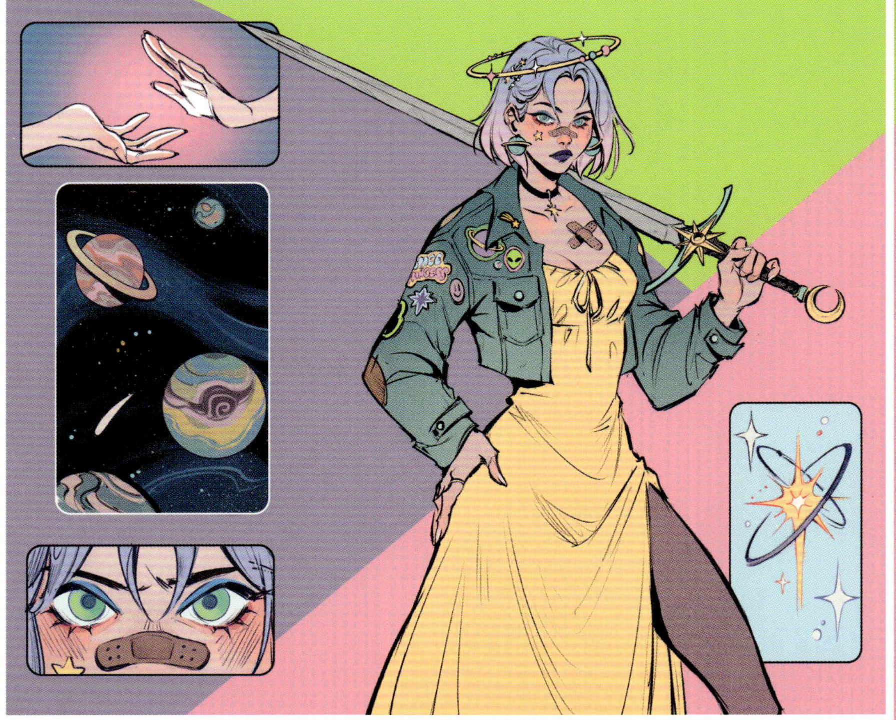

All the main elements are filled in with their base colours

Here's where things start to make a bit more sense. By picking up the colours of my initial sketch, I start filling in all the elements and figures with their corresponding colours. I like to use as few layers as possible, so I just create one for the main character and one for each panel. In this step I also use the Gradient tool to create some colour variation, on the character's cheeks and her denim jacket, for example. This makes the base colours look more natural and creates the perfect base for the next step: shadows.

I create a clipping mask for each base layer and set them to Multiply mode. I then select a light colour (in this case a pastel violet) and start shading all the elements. This is an easy and simple way to add depth to any drawing. I really dig the cel-shading effect as it reminds me of the 2000s cartoons I watched as a kid, but it's easy to create blended edges for a more realistic look by using a softer brush.

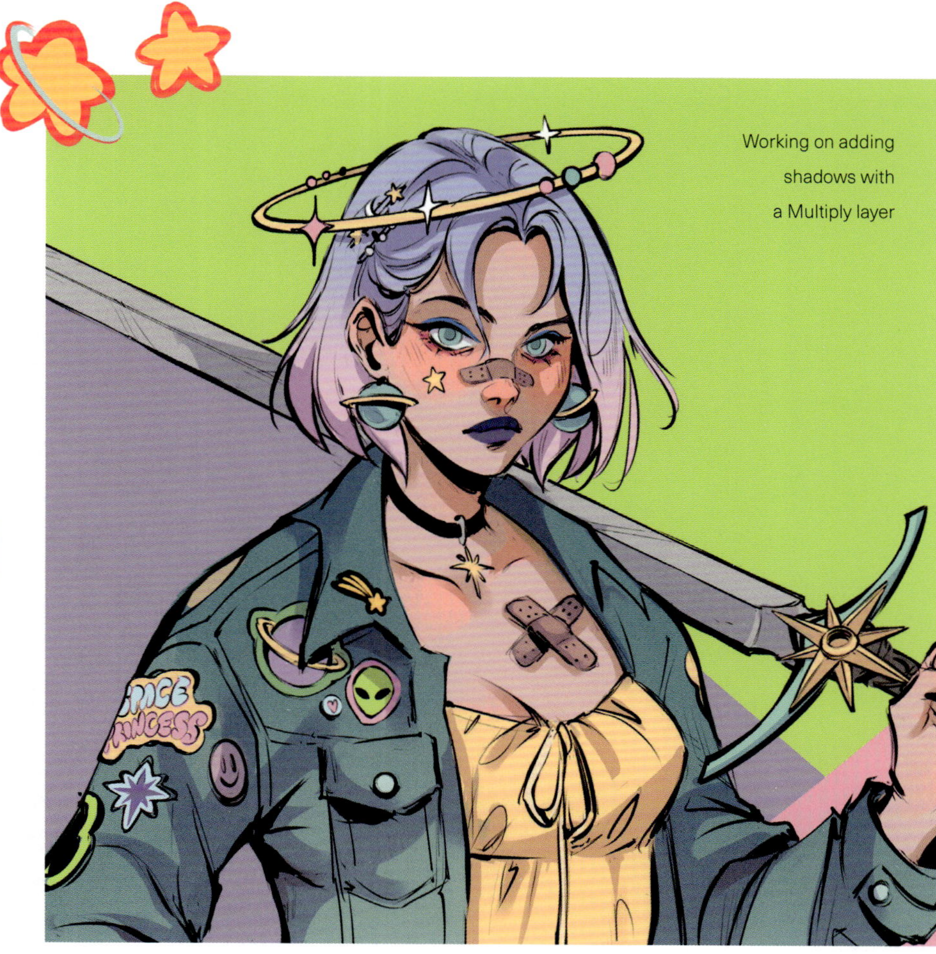

Working on adding shadows with a Multiply layer

Adding a layer of different patterns and textures to the base colours

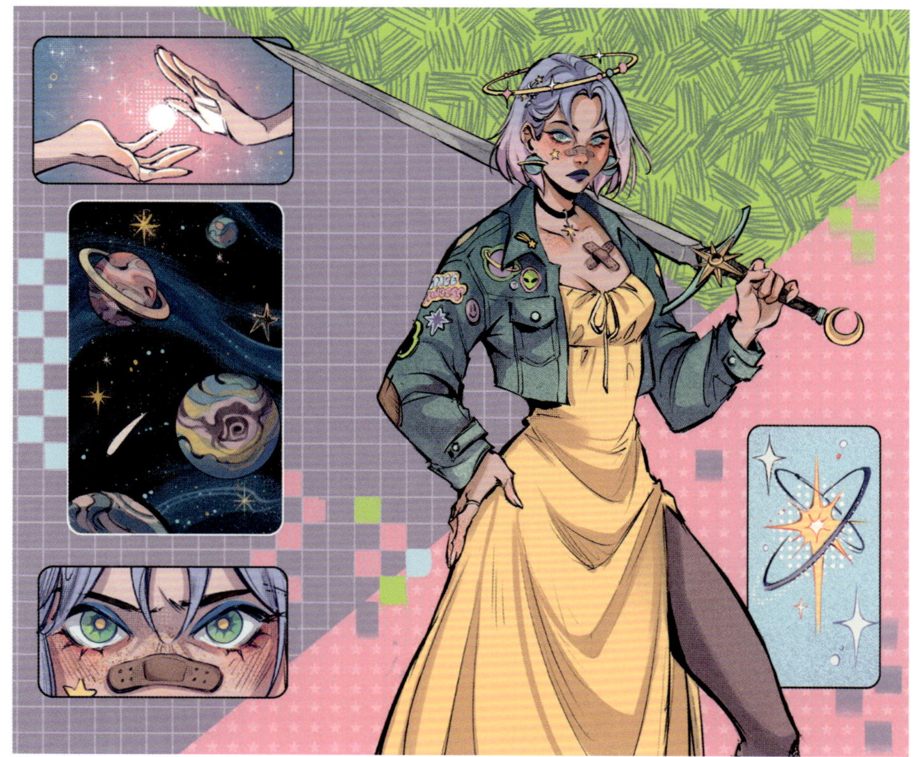

As someone who is very enthusiastic about mixed media and traditional art in general, it can sometimes be quite a challenge to be happy with my digital art. That's why I've become a huge fan of adding a lot of texture to my work over the years. Texture helps to get rid of that digital 'feel' and makes flat colours less boring, and richer. I use graphic brushes to add a variety of patterns to the background and a screentone brush with little dots to add a printed touch to the image. These elements help to strengthen my initial idea of a retro aesthetic.

Details make everything look more put together. They add complexity and storytelling, and hopefully make our eyes linger on an image for a little longer. I create a new layer on top of everything else and start rendering the drawing. I paint hair strands, highlights to accentuate volume, and fix little mistakes I find until I'm happy with the result. The white border helps to separate the character from the background and at the same time reads as though they are drawn on a scrap of paper. I also add little shapes with patterns to resemble washi tape, reinforcing the scrapbook feel I was going for.

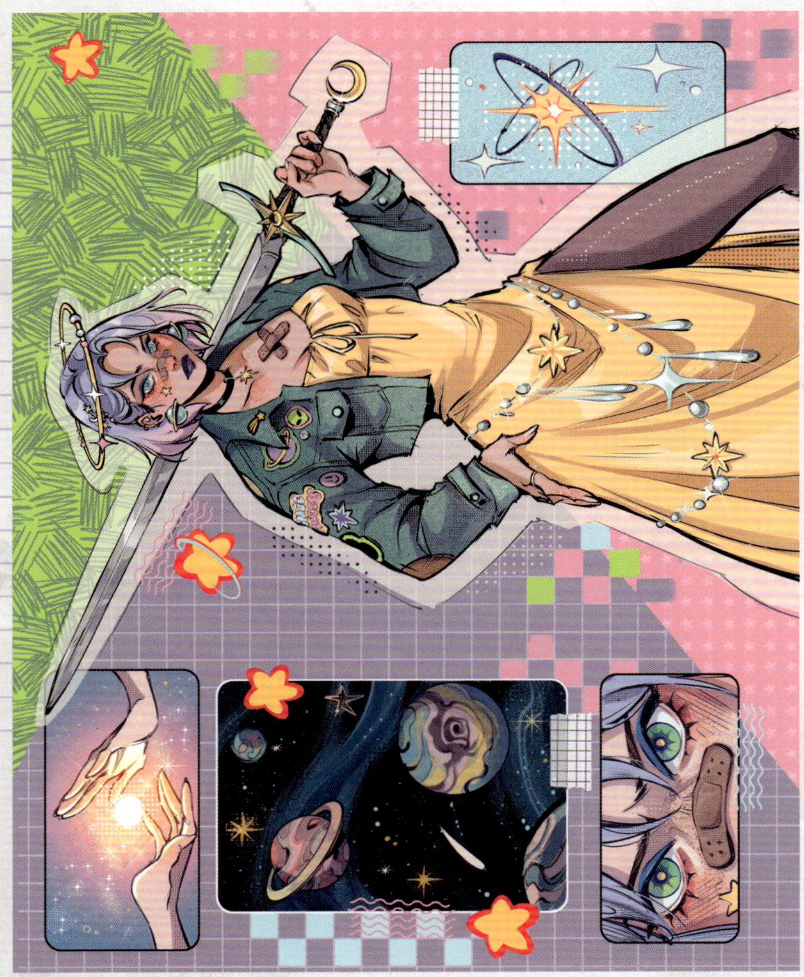

Getting into the small details and further rendering the whole image

I usually make a few adjustments in the very last step, just to make sure the colours stay as vibrant as I like them. For this, I use a mix of saturation and chromatic aberration. You can also change certain hues without affecting other colours with the Selective Colour tool, which I find incredibly helpful. Lastly, I like to lower the contrast of the whole image slightly, to further blend the colours together and give everything a softer look. And with that, the cover is done!

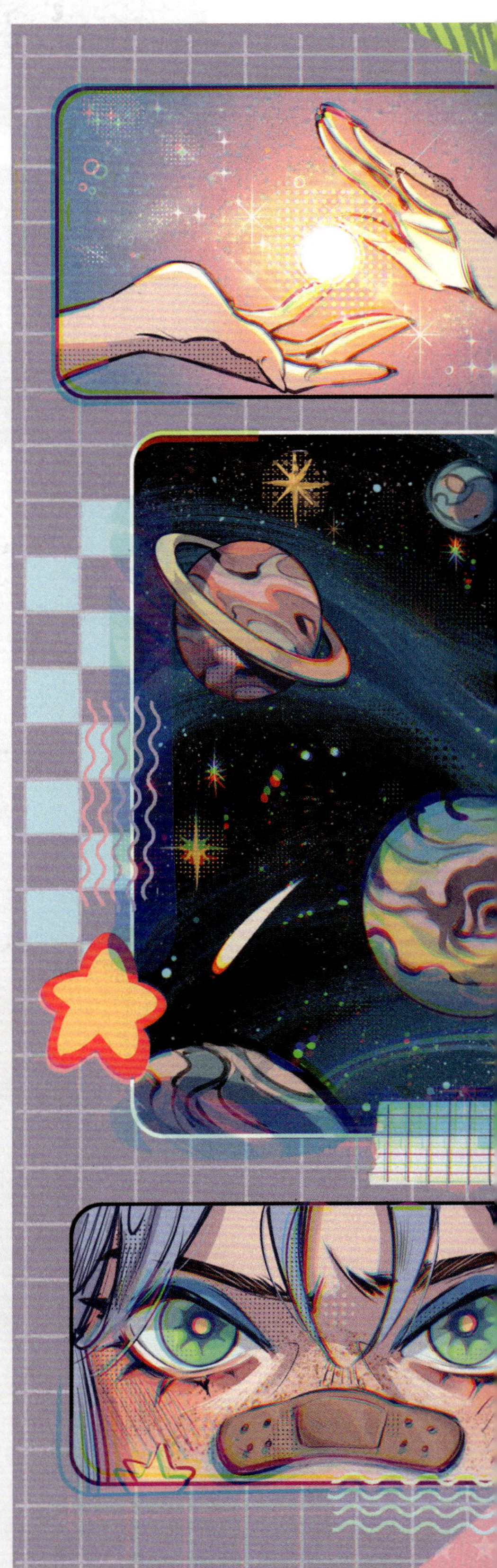

Final colour adjustments to the finished illustration

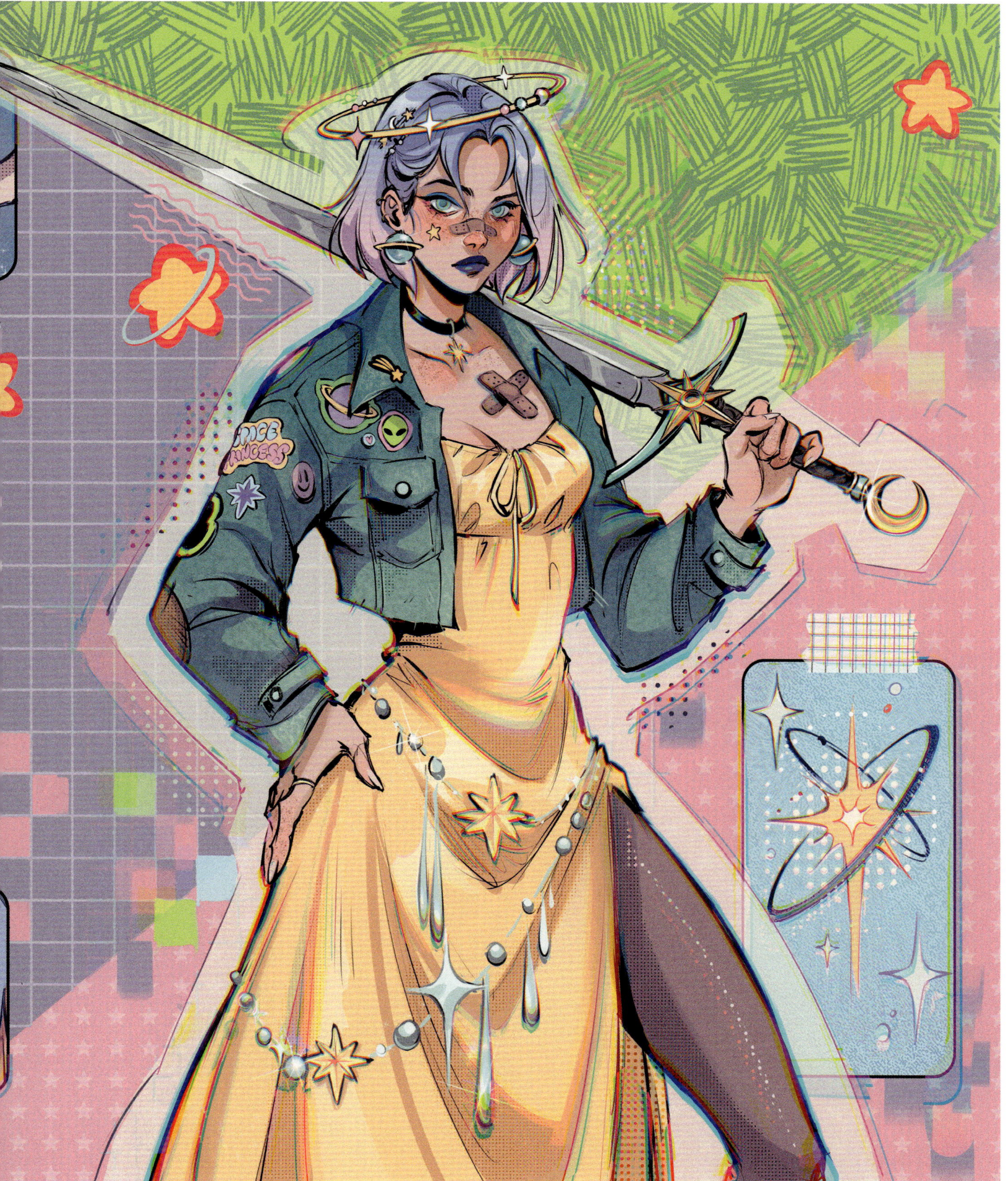

A cat for all seasons

Tessa Nelissen shows us how to make feline characters that truly stand out

I enjoy drawing what lightens my heart and puts a smile on my face, which has resulted in most of my artwork containing animal characters – and primarily cats! Why? I think many people will agree with me that animals have a pureness to them that humans lack, which makes them so endearing. When watching action movies, we often don't mourn the humans that are killed along the way, but when the dog dies... And where would any Disney character be without their animal companion?

Animals come in all shapes and sizes, and for those of us who share a bond with a pet, we know each of them has their own unique personality. In this article I will explain what inspires the animal characters that I draw, how I stylize them, and how to showcase their personality.

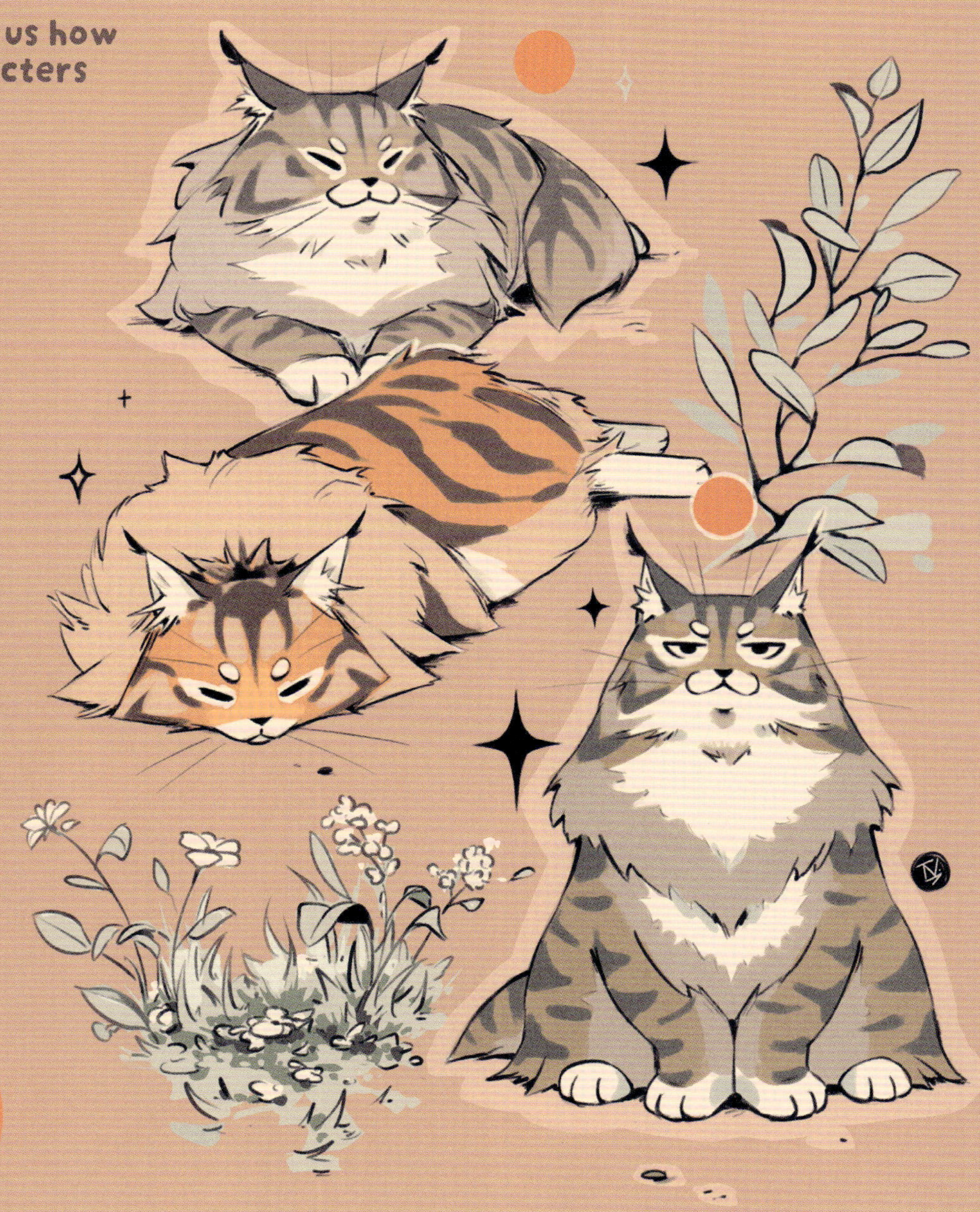

To draw compelling animal characters, it helps to actually know some! My own cats (past and present) have inspired me countless times, but if you don't have a muse at home, luckily the internet is *full* of pictures of animals – so get online and start saving some inspirational material. Keep anything that sparks your imagination: a compelling pose, a funny, relatable situation, beautiful fur patterns – it can be anything.

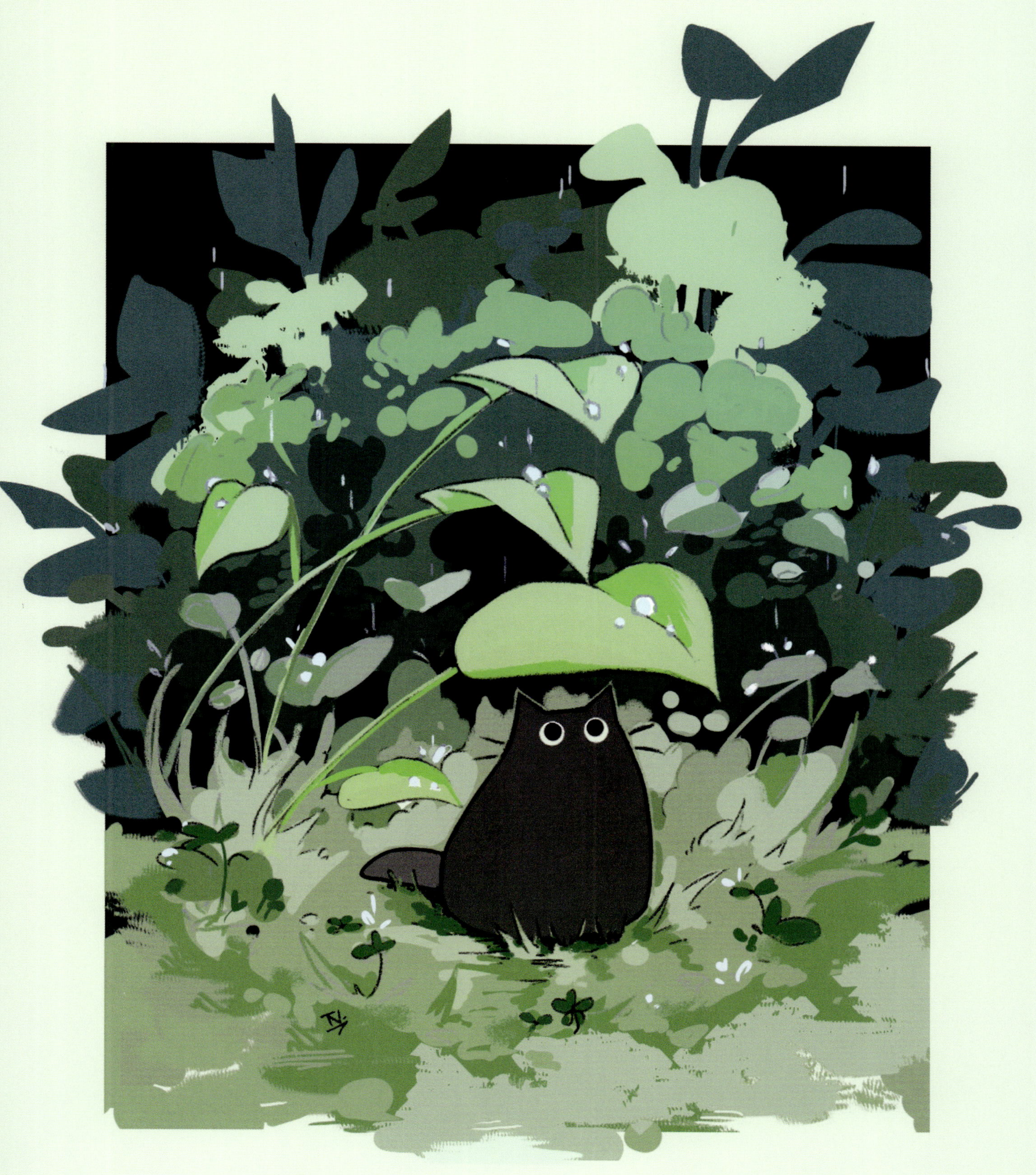

Stylizing an animal character starts by defining its main attributes. Take cats, for example: as long as they have eyes, triangular ears, whiskers, and a tail, even a blob shape will be recognizable as a cat. My character 'Pooty' is a great example of how an abstract shape can still be easily identifiable if you include the animal's main features.

All images © Tessa Nelissen

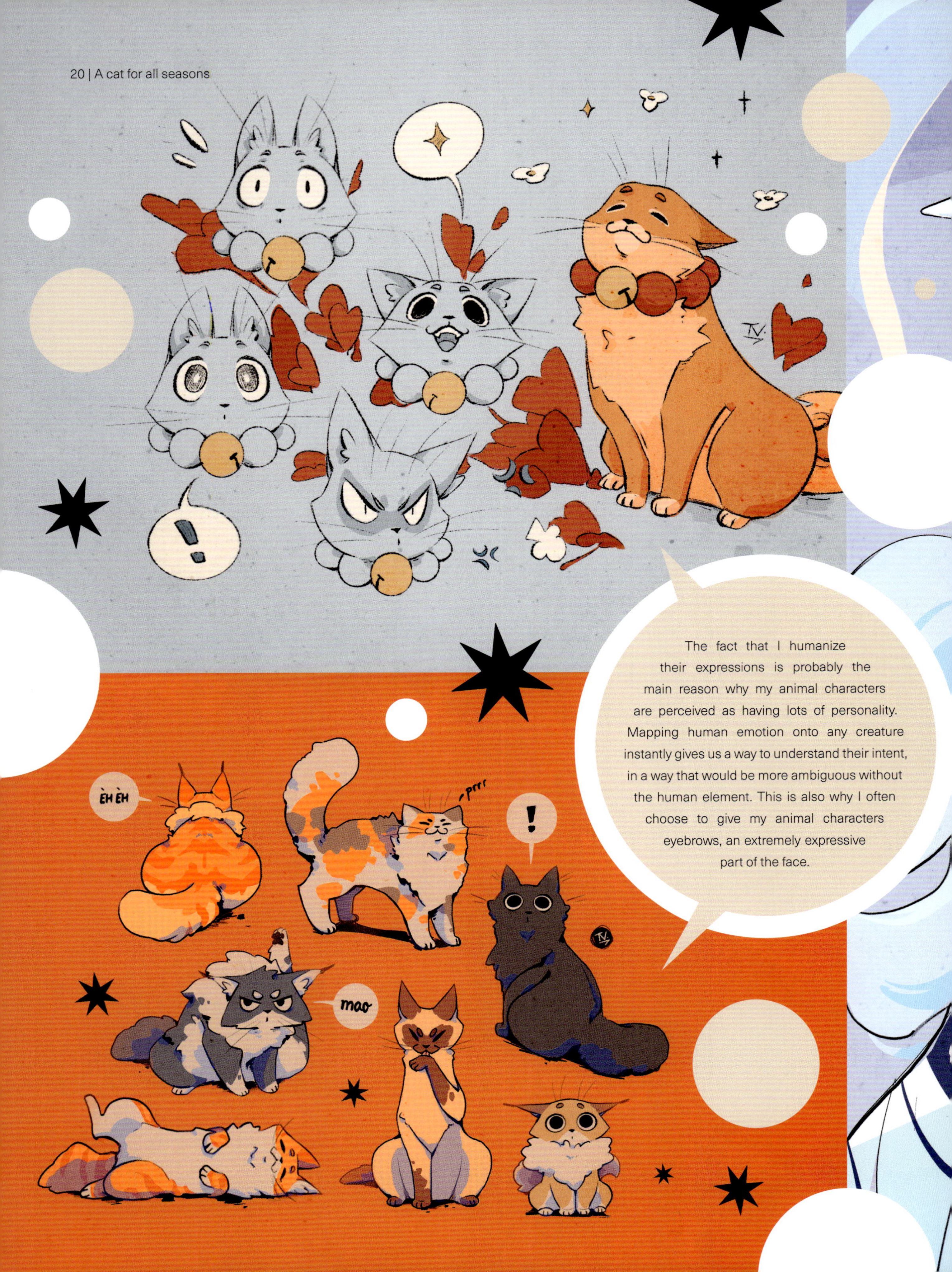
EH EH
mao
The fact that I humanize
their expressions is probably the
main reason why my animal characters
are perceived as having lots of personality.
Mapping human emotion onto any creature
instantly gives us a way to understand their intent,
in a way that would be more ambiguous without
the human element. This is also why I often
choose to give my animal characters
eyebrows, an extremely expressive
part of the face.

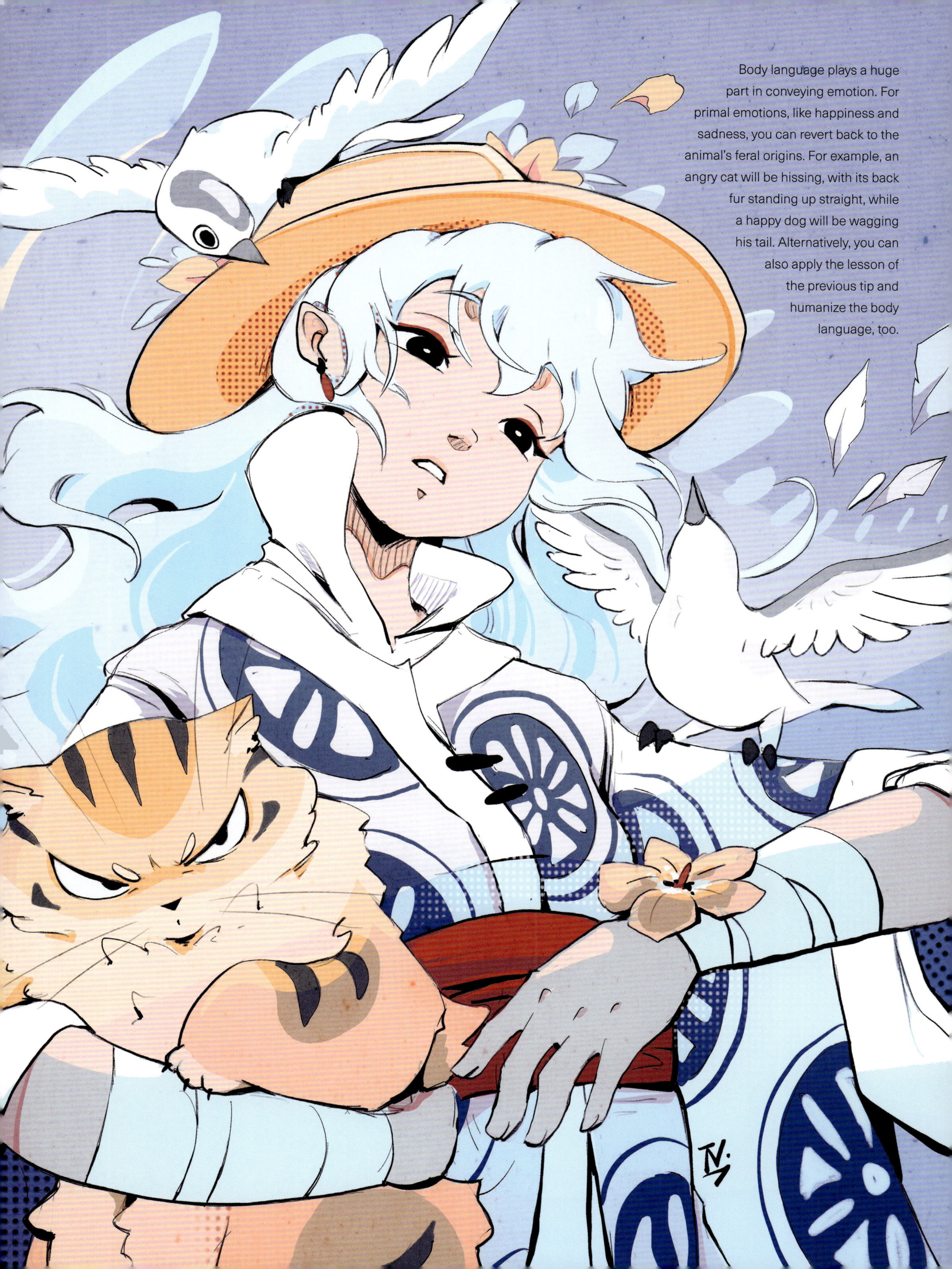
Body language plays a huge part in conveying emotion. For primal emotions, like happiness and sadness, you can revert back to the animal's feral origins. For example, an angry cat will be hissing, with its back fur standing up straight, while a happy dog will be wagging his tail. Alternatively, you can also apply the lesson of the previous tip and humanize the body language, too.

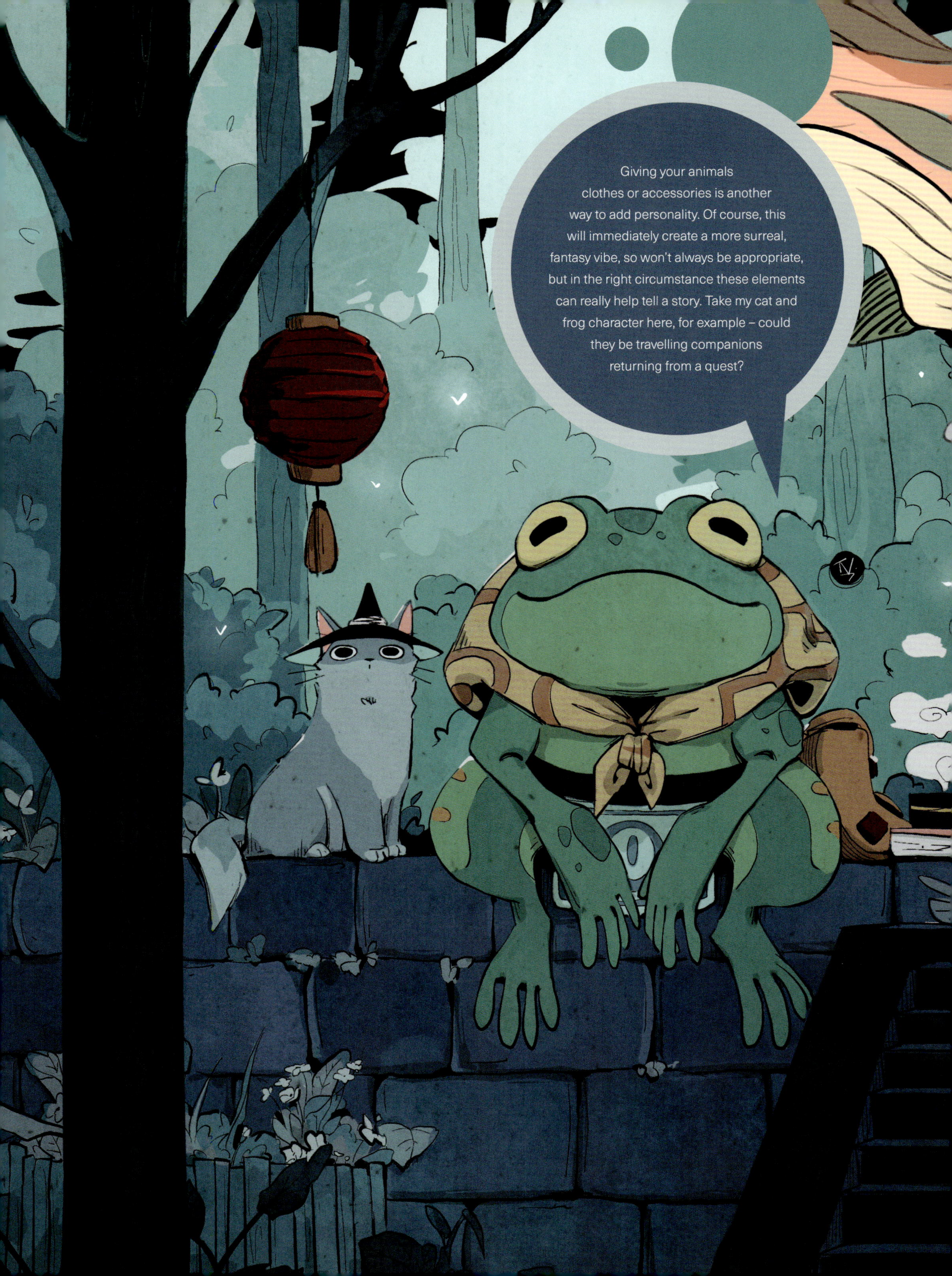

Giving your animals clothes or accessories is another way to add personality. Of course, this will immediately create a more surreal, fantasy vibe, so won't always be appropriate, but in the right circumstance these elements can really help tell a story. Take my cat and frog character here, for example – could they be travelling companions returning from a quest?

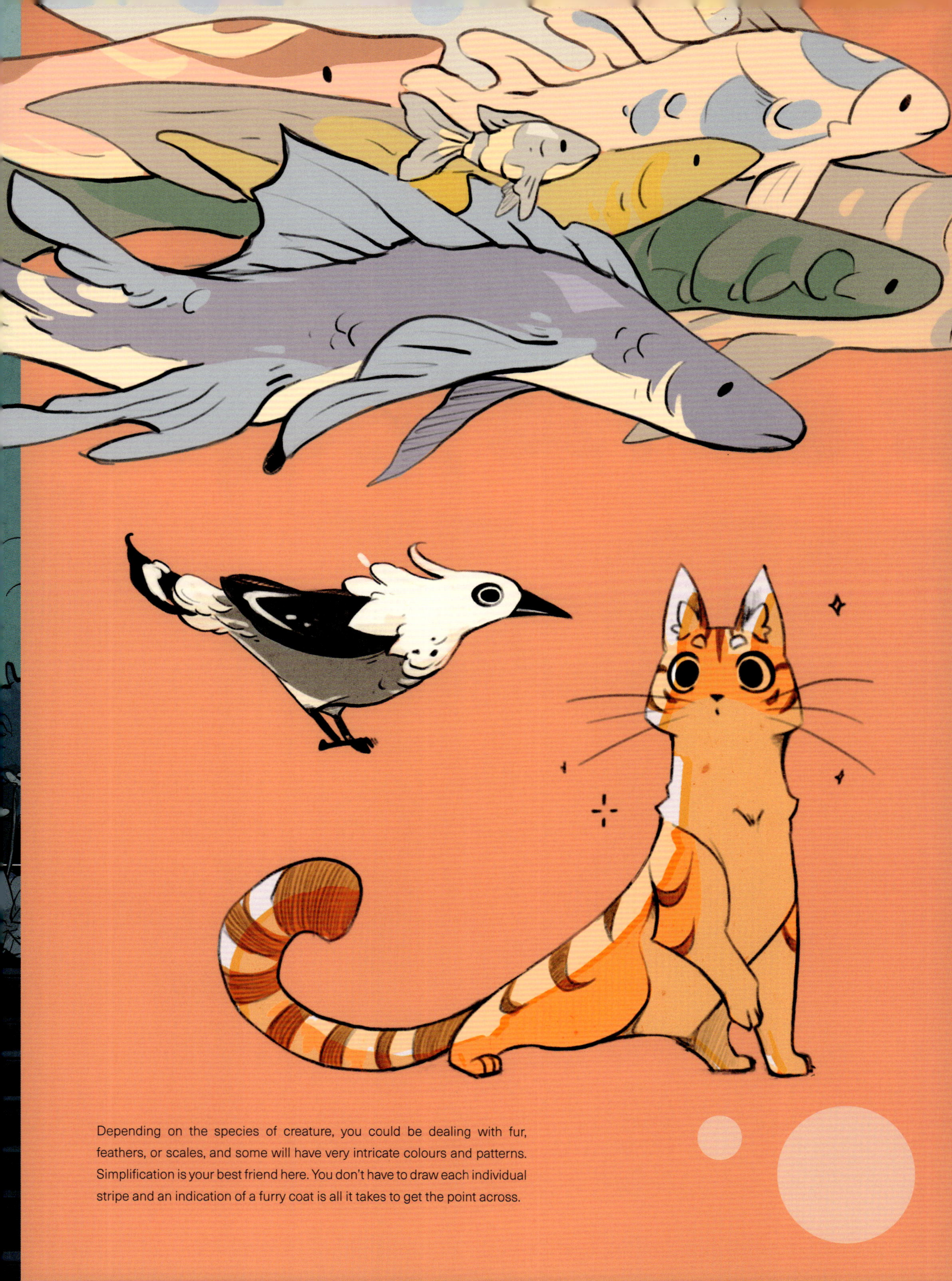

Depending on the species of creature, you could be dealing with fur, feathers, or scales, and some will have very intricate colours and patterns. Simplification is your best friend here. You don't have to draw each individual stripe and an indication of a furry coat is all it takes to get the point across.

VALENTINA GRAZIUSO

Let me take you on a deep dive into everything shape and line-focused about character design. If you're looking for some inspiration on how to go about drawing manic bats and lovable grannies, then read on!

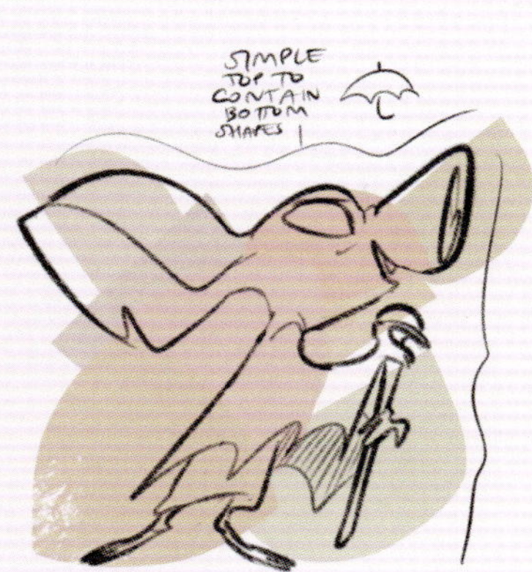

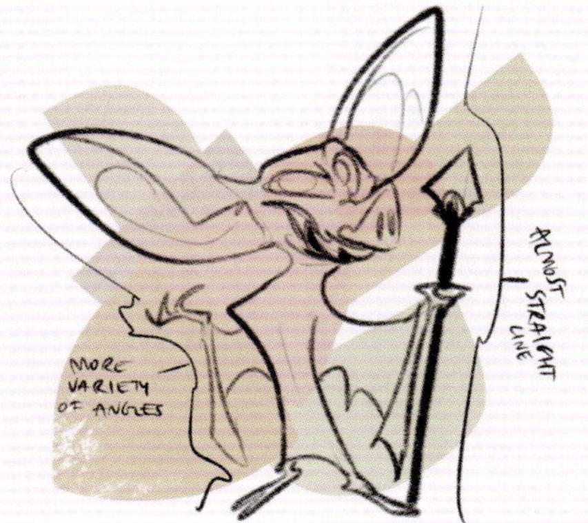

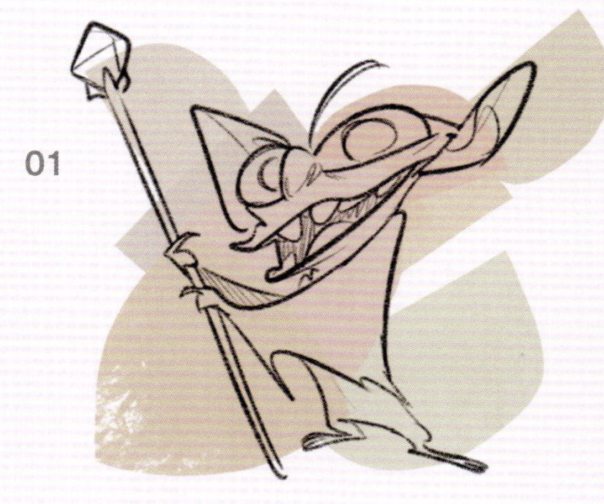

01. This stage is all about loose sketching. I often like to start off with abstract shapes on which to base my lines while keeping an eye out for clean and strong silhouettes. I always look for fun and different ways that shapes and lines can counterbalance each other and provide rhythm to the final idea – in this case, a bat seizing a sceptre and getting up to mischief!

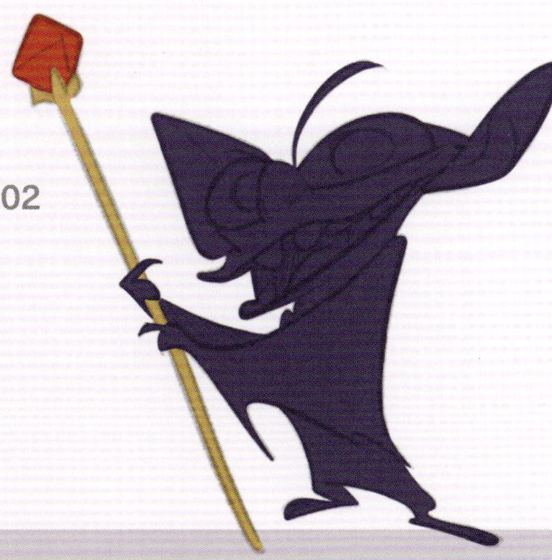

02. Once I find an interesting combination of lines and shapes, I move on to basic colour-blocking, while reducing the sketch opacity. This will allow me to isolate the main parts of the character, which will make it easier to then colour and add details in the next stages.

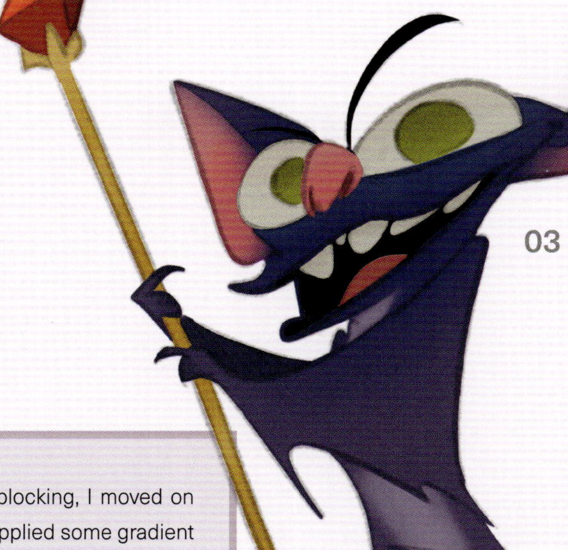

03. Thanks to the previous shape blocking, I moved on to some more detailed colouring and applied some gradient transitions – especially around the chest and ears.

All images © Valentina Graziuso

04. In the final part of the process, I added lights and shadows to better define the character's shapes. I defined some smaller details and created a background that complements the character without drawing attention away from it – even though with those ears our bat should still stand out without any problems.

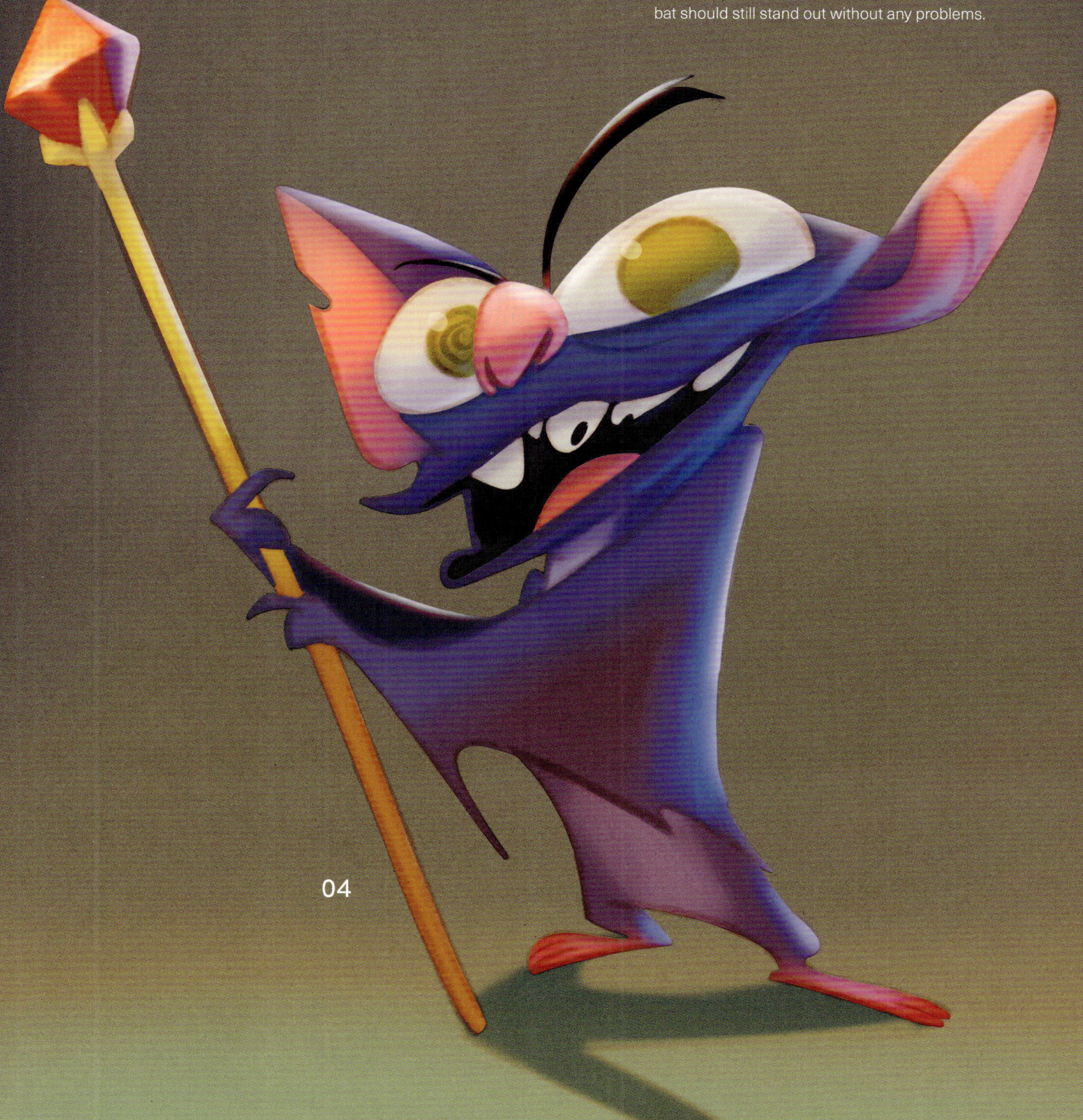

04

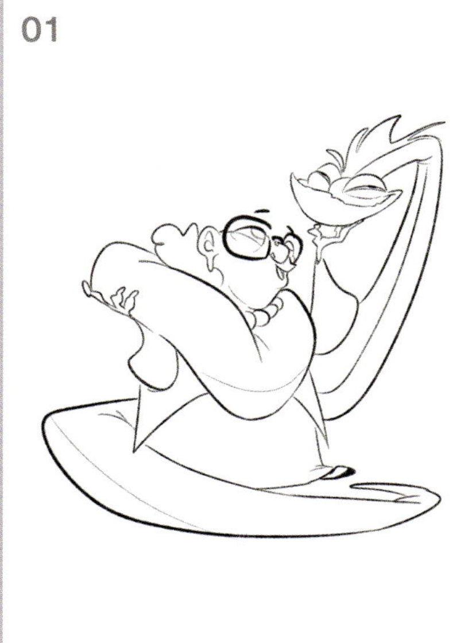

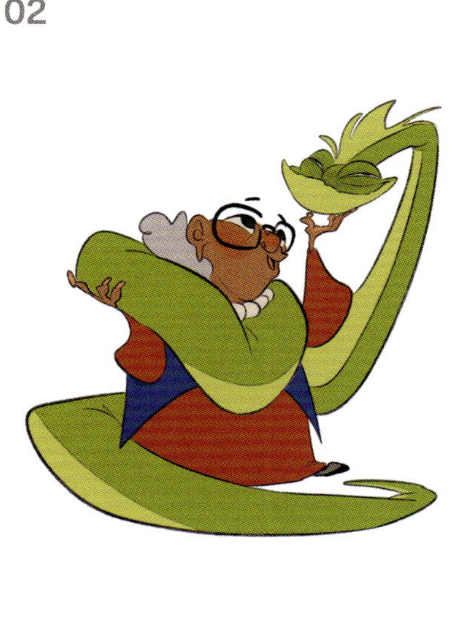

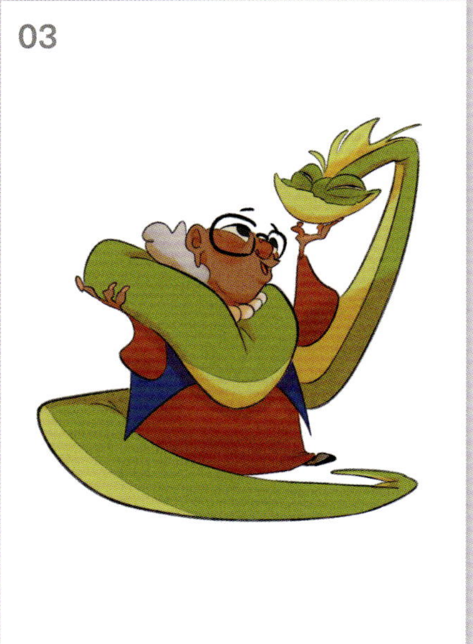

01. I love to draw grannies, especially when they swap their knitting for a lovable snake. I already had an idea in mind here, so I was mostly playing with the two characters' personalities and how they could interact with each other. Eventually, I feel like moving forward with a cuddly moment between the two.

02. This time I have pushed the colour-blocking a bit further and also defined smaller areas for both characters, while leaving the line work slightly more visible. For colouring, I mostly picked warmer hues to reflect the warmth and fuzziness of their interaction.

03. I then moved on to shading, focusing on defining the occlusion areas like noses, folds, and chubby rolls. I am already starting to define the overall lighting direction, which will eventually move the attention to the top part of the design, where our characters' faces are drawn together.

04. I added more lighting, a complementary background, and a subtle gradient shade that leaves the lower part of the design slighty out of focus, in favour of the top area where we have this sweet moment between our granny and fuss-loving snake.

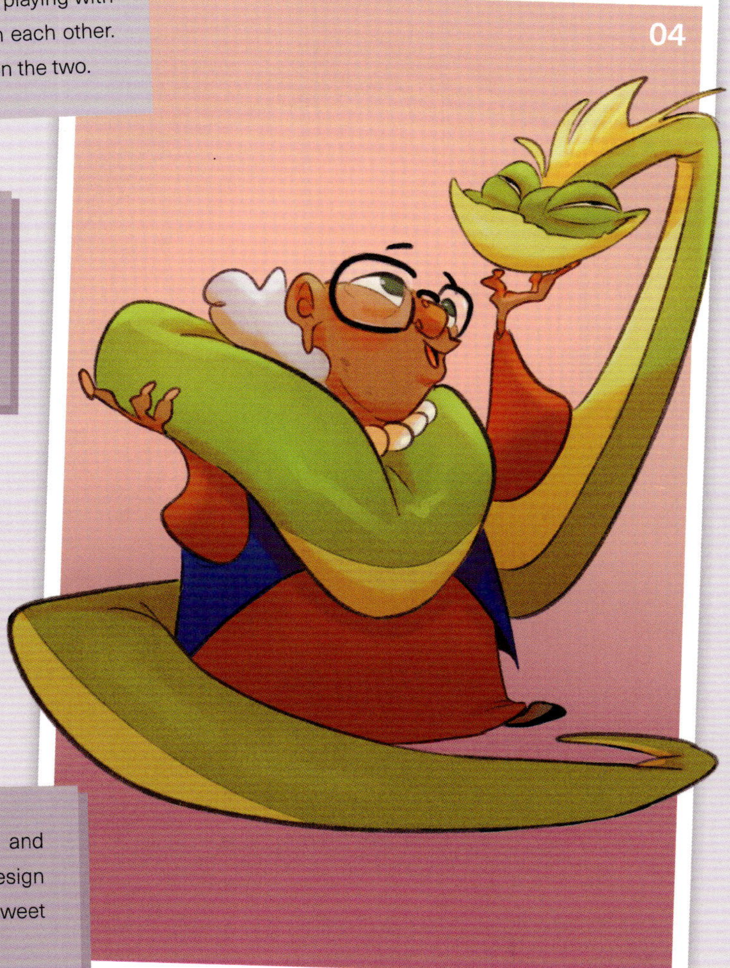

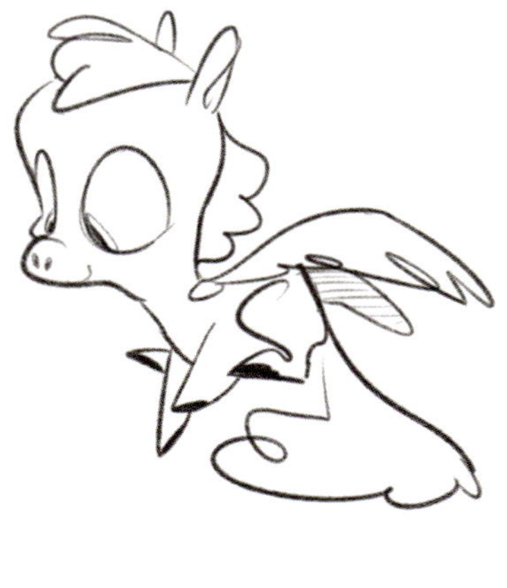

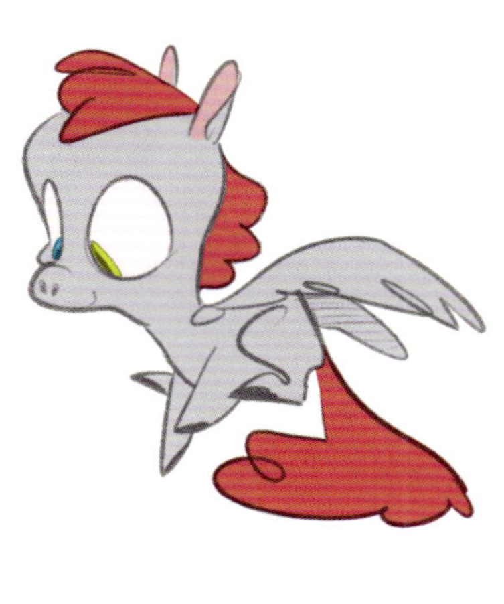

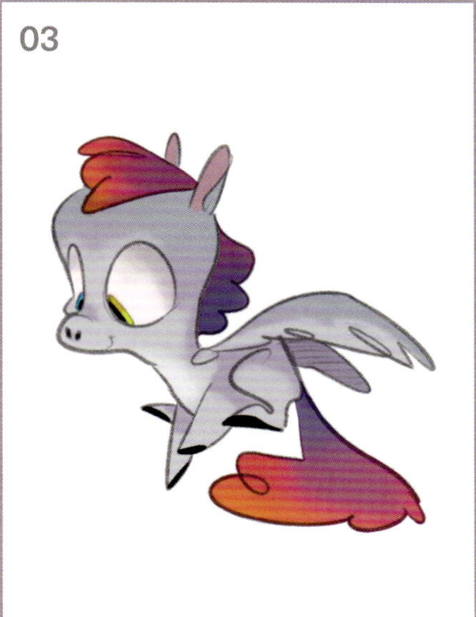

01. I wanted to save an overload of cuteness for last, so here I am playing around with more fun shapes to find the cutest (and slightly silly) winged horse. As I was aiming for cuteness, I used round features and mostly focused on proportions where the head is more prominent than the rest of the body. However, I am also looking for a spark of personality, so I decided to go for this design where there's a bit of curiosity about what lies below.

02. With a design chosen, I moved on to the usual colour blocking where I can already start thinking of a general direction for the colours: our little fellow will definitely deserve some rainbow, heterochromic vibes!

03. This step is all about shape definition, with some cool shading, as well as better defining those rainbow vibes we mentioned earlier.

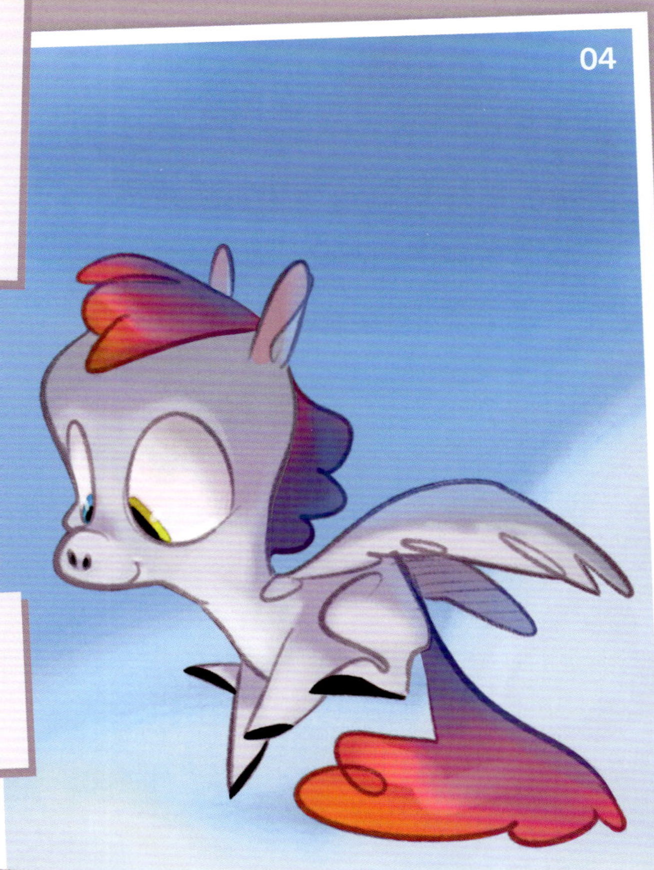

04. We are now at the end of the process, where highlights are added along with coloured line art to bring more vibrancy to the final design. I also needed to draw a background of blue skies and fluffy clouds, so I added some nice blueish bounce light, tying together background and character.

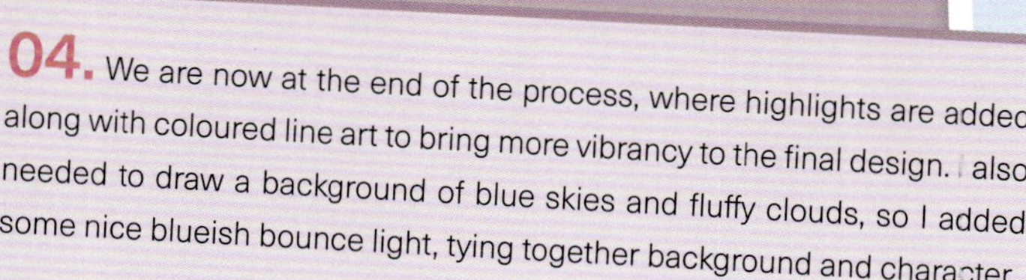

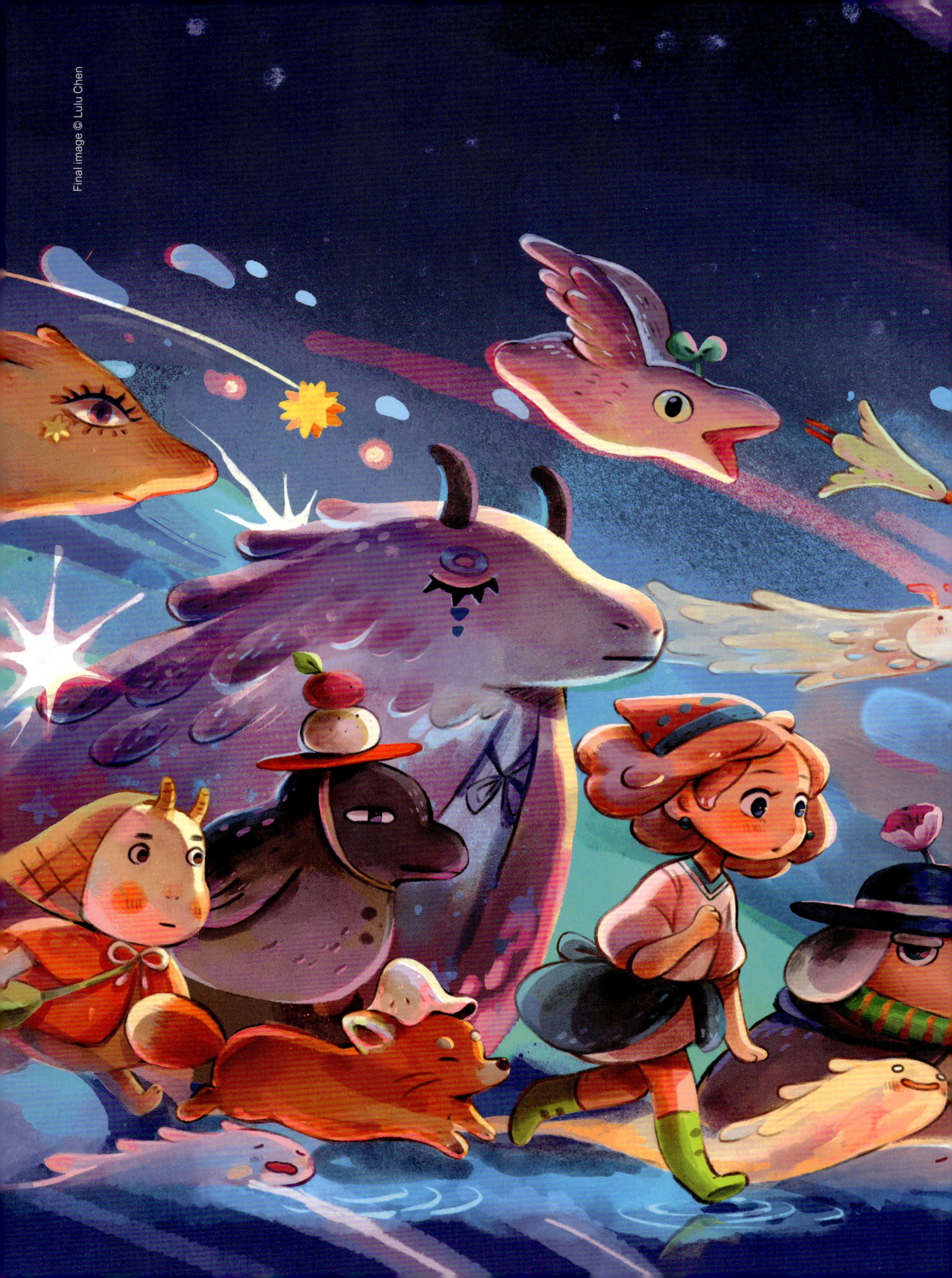
Final image © Lulu Chen

The Market

Lulu Chen

Lulu Chen shows us how she created a colourful scene from her award-winning film *The Market*

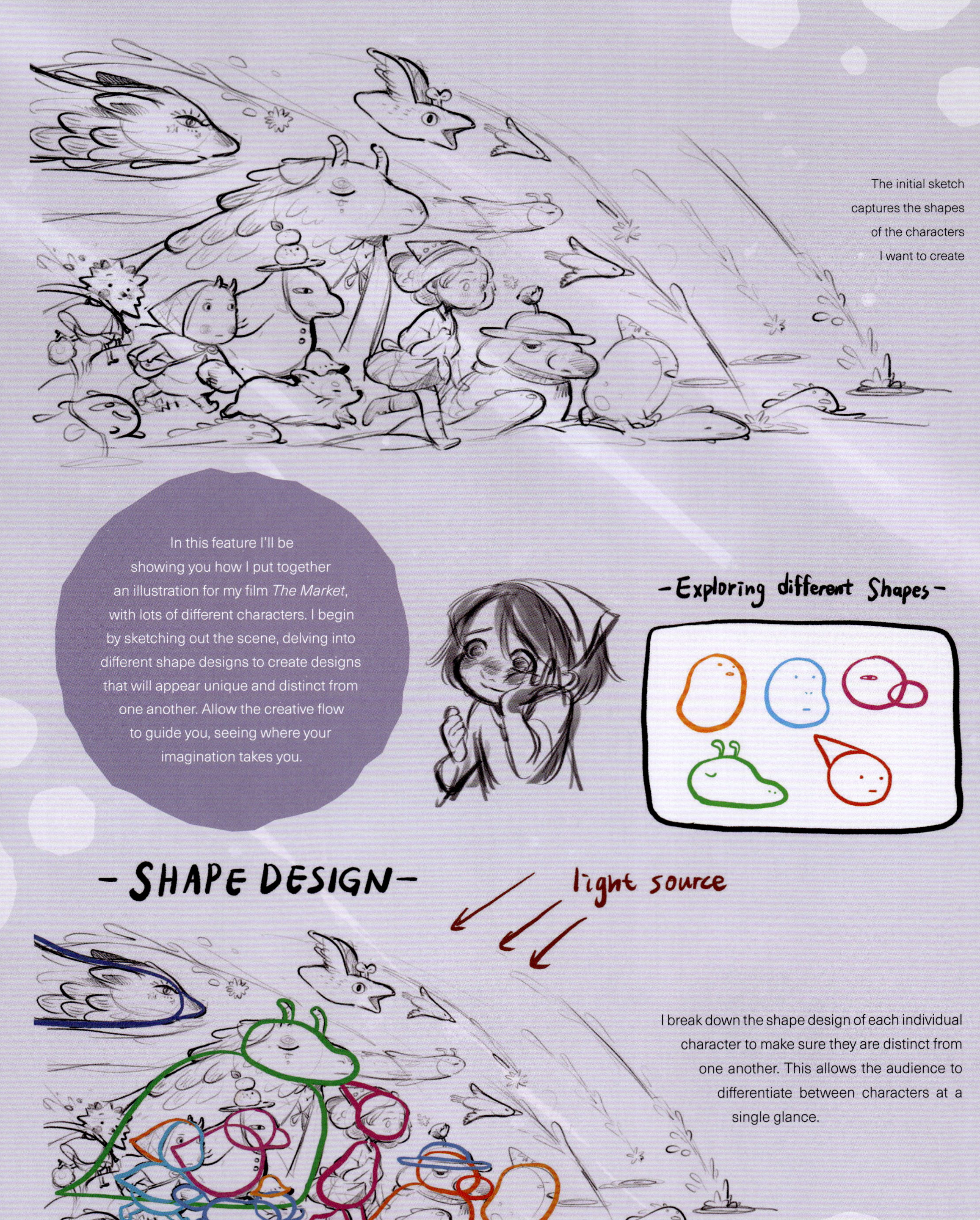

The initial sketch captures the shapes of the characters I want to create

In this feature I'll be showing you how I put together an illustration for my film *The Market*, with lots of different characters. I begin by sketching out the scene, delving into different shape designs to create designs that will appear unique and distinct from one another. Allow the creative flow to guide you, seeing where your imagination takes you.

- Exploring different Shapes -

- SHAPE DESIGN -

light source

flow

I break down the shape design of each individual character to make sure they are distinct from one another. This allows the audience to differentiate between characters at a single glance.

With my sketch complete, I now try different colour schemes, experimenting with cool, warm tones, and saturated tones. Don't be afraid to push your ideas as far as you can, no matter how crazy they may seem. You might surprise yourself with what you come up with.

Trying different colour schemes for the full image

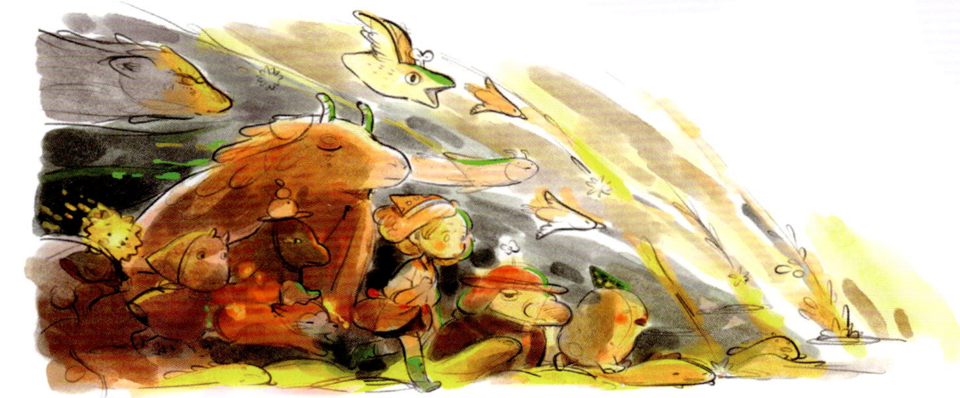

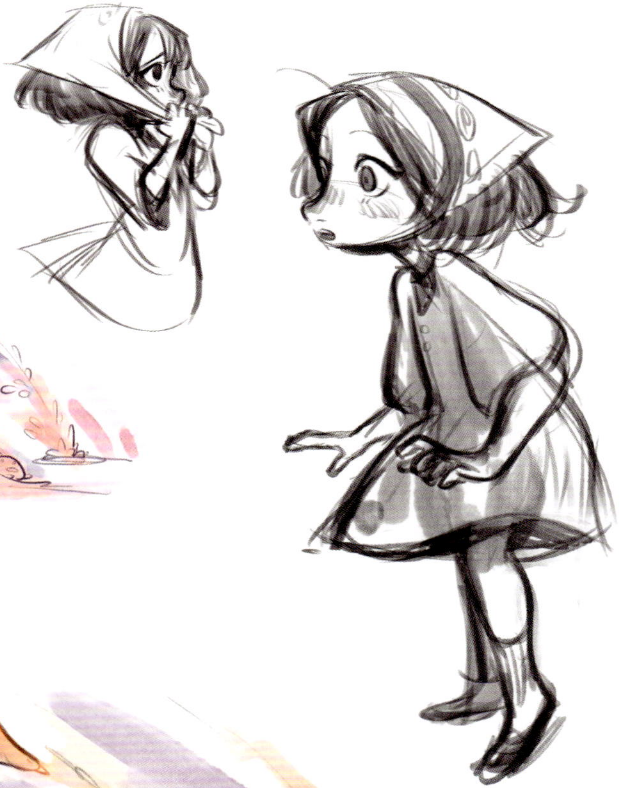

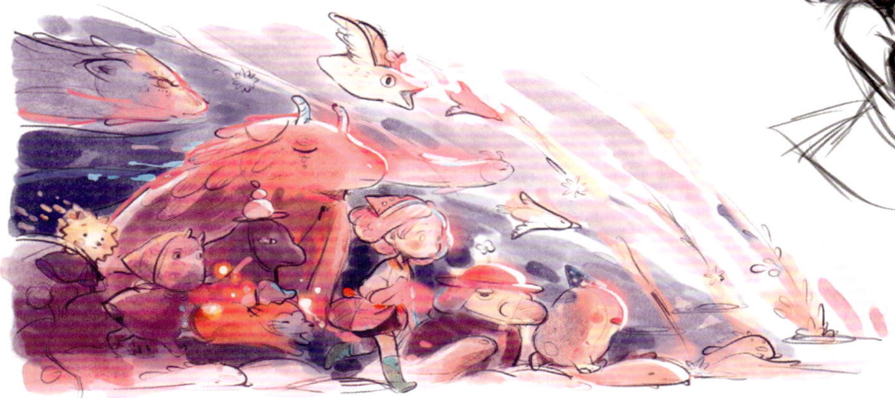

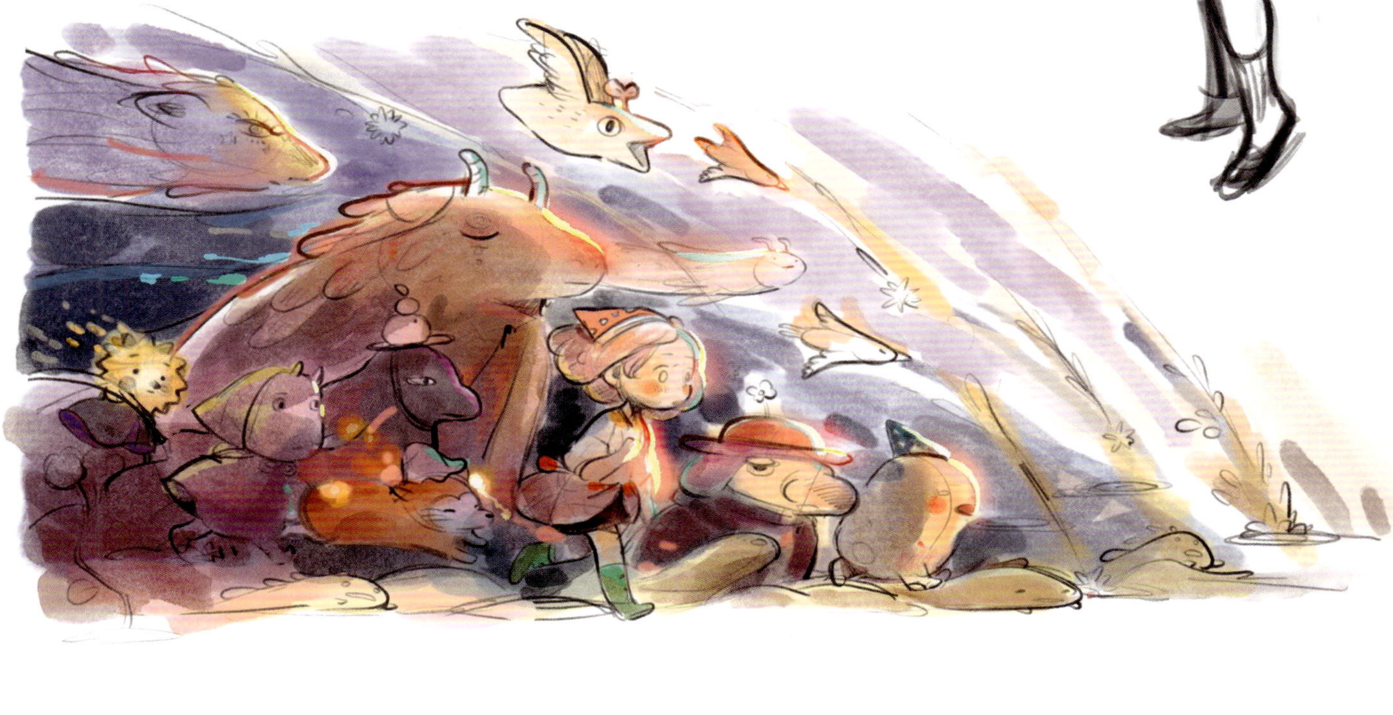

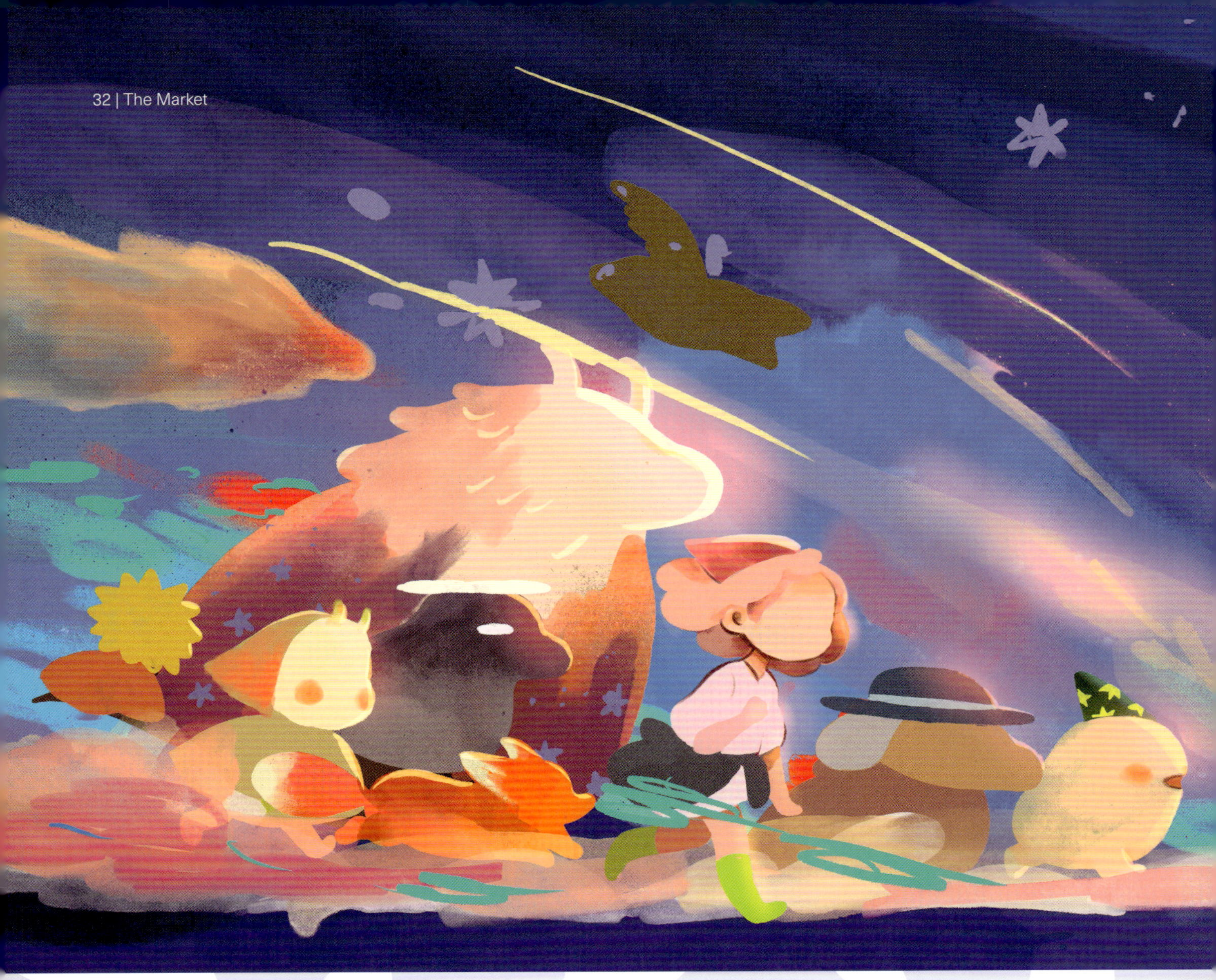

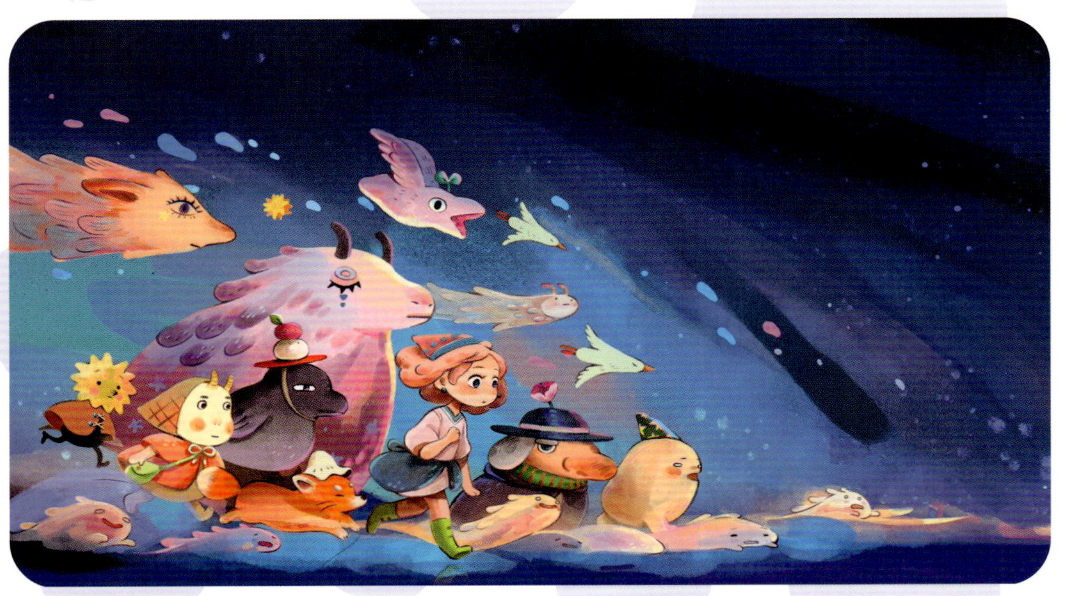

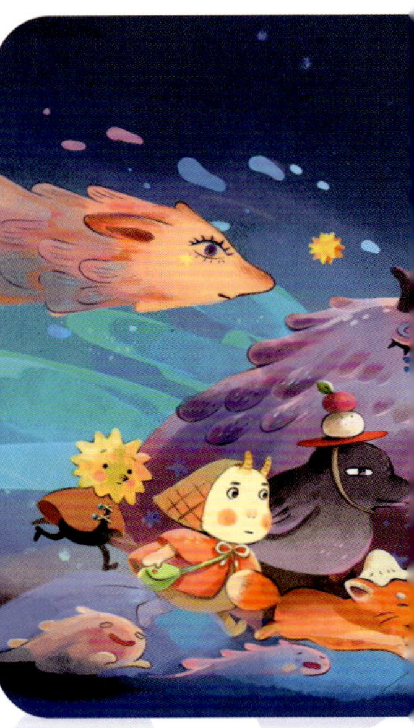

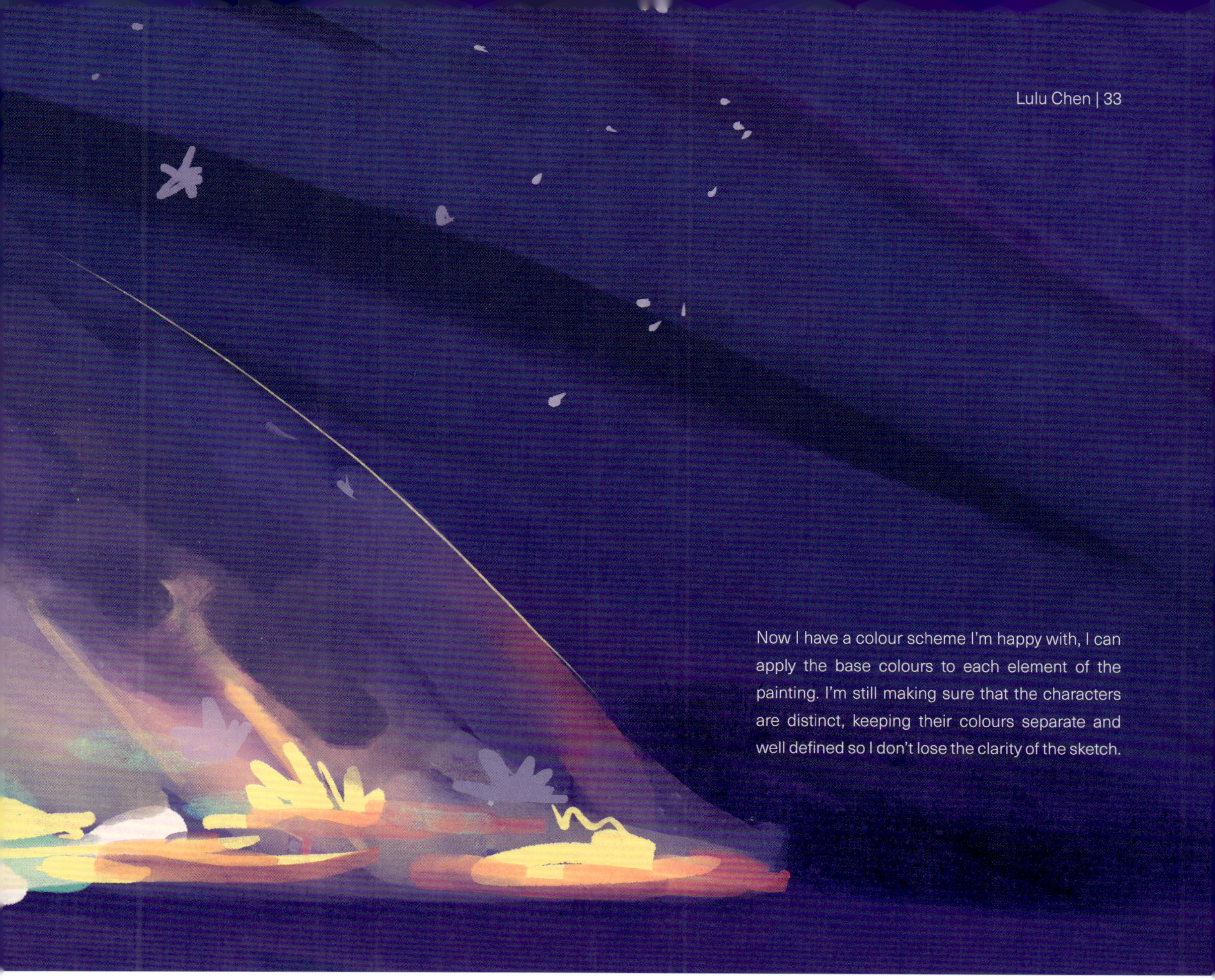

Now I have a colour scheme I'm happy with, I can apply the base colours to each element of the painting. I'm still making sure that the characters are distinct, keeping their colours separate and well defined so I don't lose the clarity of the sketch.

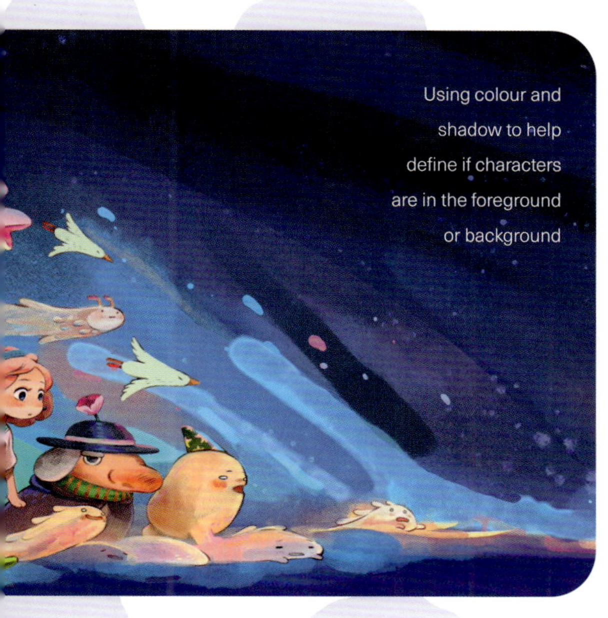

Next, I add depth to the design. Adding shadows to the background characters separates them from those in the foreground. I also try to use only cooler tones on the background characters and then add strong colours, like orange and red, to those in the foreground, like the little fox.

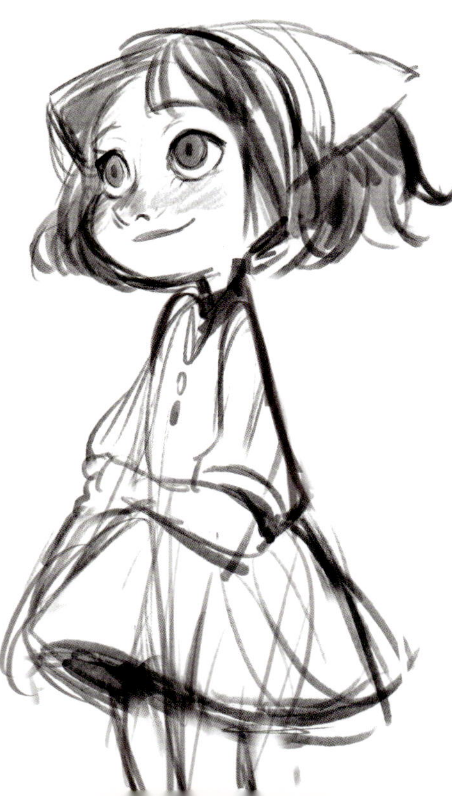

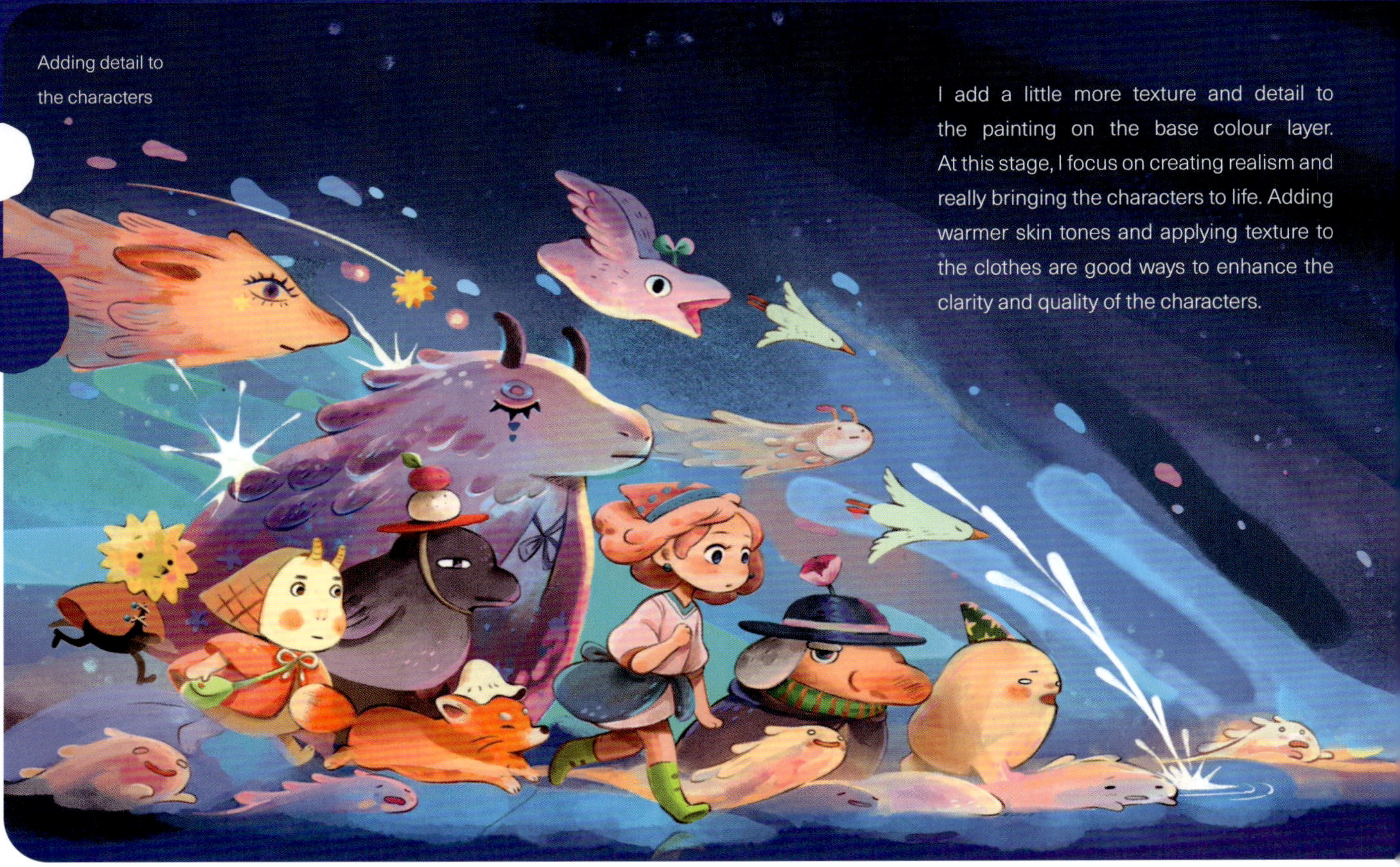

Adding detail to
the characters

I add a little more texture and detail to the painting on the base colour layer. At this stage, I focus on creating realism and really bringing the characters to life. Adding warmer skin tones and applying texture to the clothes are good ways to enhance the clarity and quality of the characters.

Next, I decide where in the image the main light source will be. Based on that, I apply another layer of shadows to every character. At this stage, I blend the characters with the background to make the whole scene more harmonious. I add the atmospheric light projecting from a shooting star and the bounce light, which is a complementary colour to the cool tones of the main light. I'm happy with the warm tones bouncing off the ground and onto the character's skin – it creates such a visually interesting colour combination.

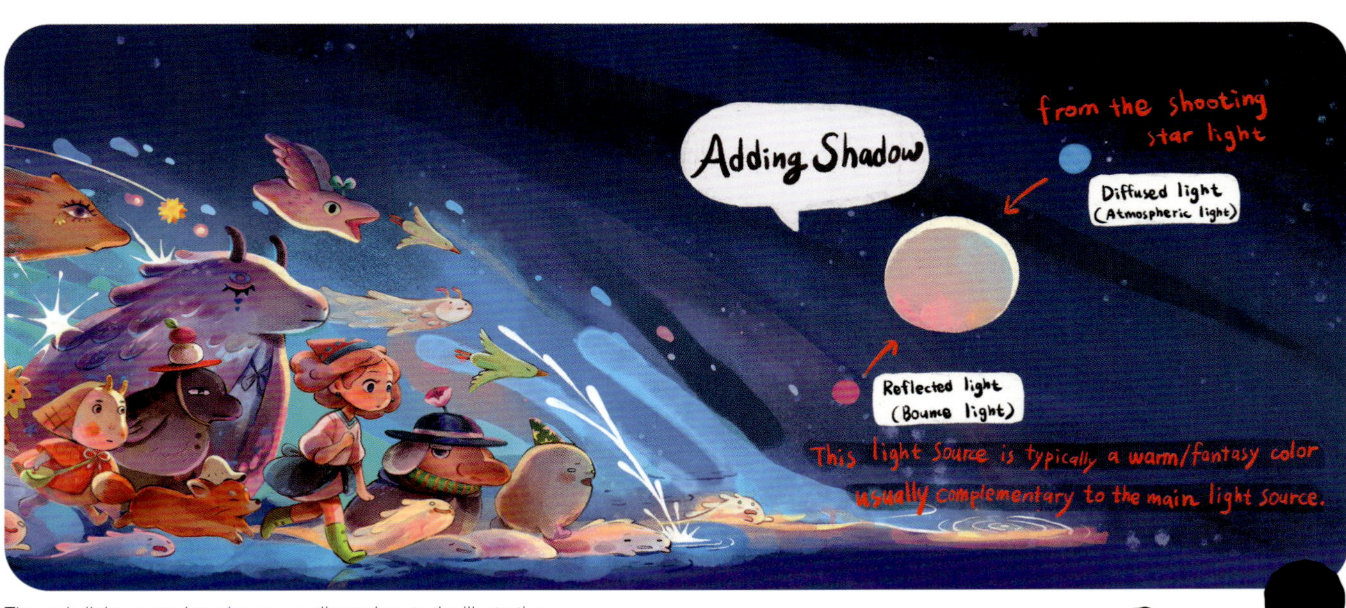

The main light source introduces new dimensions to the illustration

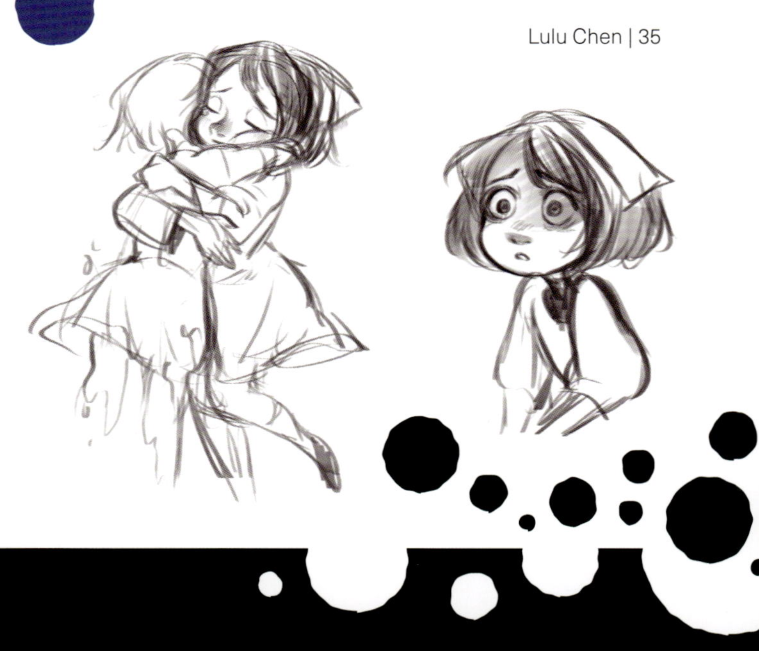

> **'ADDING WARMER SKIN TONES AND APPLYING TEXTURE TO THE CLOTHES ARE GOOD WAYS TO ENHANCE THE CLARITY AND QUALITY OF THE CHARACTERS'**

For the final touches, I play around with the balance of the painting. Since there are many characters in the scene and a lot happening in the background, I emphasize the contrast between each section, considering where I want the audience to look first, second, and so on. I enjoy playing around with how the different light sources bounce off one another. Because the background lighting is so fantastical and vibrant, it allows me to be creative with the light.

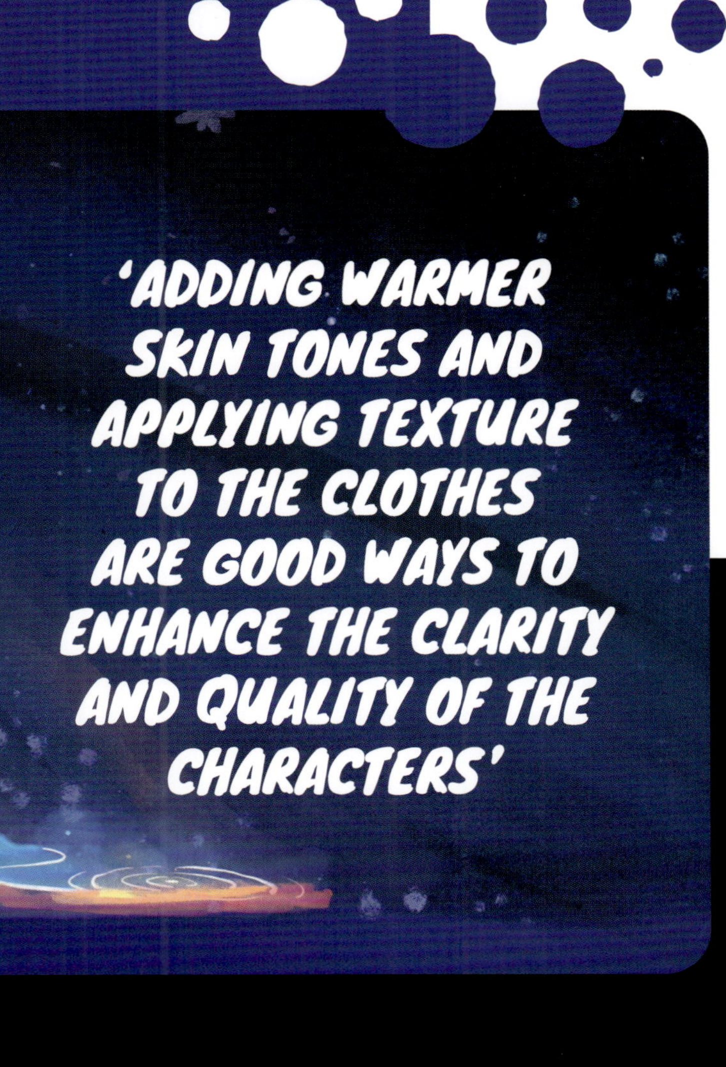

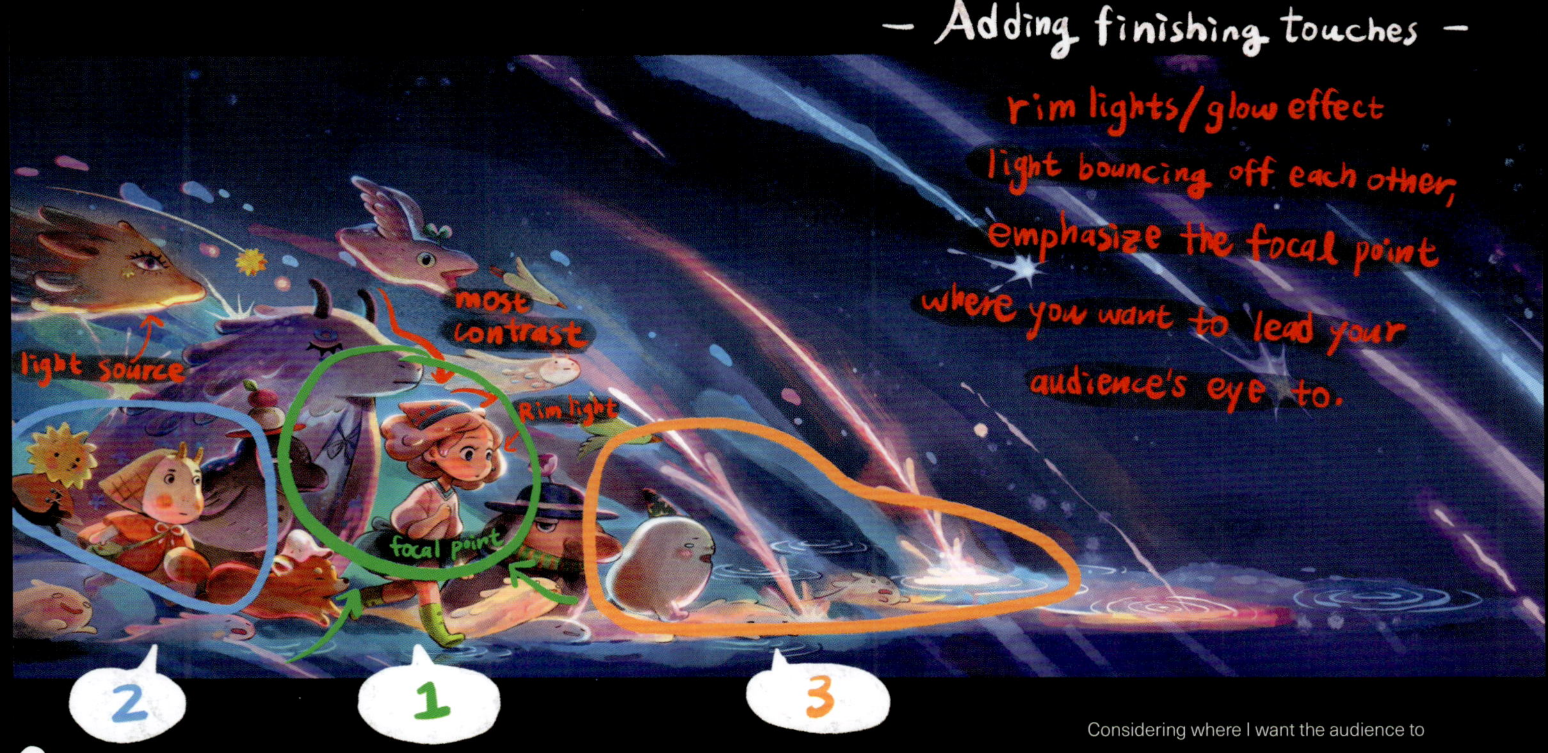

Considering where I want the audience to look first is a key part of the final design

Making this mixed-media film was honestly a dream come true, something I've imagined since I was a 'tiny potato', obsessing over Studio Ghibli films and soaking up inspiration during my time in the UK. I combined 2D and 3D techniques to create the hand-drawn, storybook vibe I've always loved while still enjoying the speed and flexibility of 3D. A big turning point for me was during my internship at Sony Pictures Imageworks, where I got to work on *Spider-Man: Across the Spider-Verse*. That's where I learned how to hand-paint 3D textures to look like 2D illustrations, and it completely changed the way I approached this film.

The process, though? Oh boy. Our professors told us not to bite off more than we could chew – no crowd shots, no running scenes, no films over a minute long. I broke every one of those 'rules'. I knew my story needed running sequences for the emotional weight to land and I wanted to fill the world with characters to make it feel alive. I won't lie, it was brutal at times (I once hand-painted six characters in one day), but I kept pushing because this story means so much to me. Tools like Blender, Toon Boom, and Procreate became my best friends, and I learned the hard way that having a well-planned project pipeline is the secret to surviving an ambitious film like this.

Final image © Lulu Chen

One of the absolute highlights of the process was asking Hayato Sumino (a famous Japanese pianist) if I could use his song 'Recollection' for the premiere – and he actually said yes! I literally screamed and cried in my bedroom when I got his reply. It still feels surreal. In the end, making this film in just one year was ridiculously hard, but I wouldn't change a thing. I got to tell a story that's so personal to me, and I hope it resonates with anyone who's ever struggled with childhood trauma, PTSD, or just needed a little extra magic in their life.

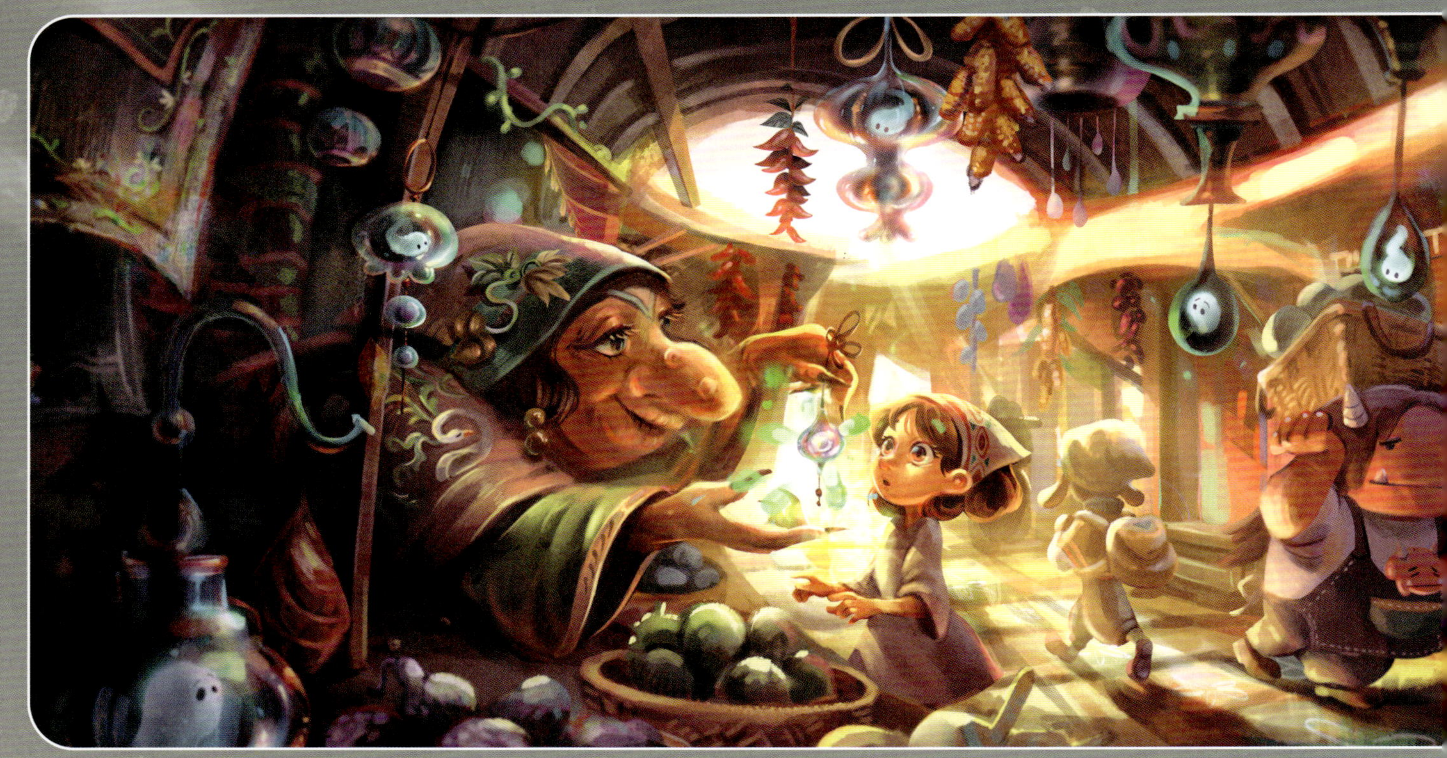

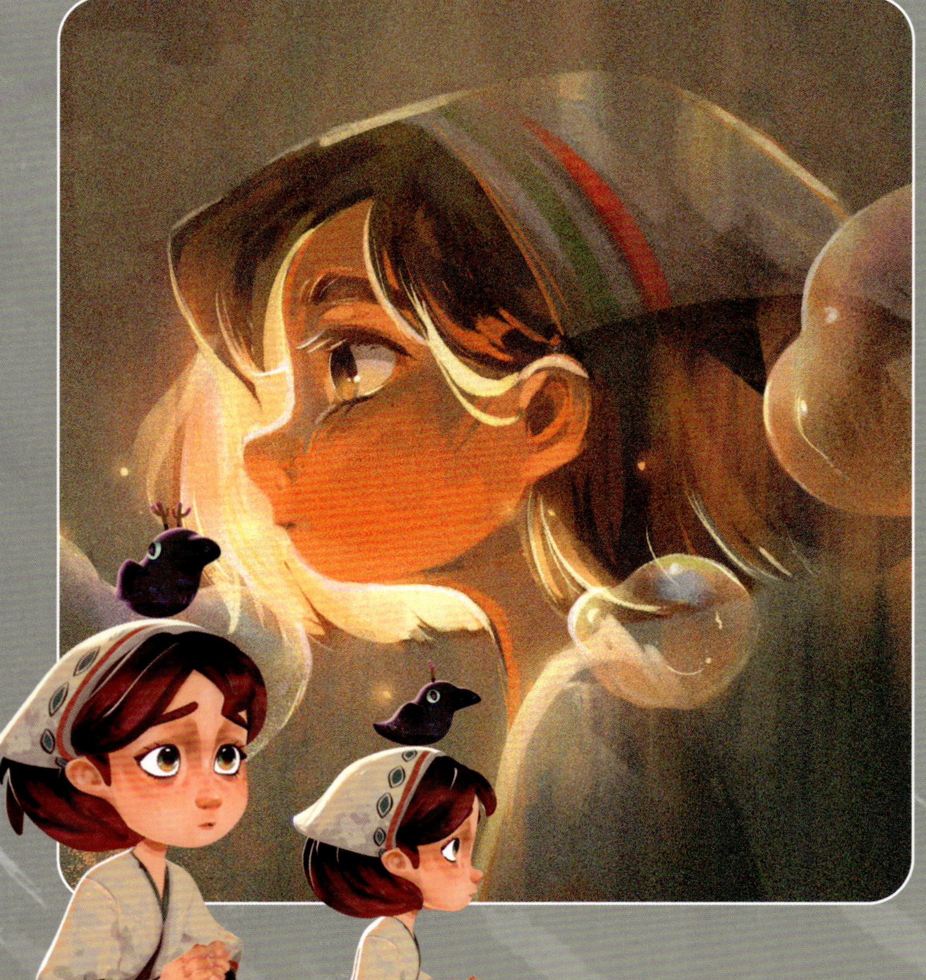

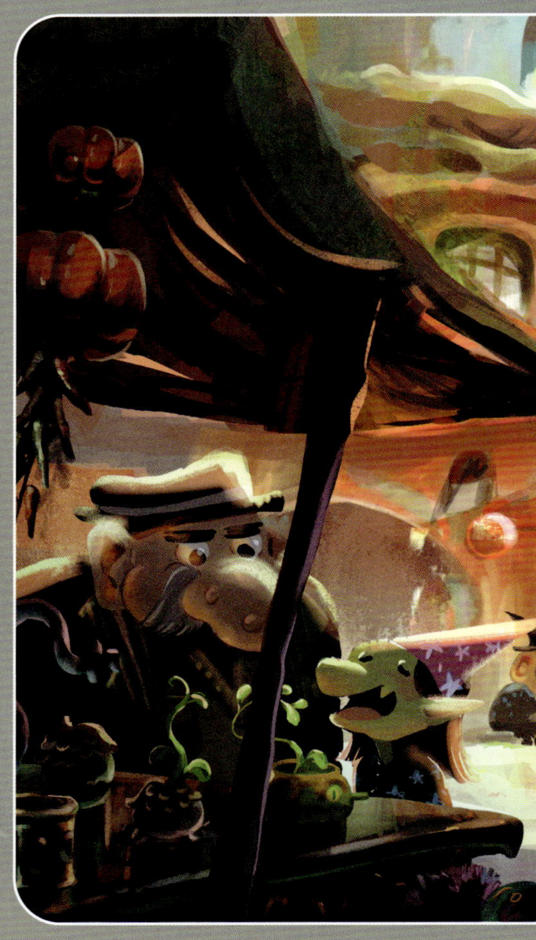

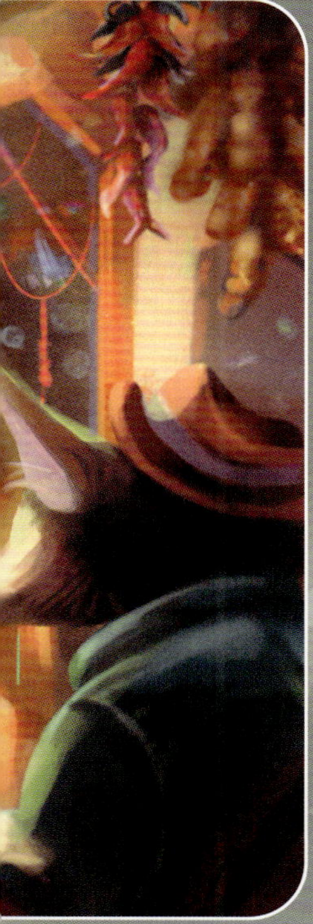

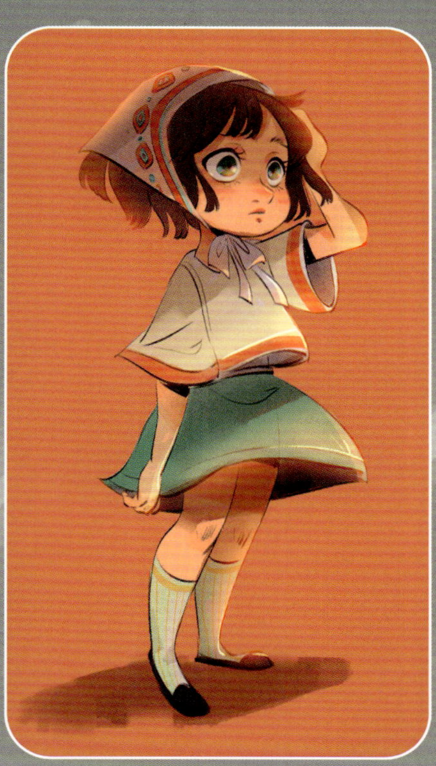

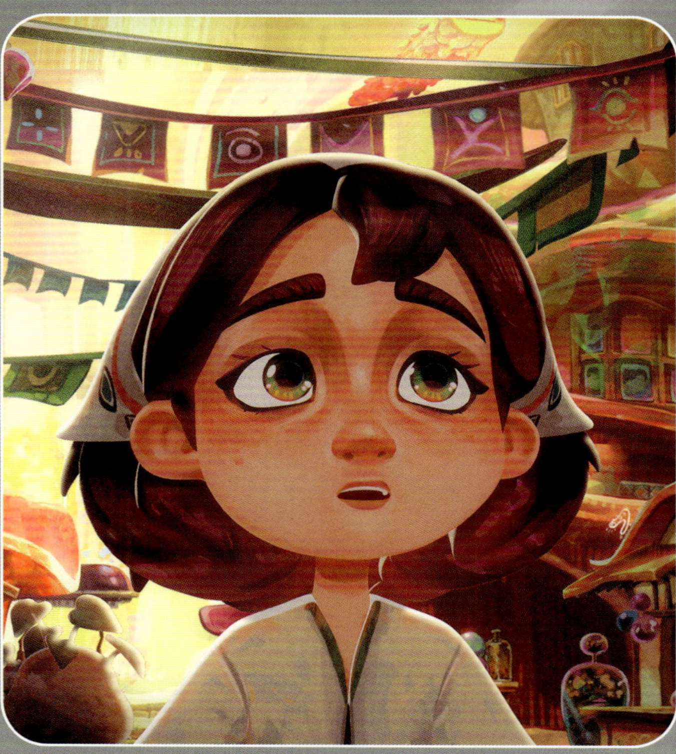

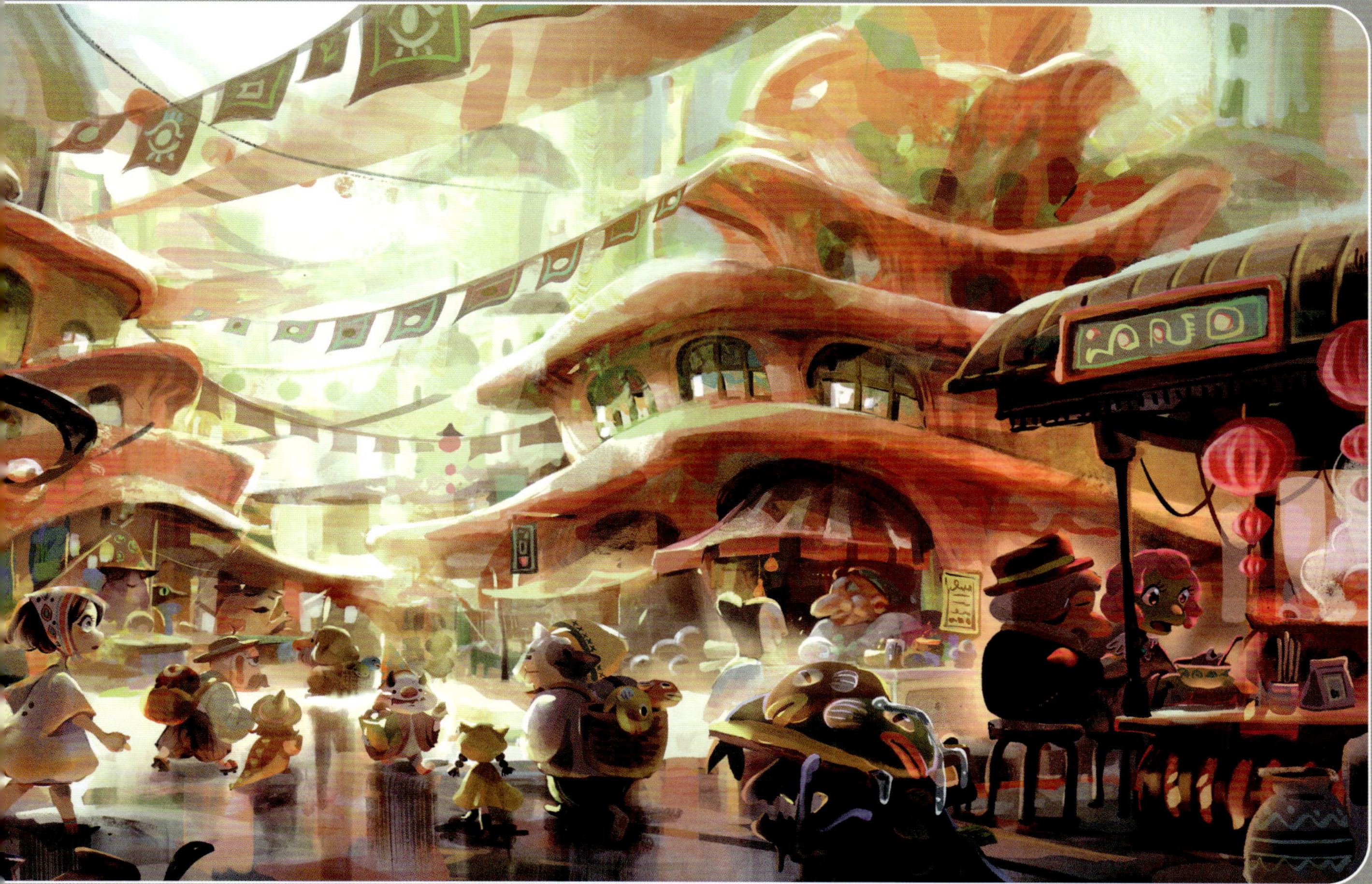

Various scenes and characters from *The Market*

WARRIOR PRINCESS

For this tutorial we will be creating a character design inspired by a historical figure, Saint Margaret of Antioch. I will use Procreate on an iPad throughout the process. I tend to always use a textured brush for drawing because I believe it leaves room for more creativity. When sketching out ideas, a general rule of thumb is the more textured the brush, the better. Using longer and more confident brush strokes when drawing adds charm and life to a design.

The character, a teenage Saint Margaret, is inspired by an historical religious figure, which means we have a lot of references available. I start my character exploration by drawing some sketches loosely based on these references. I focus on one sketch that shows her as a saintly princess and another that shows her as a warrior.

I sketch facial expressions to find the right personality for my character. I want to convey an elegant and poised expressiveness, with no contorting of her facial features that would be considered 'unladylike' or 'impolite'.

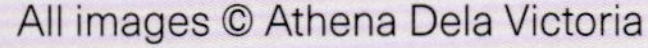

All images © Athena Dela Victoria

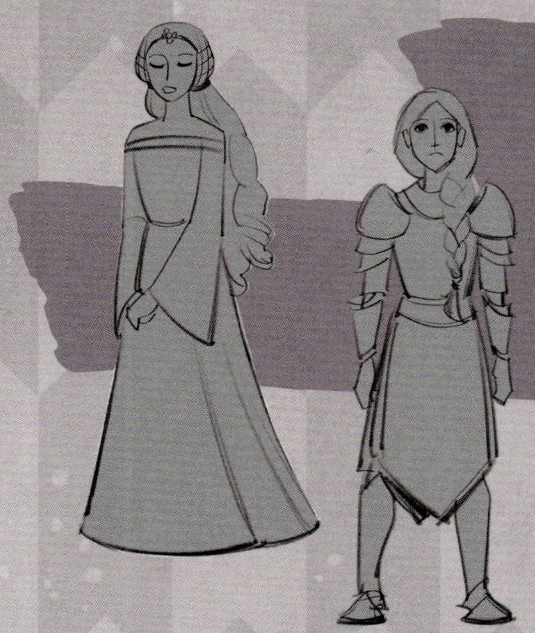

Next, I decide on the character's shape language. I experiment with different body structures, hairstyles, and clothing to create an interesting silhouette.

Clothing should also show the personality of the character. Saint Margaret wears four different crests to signify the different banners she represents. It's important to include contrasting colours as this will help the design read as more interesting.

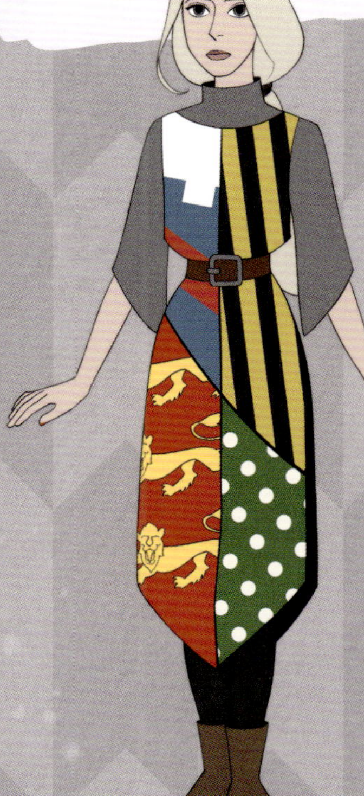

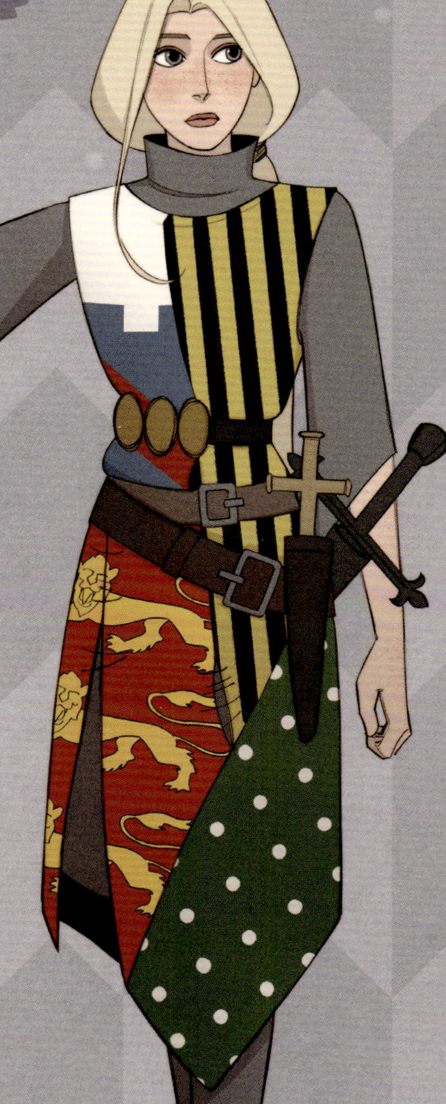

With the silhouette and clothing all set, I now move forward by making a few stylistic choices to further portray Margaret's motivations. A badly sewn surcoat and lopsided belts showcase her amateur skills and youth. A low ponytail balances the chaos of the clothing.

I like to end the process of designing a character by drawing a full-body model for reference, with the final choices on display. Saint Margaret's completed design is a battle-ready teenage girl who looks like she's barely still on commission as a knight.

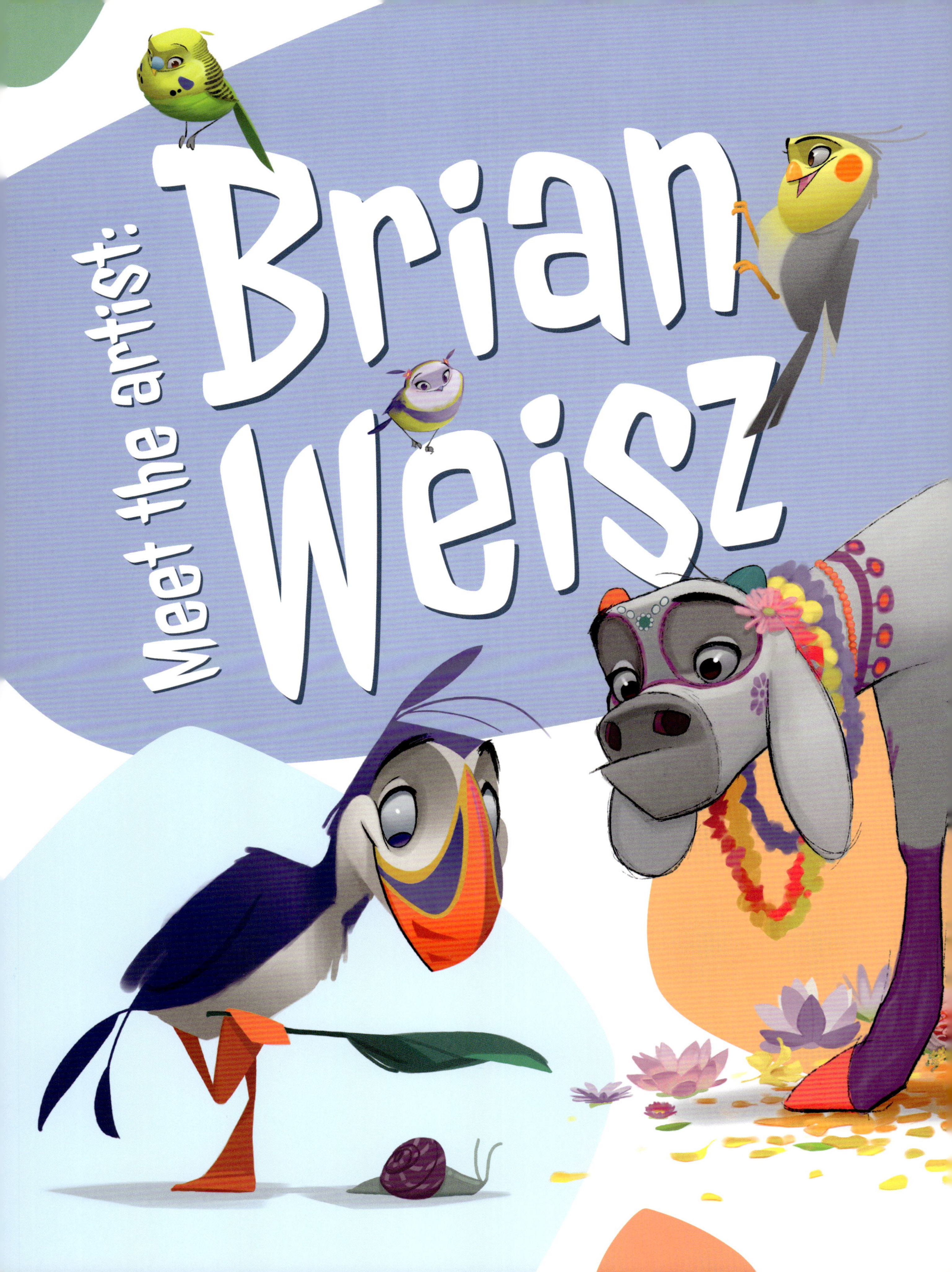

Meet the artist:
Brian Weisz

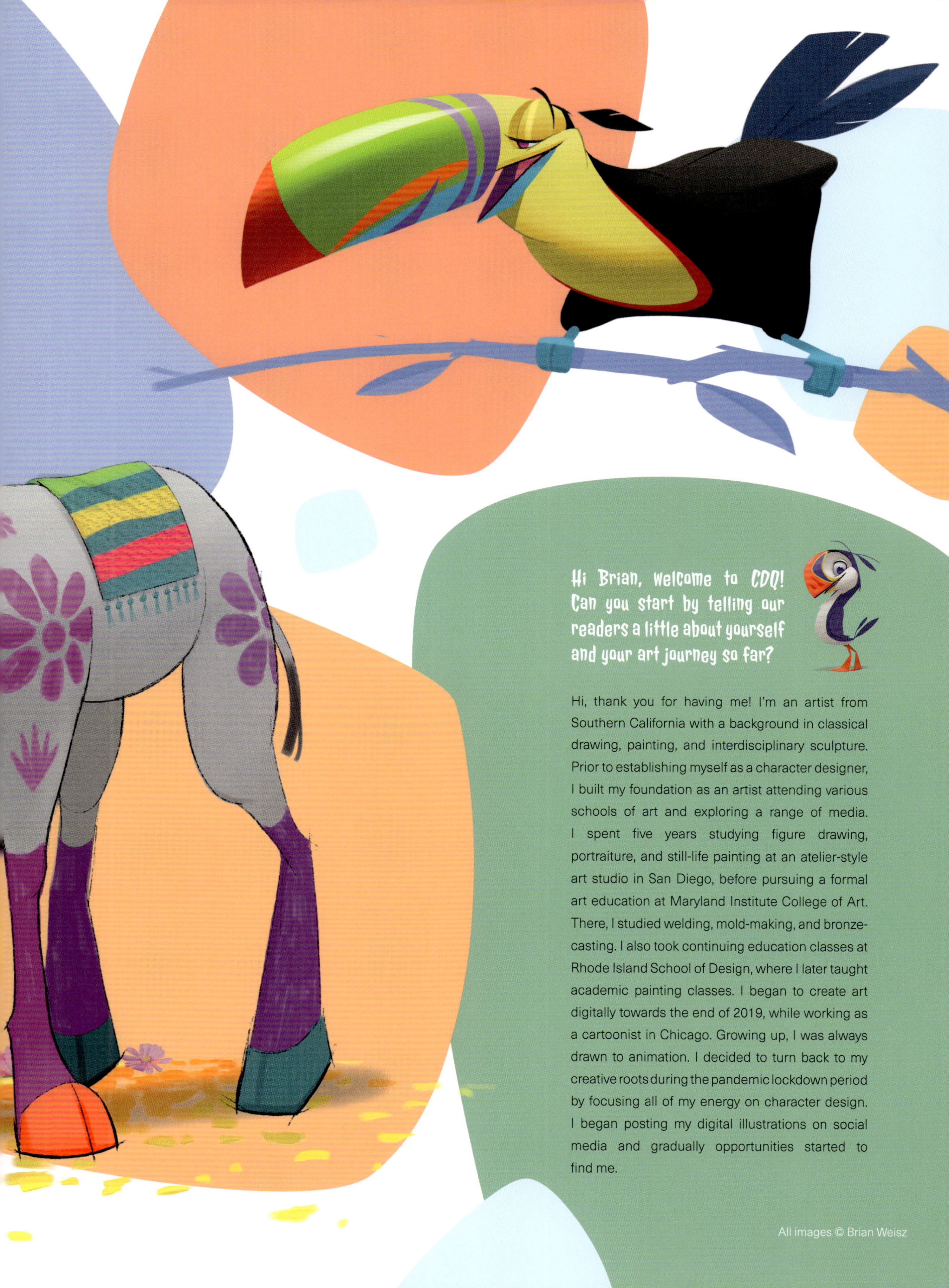

Hi, thank you for having me! I'm an artist from Southern California with a background in classical drawing, painting, and interdisciplinary sculpture. Prior to establishing myself as a character designer, I built my foundation as an artist attending various schools of art and exploring a range of media. I spent five years studying figure drawing, portraiture, and still-life painting at an atelier-style art studio in San Diego, before pursuing a formal art education at Maryland Institute College of Art. There, I studied welding, mold-making, and bronze-casting. I also took continuing education classes at Rhode Island School of Design, where I later taught academic painting classes. I began to create art digitally towards the end of 2019, while working as a cartoonist in Chicago. Growing up, I was always drawn to animation. I decided to turn back to my creative roots during the pandemic lockdown period by focusing all of my energy on character design. I began posting my digital illustrations on social media and gradually opportunities started to find me.

All images © Brian Weisz

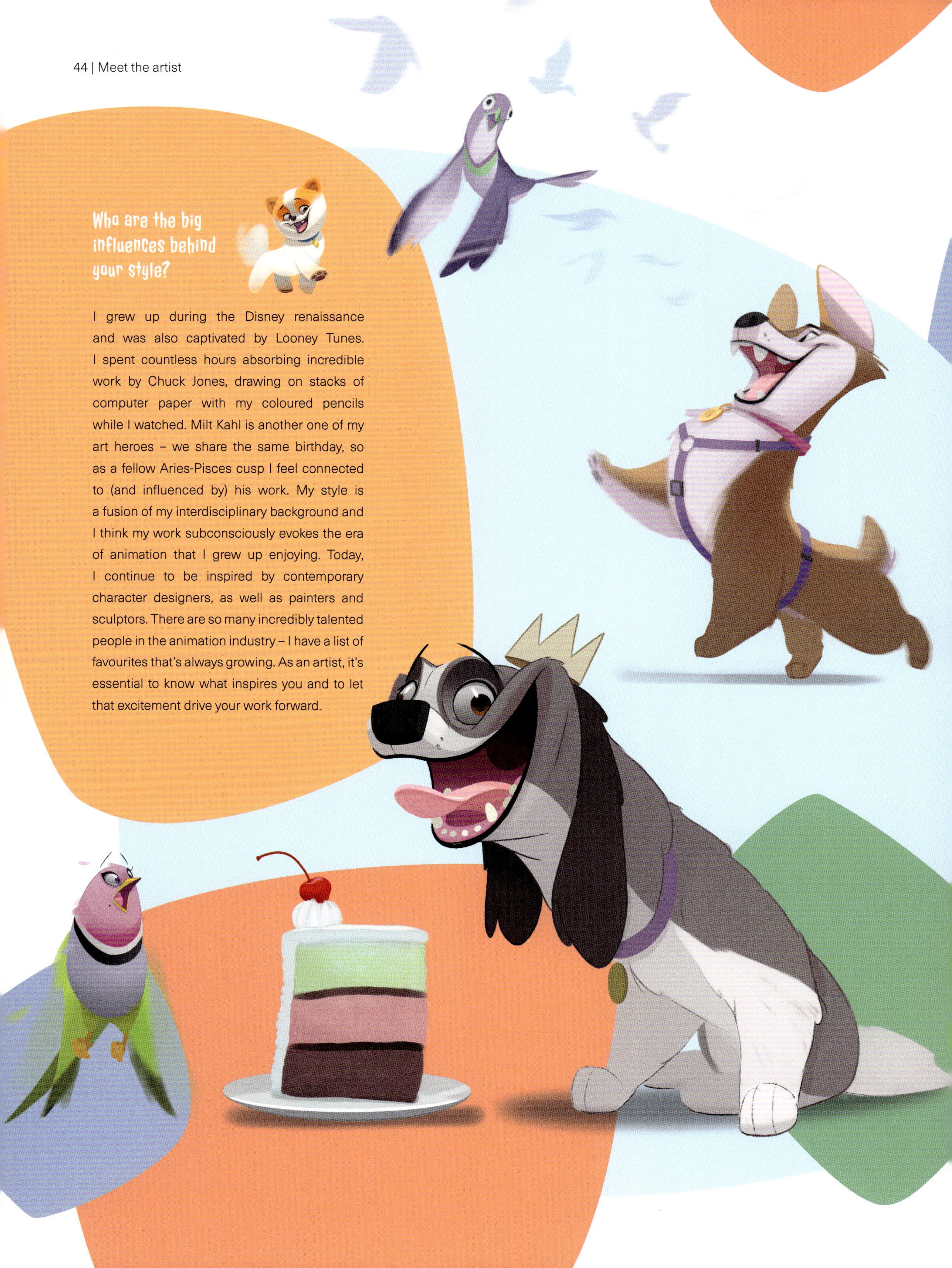

Who are the big influences behind your style?

I grew up during the Disney renaissance and was also captivated by Looney Tunes. I spent countless hours absorbing incredible work by Chuck Jones, drawing on stacks of computer paper with my coloured pencils while I watched. Milt Kahl is another one of my art heroes – we share the same birthday, so as a fellow Aries-Pisces cusp I feel connected to (and influenced by) his work. My style is a fusion of my interdisciplinary background and I think my work subconsciously evokes the era of animation that I grew up enjoying. Today, I continue to be inspired by contemporary character designers, as well as painters and sculptors. There are so many incredibly talented people in the animation industry – I have a list of favourites that's always growing. As an artist, it's essential to know what inspires you and to let that excitement drive your work forward.

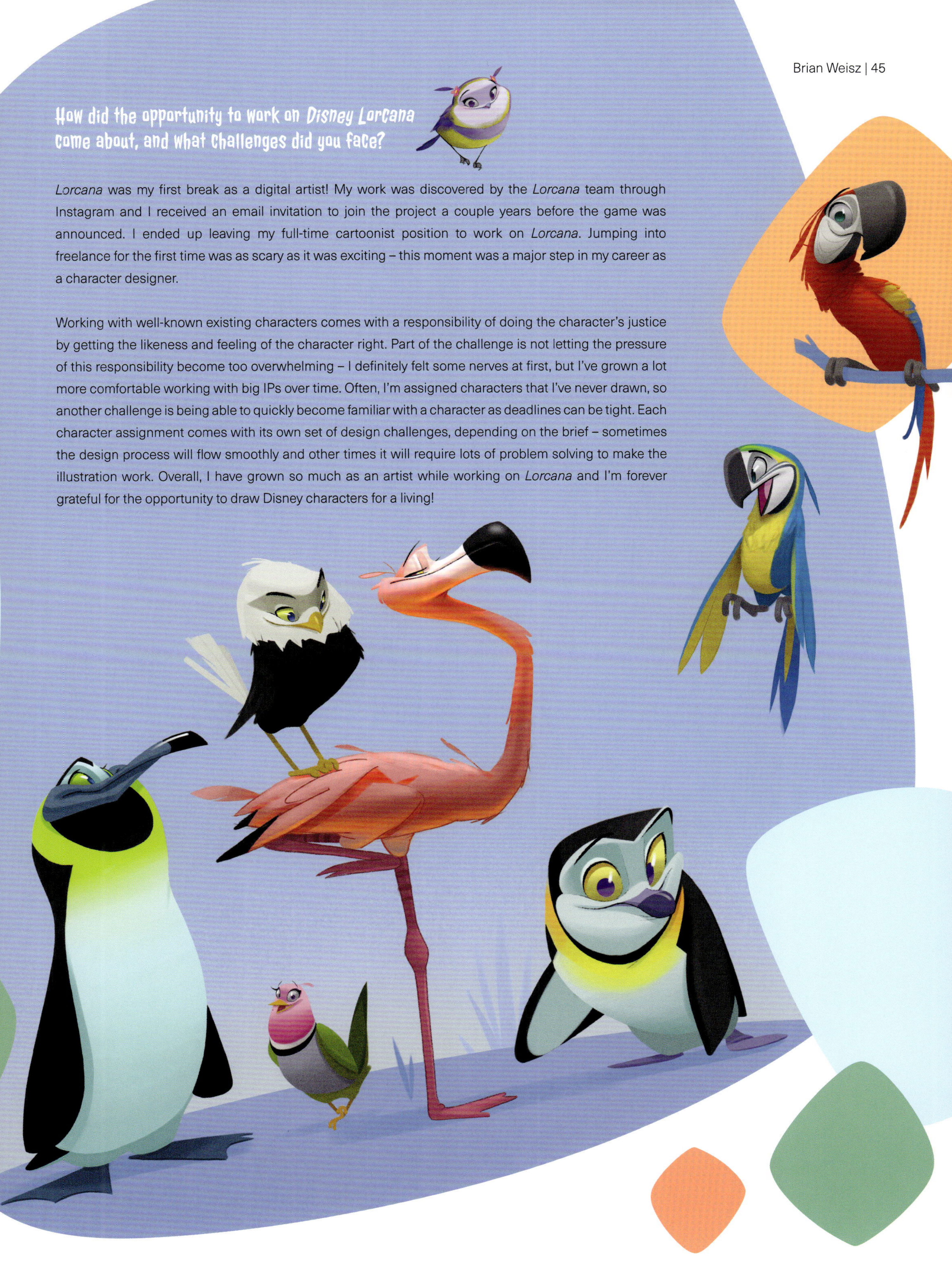

How did the opportunity to work on *Disney Lorcana* come about, and what challenges did you face?

Lorcana was my first break as a digital artist! My work was discovered by the *Lorcana* team through Instagram and I received an email invitation to join the project a couple years before the game was announced. I ended up leaving my full-time cartoonist position to work on *Lorcana*. Jumping into freelance for the first time was as scary as it was exciting – this moment was a major step in my career as a character designer.

Working with well-known existing characters comes with a responsibility of doing the character's justice by getting the likeness and feeling of the character right. Part of the challenge is not letting the pressure of this responsibility become too overwhelming – I definitely felt some nerves at first, but I've grown a lot more comfortable working with big IPs over time. Often, I'm assigned characters that I've never drawn, so another challenge is being able to quickly become familiar with a character as deadlines can be tight. Each character assignment comes with its own set of design challenges, depending on the brief – sometimes the design process will flow smoothly and other times it will require lots of problem solving to make the illustration work. Overall, I have grown so much as an artist while working on *Lorcana* and I'm forever grateful for the opportunity to draw Disney characters for a living!

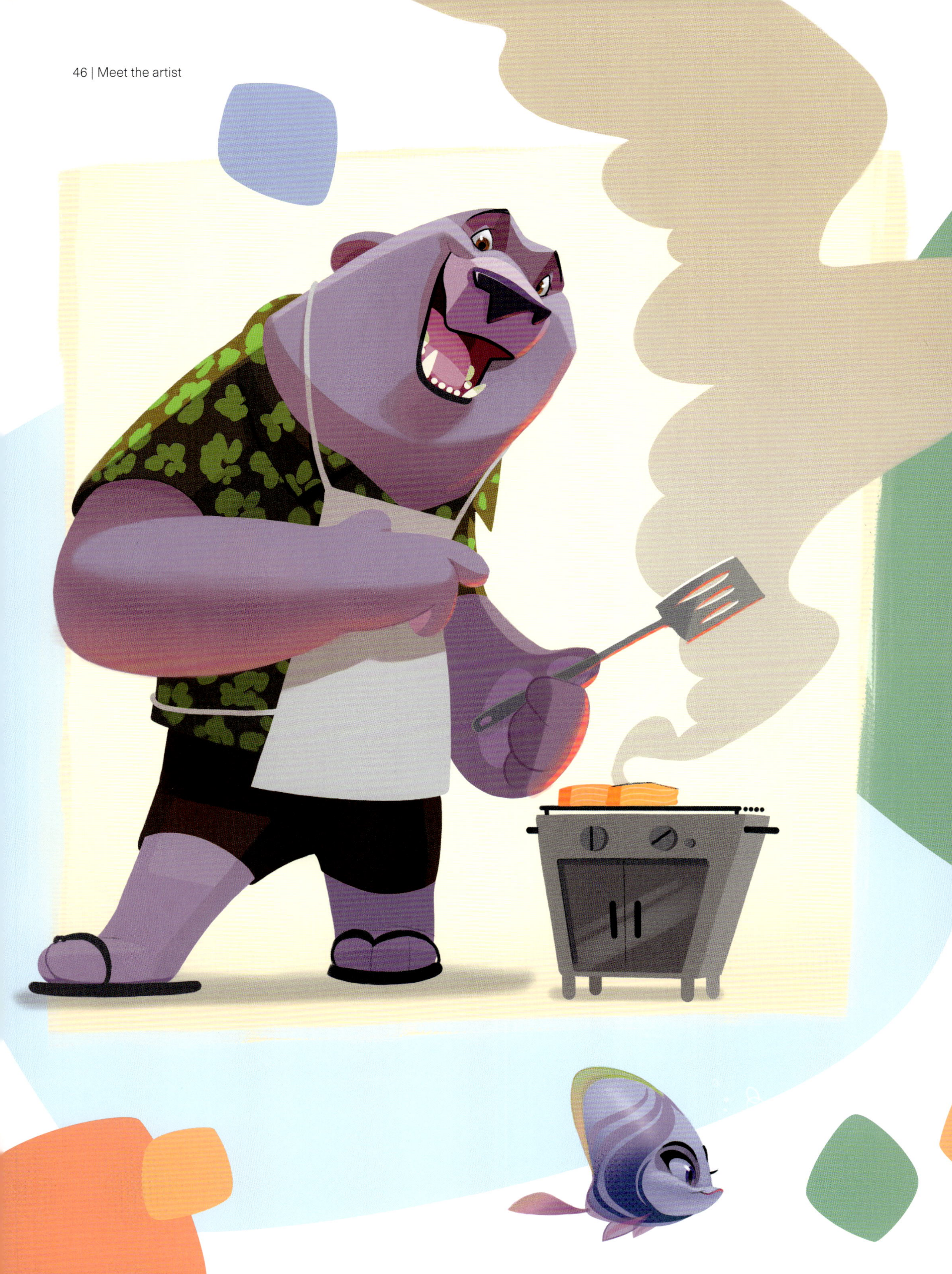

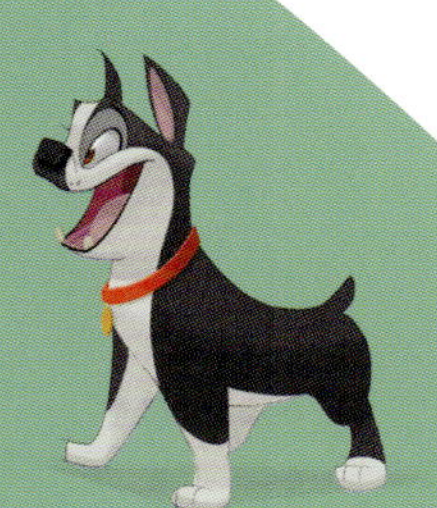

Both types of work have their own set of guidelines, challenges, and expectations. Creating characters for animation is similar to concept work, whereas *Lorcana* and similar projects are more like illustration assignments. Developing characters from scratch allows artists to have more overall creative freedom to search and discover the physical look and feel that embodies a new character or line up. This process involves more character exploration and risk taking which is a lot of fun! In this type of work, it's best to produce as many ideas as possible, as the majority of the drawings will more than likely be thrown out or simply not used. As a result, sketching quickly is the most efficient way to work in this setting. It's better to have lots of loose character sketch ideas, rather than presenting fewer tighter drawings for the creative team to choose from.

Having said that, there is still a fair amount of room to explore design possibilities with *Lorcana* and similar projects, as artists are tasked with developing fully realized compositions with backgrounds that result in full-colour illustrations.

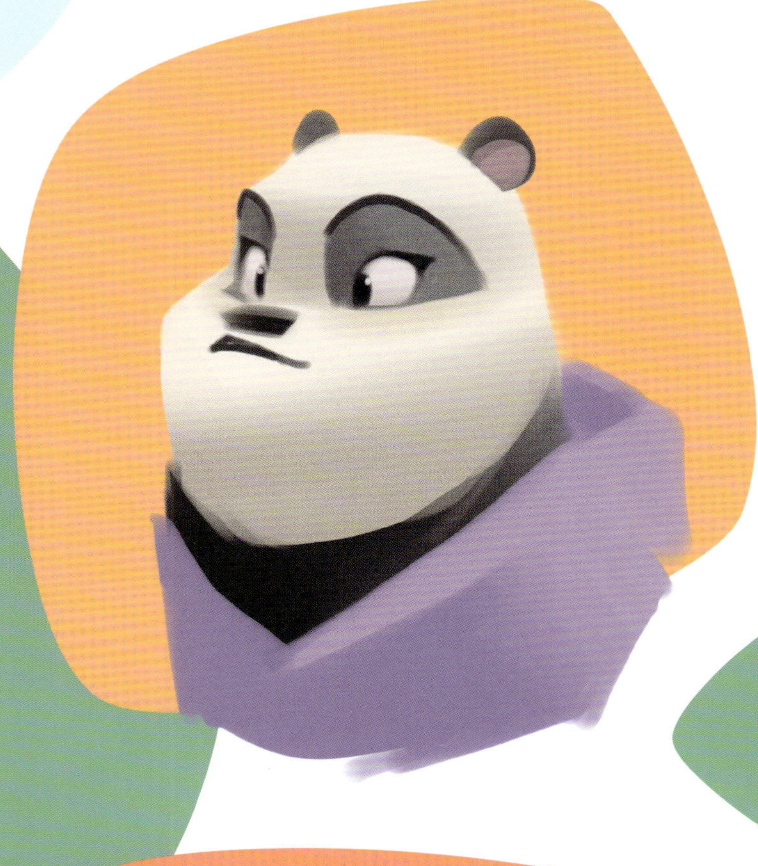

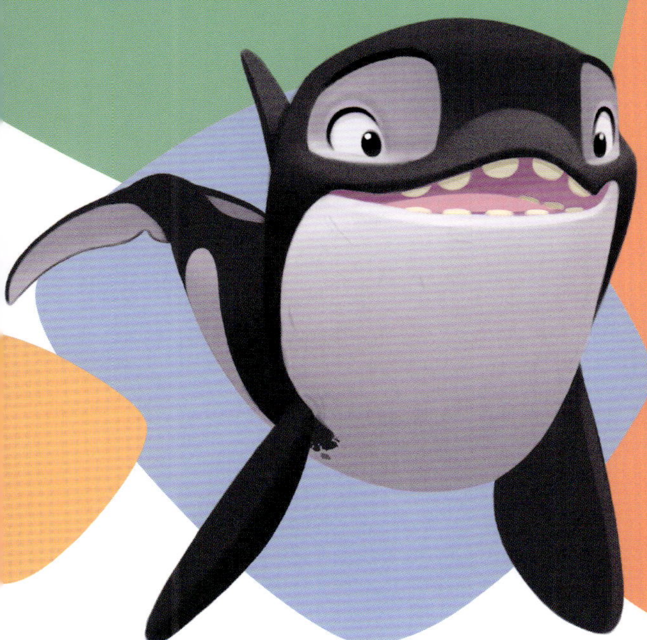

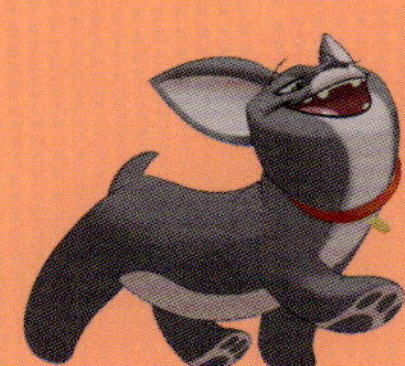

For years I studied portrait painting and found that I really enjoyed capturing the intricacies of facial expressions, drawing the audience in with their warmth. Facial structure and organization are what will make a character's face look uncluttered – the emotions and expressions are supported by the base structure of the design. I've always enjoyed drawing characters with big emotions. I tend to draw characters that are smiling because the act of drawing makes me happy. As a kid I would draw characters with gigantic smiles that would spread from ear to ear, so even then I was drawing bold expressions, even if they were kind of grotesque and strange looking. I like to place emphasis on the eyes – after all, they are the windows to the soul. Another great way to convey emotions in character design is to think about using empathy as a drawing tool. If you are able to briefly live in the mind of your characters while you are drawing them you will be able to better convey their emotional state.

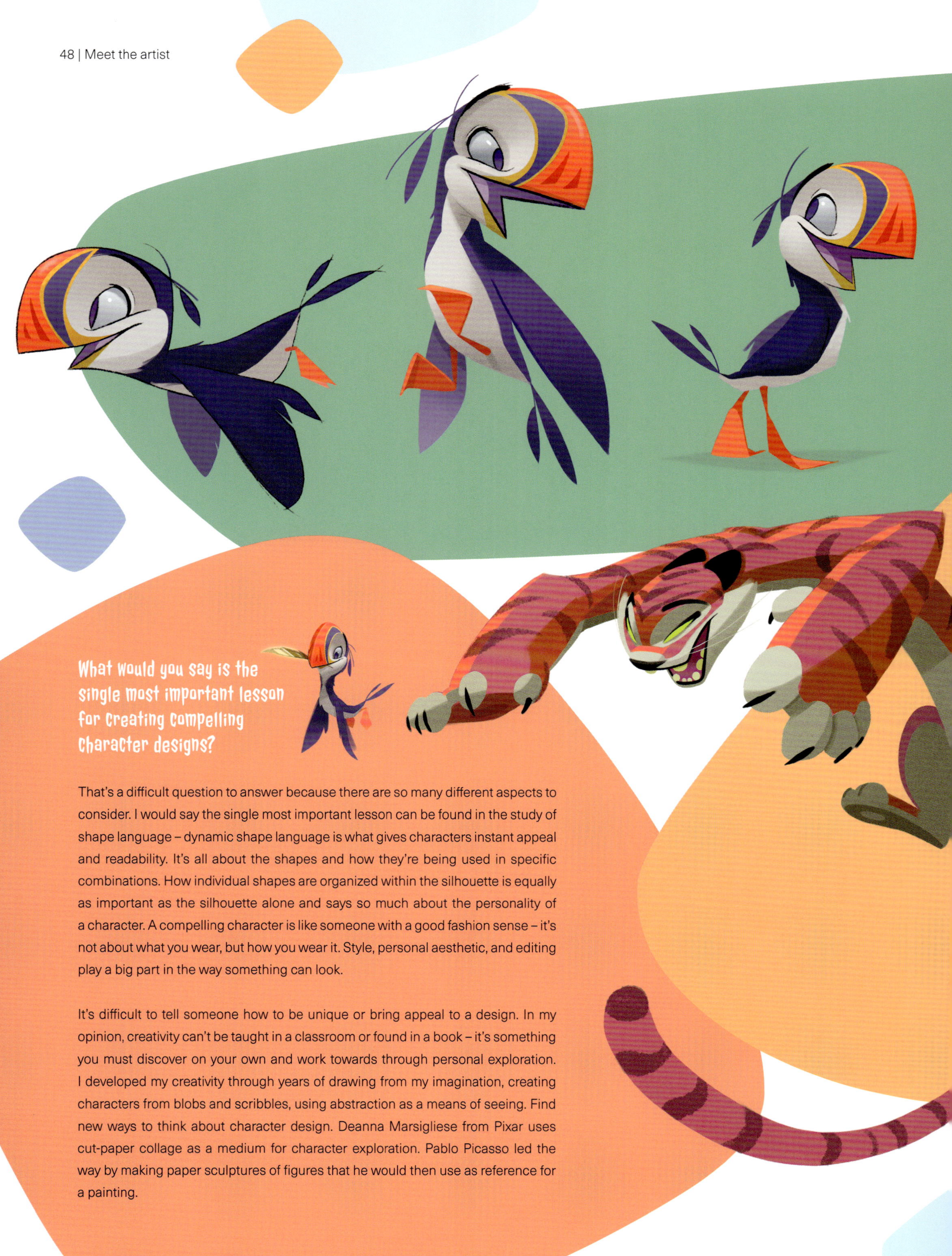

That's a difficult question to answer because there are so many different aspects to consider. I would say the single most important lesson can be found in the study of shape language – dynamic shape language is what gives characters instant appeal and readability. It's all about the shapes and how they're being used in specific combinations. How individual shapes are organized within the silhouette is equally as important as the silhouette alone and says so much about the personality of a character. A compelling character is like someone with a good fashion sense – it's not about what you wear, but how you wear it. Style, personal aesthetic, and editing play a big part in the way something can look.

It's difficult to tell someone how to be unique or bring appeal to a design. In my opinion, creativity can't be taught in a classroom or found in a book – it's something you must discover on your own and work towards through personal exploration. I developed my creativity through years of drawing from my imagination, creating characters from blobs and scribbles, using abstraction as a means of seeing. Find new ways to think about character design. Deanna Marsigliese from Pixar uses cut-paper collage as a medium for character exploration. Pablo Picasso led the way by making paper sculptures of figures that he would then use as reference for a painting.

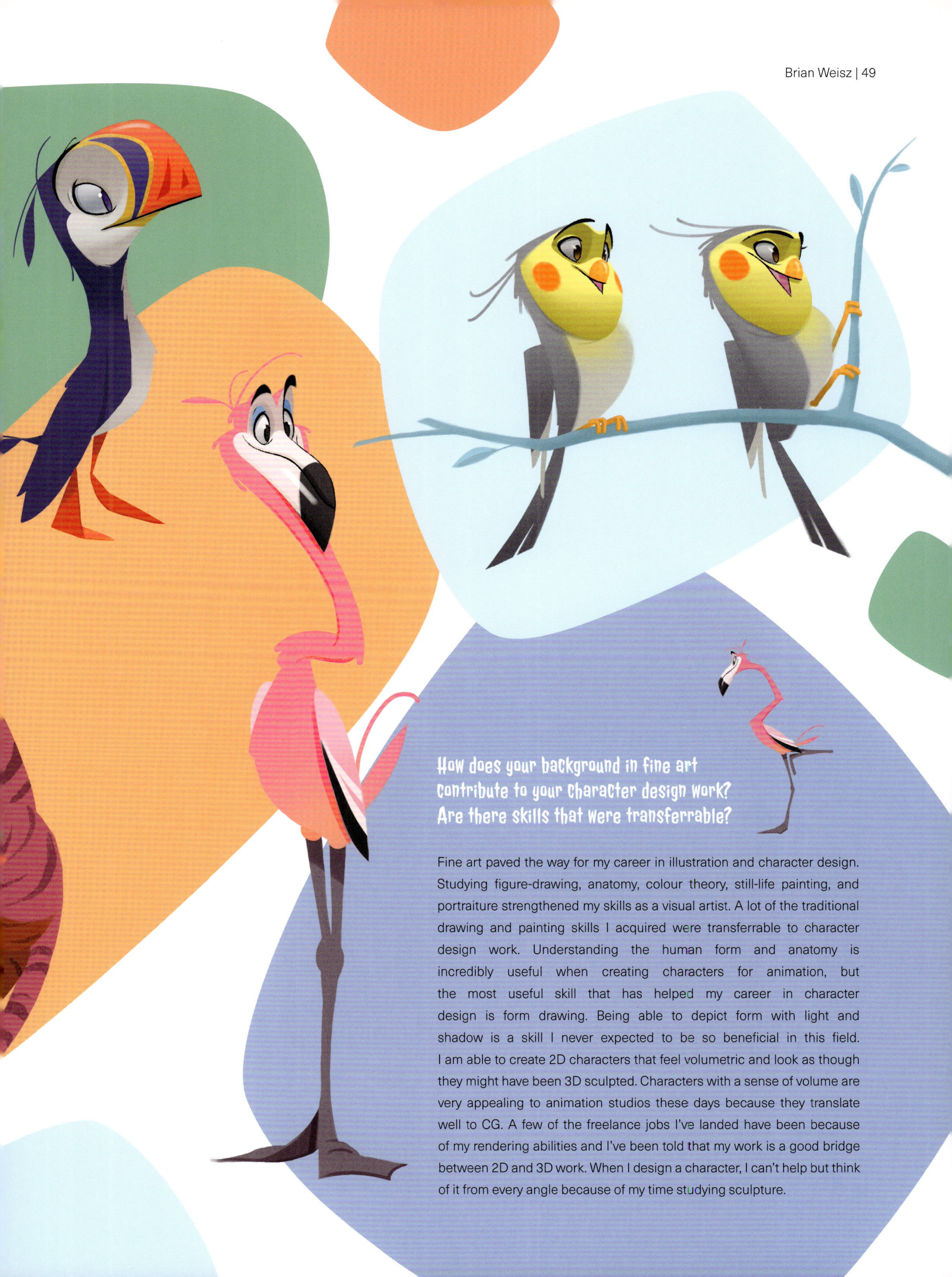

How does your background in fine art contribute to your character design work? Are there skills that were transferrable?

Fine art paved the way for my career in illustration and character design. Studying figure-drawing, anatomy, colour theory, still-life painting, and portraiture strengthened my skills as a visual artist. A lot of the traditional drawing and painting skills I acquired were transferrable to character design work. Understanding the human form and anatomy is incredibly useful when creating characters for animation, but the most useful skill that has helped my career in character design is form drawing. Being able to depict form with light and shadow is a skill I never expected to be so beneficial in this field. I am able to create 2D characters that feel volumetric and look as though they might have been 3D sculpted. Characters with a sense of volume are very appealing to animation studios these days because they translate well to CG. A few of the freelance jobs I've landed have been because of my rendering abilities and I've been told that my work is a good bridge between 2D and 3D work. When I design a character, I can't help but think of it from every angle because of my time studying sculpture.

Is there a dream project you'd like to work on?

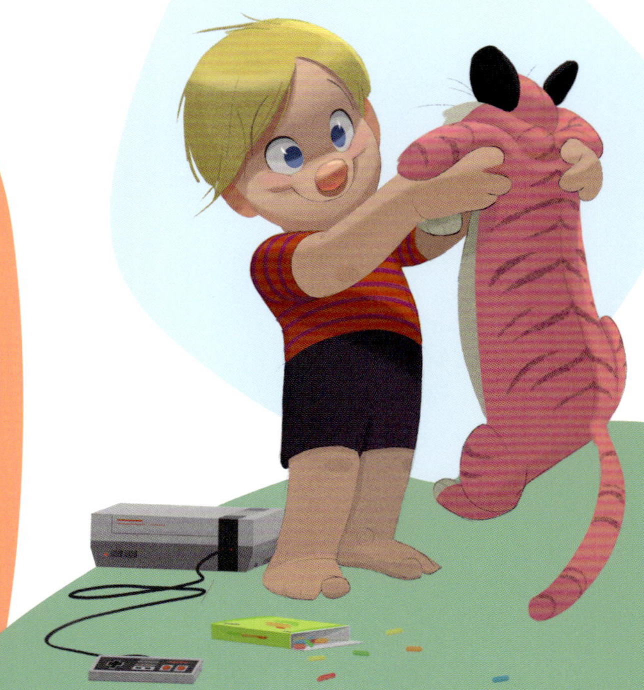

A dream project for me would be getting the opportunity to work on a feature film with a major animation company. I would love to get the experience of working in a studio someday. I want to be surrounded by other creative people in the industry and learn from their experience in person. Don't get me wrong, working from home as a freelance illustrator isn't too bad, but one thing I took away from art school is how important being surrounded by creative people can be for learning. I gained just as much from my peers as I did from the art professors leading the classes. Starting characters from scratch with a team to eventually see them on the big screen would be a dream come true for me.

Do you have any advice for reader's looking to make it in the industry?

You have to be passionate about learning. Understand that progress will happen in small steps over time – practising every day can be the most impactful thing for your career if you choose to commit yourself. Build on your strengths but also make time to study the areas that might be a gap in your skillset. Aside from drawing there are many things you can do to develop professional practices and take steps toward your career goals. First and foremost, you must promote your artwork online. Consider yourself your own marketing manager – if you don't put your artwork out into the world, no one is going to see it. Be professional and pleasant online and start building friendships and a network within the industry. Make sure you have an up-to-date resume and an online portfolio of your best work. If you haven't already, I would recommend creating a profile on LinkedIn. This platform is more of a professional space to display your experiences, resume, and a link to your portfolio website, and there are lots of job opportunities and industry professionals on there. I try to only post my best work on LinkedIn and like to create posts sharing milestone artistic achievements. For example, I was asked to collaborate on a storybook called *The Troll & The Puffin* with a group of talented artists in the industry that I look up to. This was a meaningful experience to me and a big step in my career as a character designer. I made a post on LinkedIn sharing my experience and work on the project and it seemed to generate a lot of interest and positive engagement. So, in a nutshell, on top of making stellar artwork, make sure you represent yourself online in a professional manner.

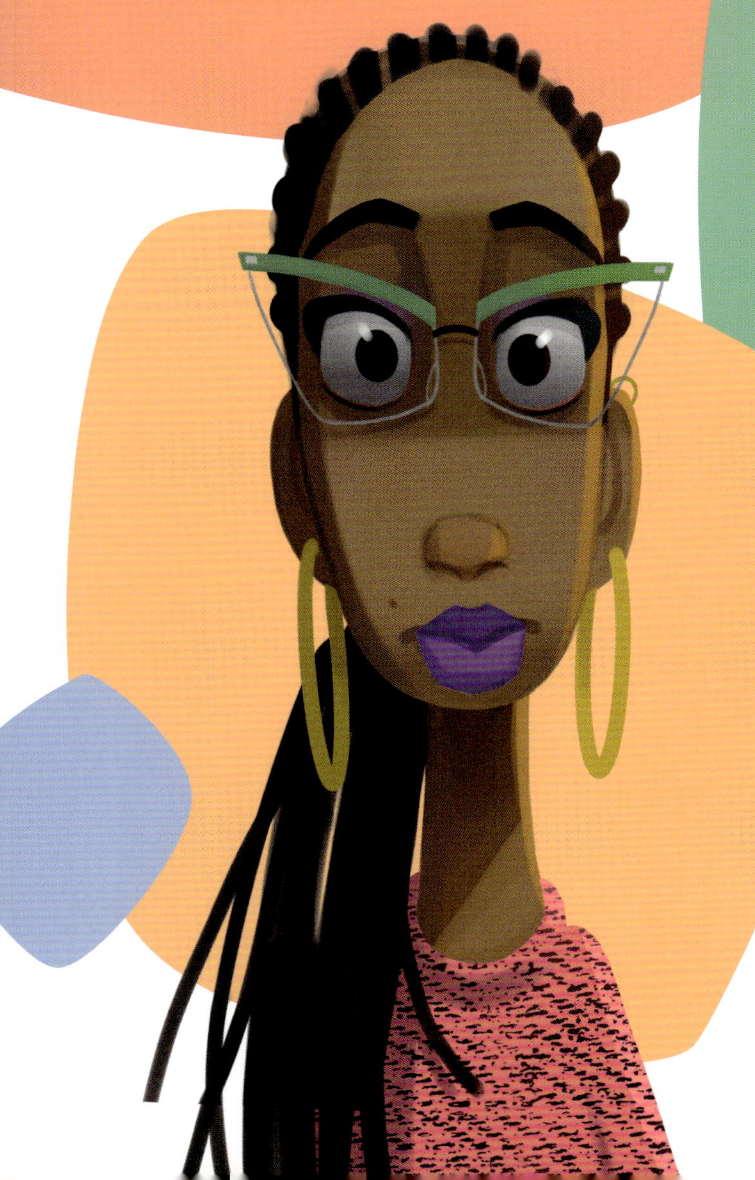

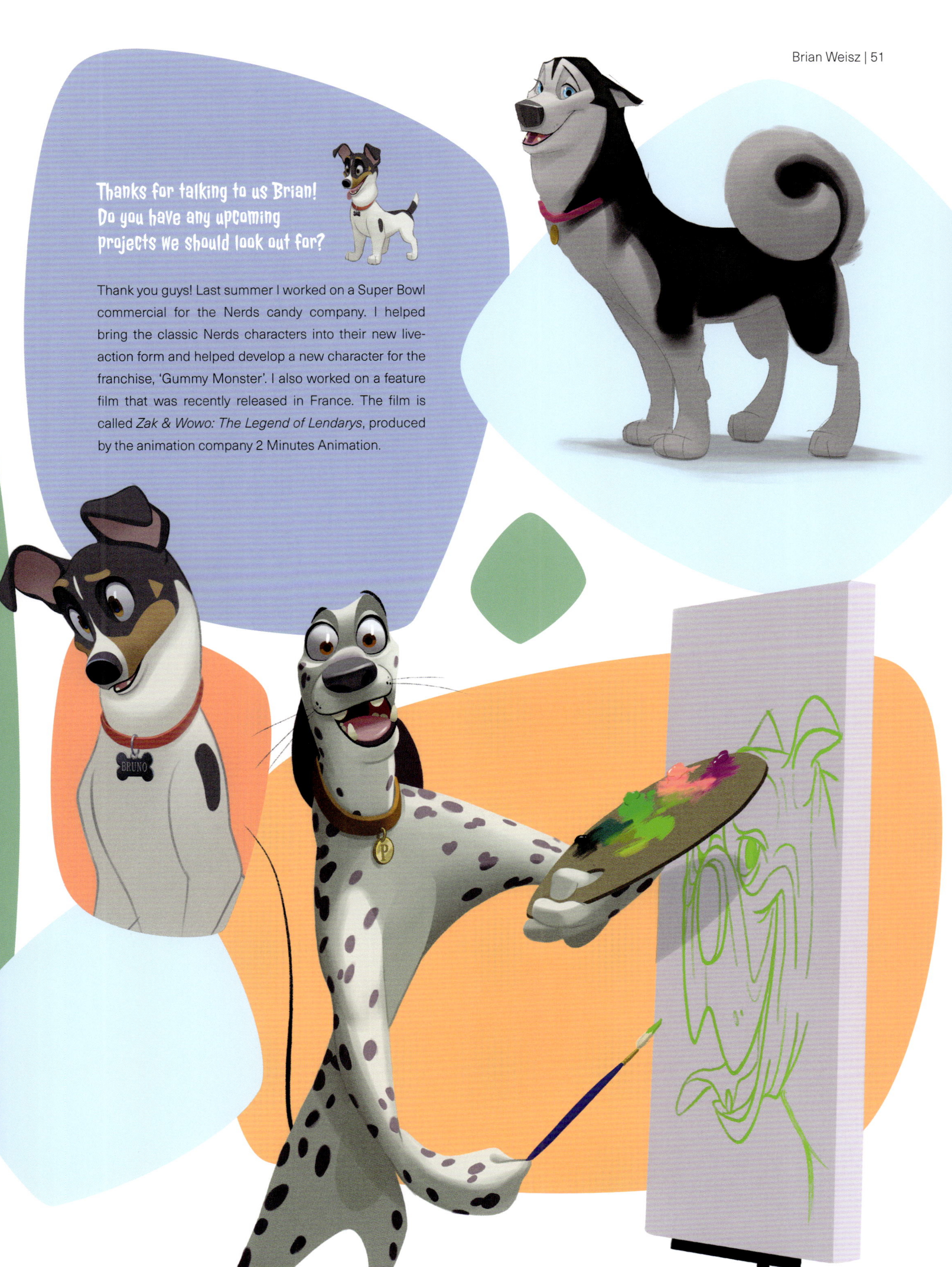

Thanks for talking to us Brian! Do you have any upcoming projects we should look out for?

Thank you guys! Last summer I worked on a Super Bowl commercial for the Nerds candy company. I helped bring the classic Nerds characters into their new live-action form and helped develop a new character for the franchise, 'Gummy Monster'. I also worked on a feature film that was recently released in France. The film is called *Zak & Wowo: The Legend of Lendarys*, produced by the animation company 2 Minutes Animation.

French Fancy

Creating characters that are visually striking requires a combination of design elements, including concepting, shape language, colour design, and costume design. I choose to draw a Parisian-inspired French Bulldog that plays off a French aesthetic and doubles down on French stereotypes. Humour is one of the best tools for character design, so let your wit and personality shine through in your design choices.

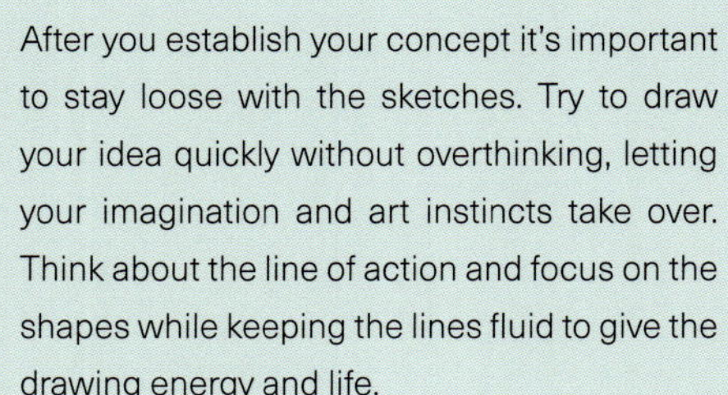

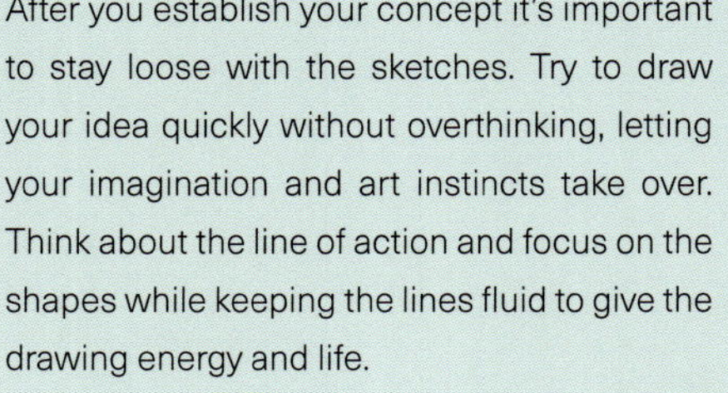

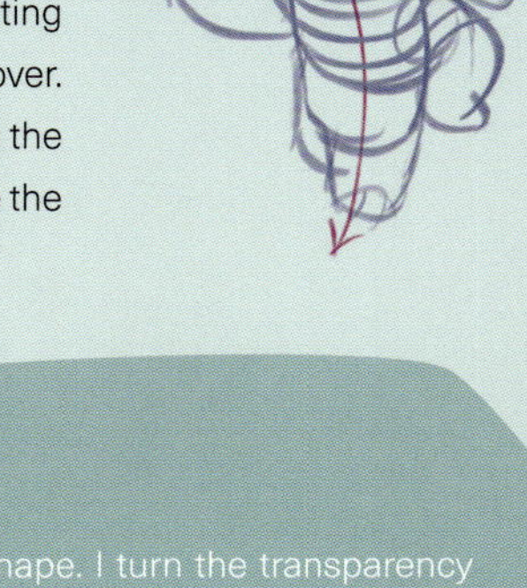

After you establish your concept it's important to stay loose with the sketches. Try to draw your idea quickly without overthinking, letting your imagination and art instincts take over. Think about the line of action and focus on the shapes while keeping the lines fluid to give the drawing energy and life.

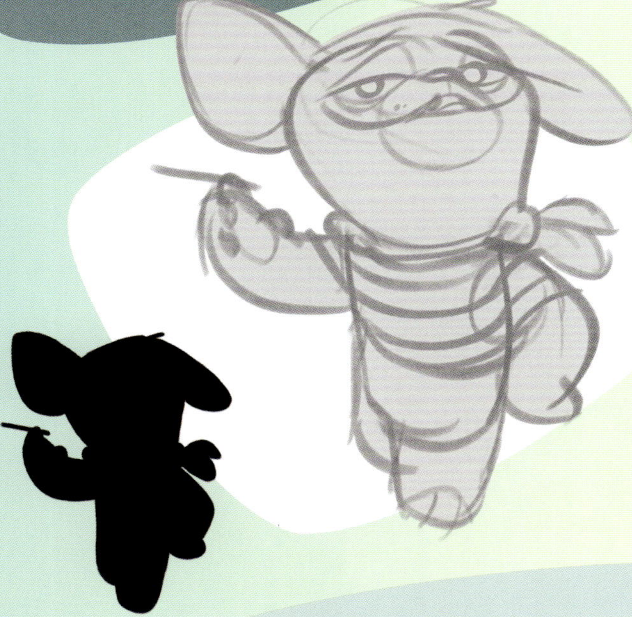

Fill in the silhouette as a solid shape. I turn the transparency down on my line work so I can create clean edges when filling in the shape. Make a copy of the silhouette layer and adjust the colour to black to see if the shape matches your design. With one ear underneath the beret, I am using the shape of the hat to balance the asymmetry of the design.

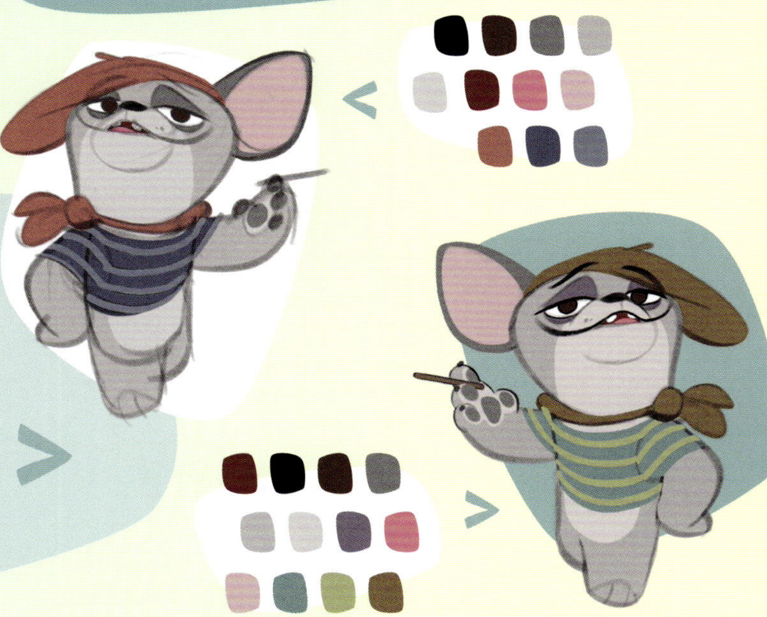

Start exploring colour choices by blocking in flat shapes of colour and separate the internal structure of the character. Experiment with colour combinations to find what works best. Colour is a big part of storytelling which can determine the mood of your character. I gave this character a vintage feel by exploring colours that imply a bygone era.

All images © Brian Weisz

At this stage it's a good idea to slow down and look at your drawing critically. Clean up the line work and make adjustments to the character wherever necessary. Double check the structure of your character and make sure the anatomy makes sense. I had to adjust the Frenchie's back foot to be more grounded. Continue to explore colour until you are satisfied with the way it looks and feels. Colour is a lot like flavour and is a great way to bring out the personality of your character.

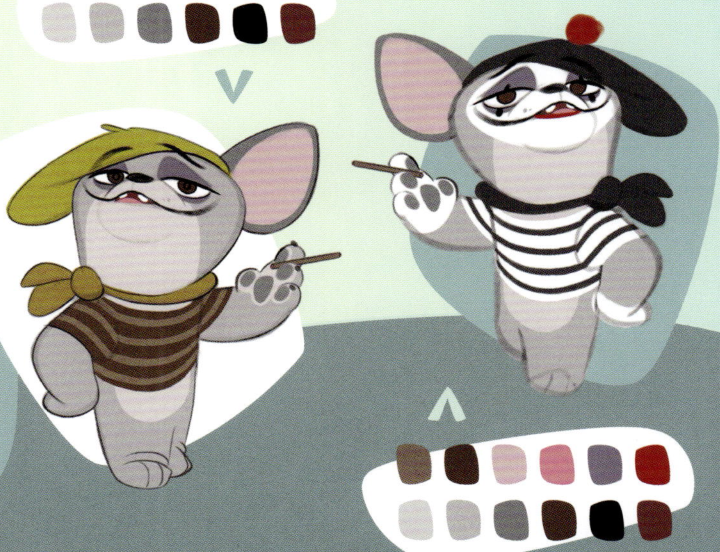

During my design process, everything is subject to change, for the sake of the art and final design of the character. As I bring this design to completion, I wonder what the character would look like with elements of a French mime artist incorporated. Making major changes to a design doesn't always work out, but you won't know unless you try. Ultimately, I want this character to have more flare – the cigarette extender and mime costume give the character the visual impact I was originally searching for.

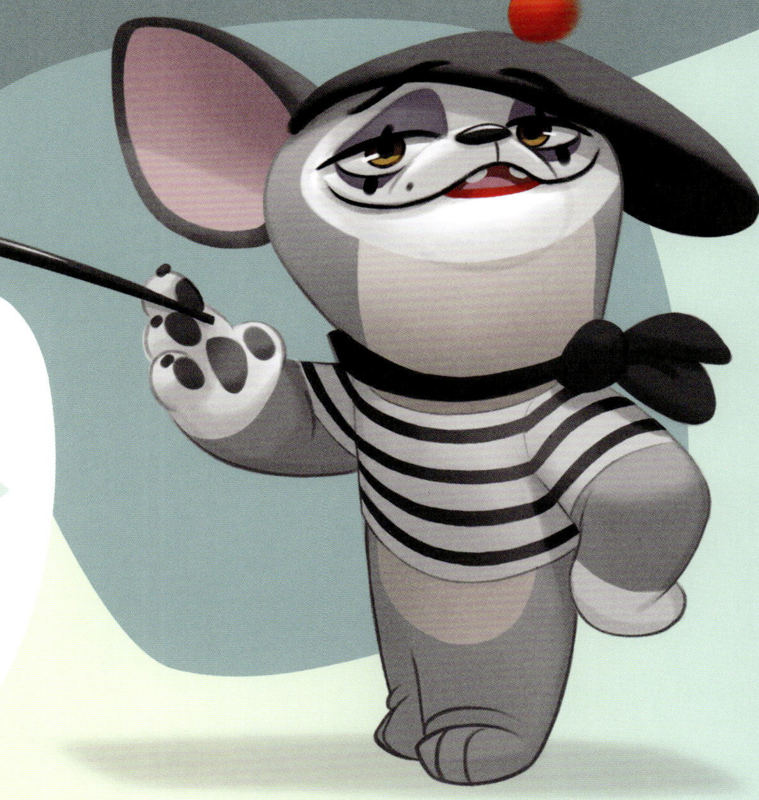

Finally, start developing the form of the character and give it some lighting. I keep all of the individual parts of my character on separate layers – this allows me to have full control of the design and makes adjusting any part relatively easy. In this case, the grey body shape, the tan tummy, and pink ear shape are each on separate layers. Use the Select tool to target one section at a time and use a large brush to add the shading. The large brush will allow for sweeping tones to look smooth.

AGATHE MOLIN

Like many others, I've drawn for as long as I can remember. My inspirations are varied and often influenced by events in my daily life, but I also like to create from prompts, which allow me to draw outside my comfort zone. In my designs, I try to play with lines of force, movement, and shapes, but I think my favourite part is colour – it's what gives my characters life and personality.

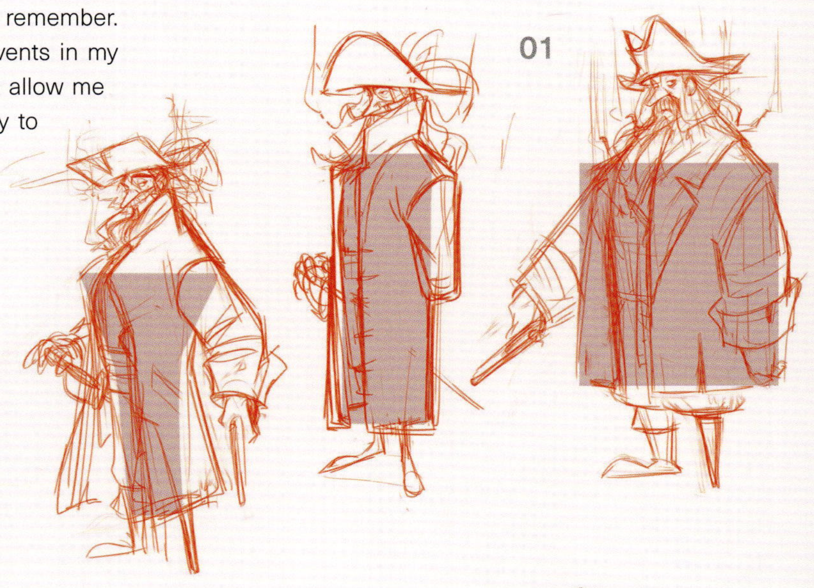

01. I was going through a phase of drawing pirates – this is Blackbeard. I had a vague idea of what I wanted him to look like, so I tried out different shapes to see which worked best, before settling on a design.

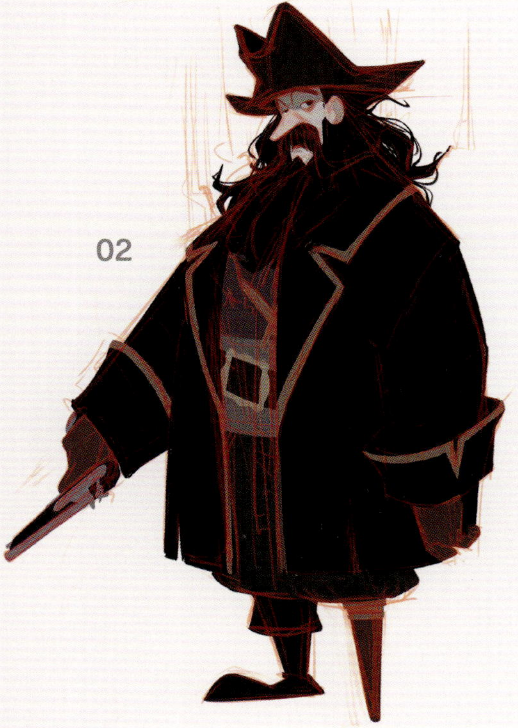

02. Once I'd made up my mind, I went straight to applying the first colours. I gave him a sickly pale skin to contrast with the dark colours of his clothes.

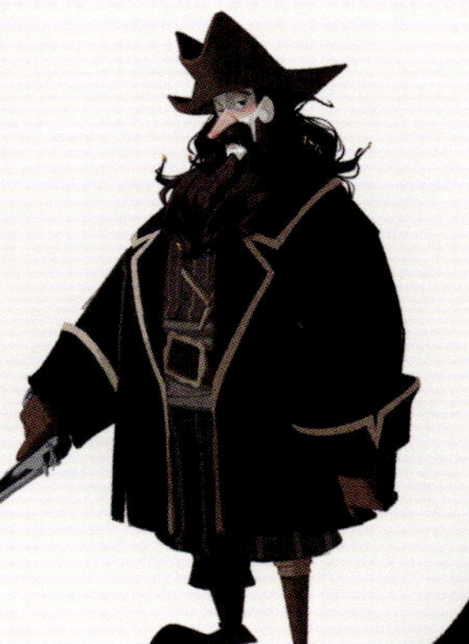

03. At this point I worked on volumes and the first details of the garments. I also drew a few lines to emphasize certain shapes and folds.

All images © Agathe Molin

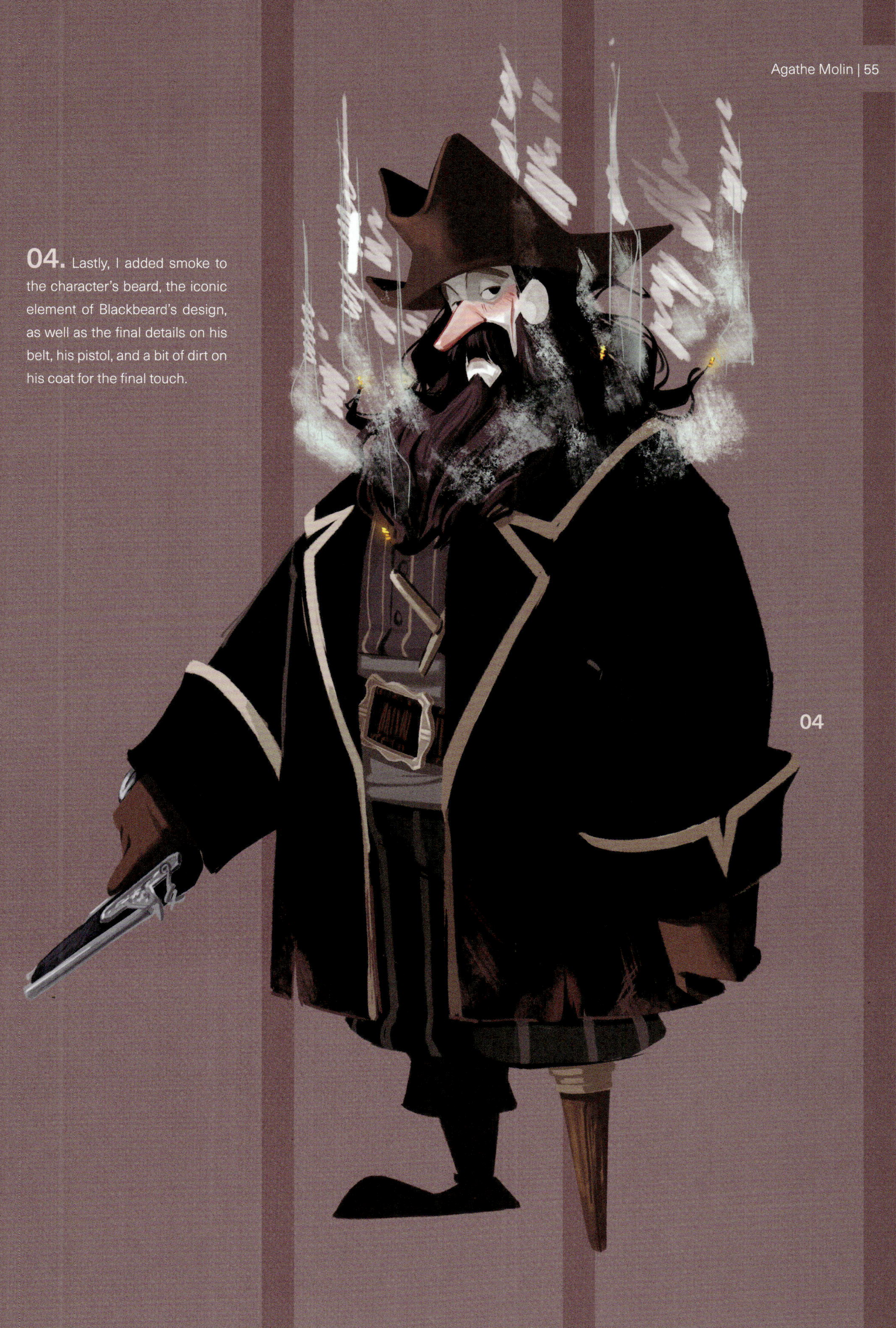

04. Lastly, I added smoke to the character's beard, the iconic element of Blackbeard's design, as well as the final details on his belt, his pistol, and a bit of dirt on his coat for the final touch.

04

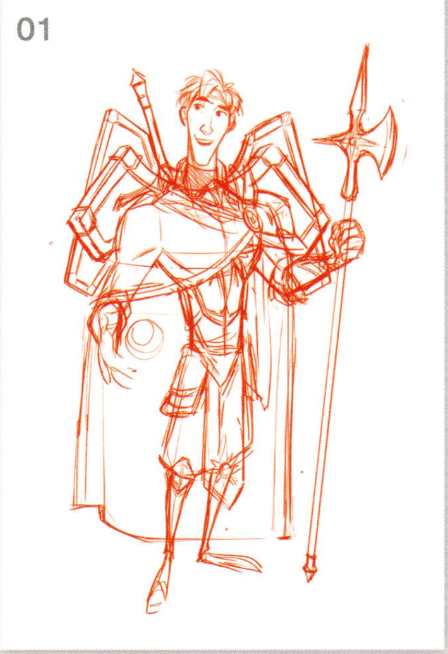

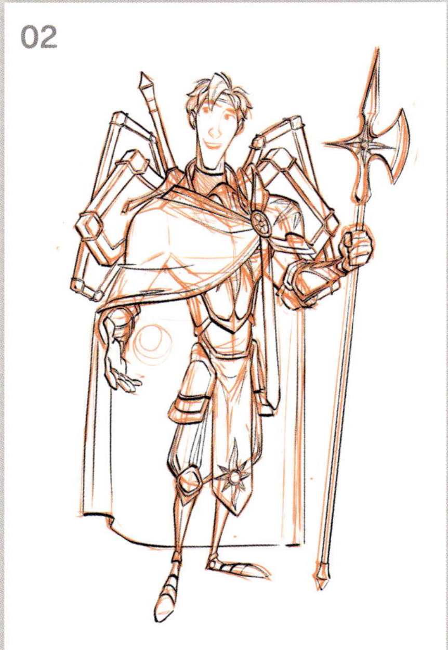

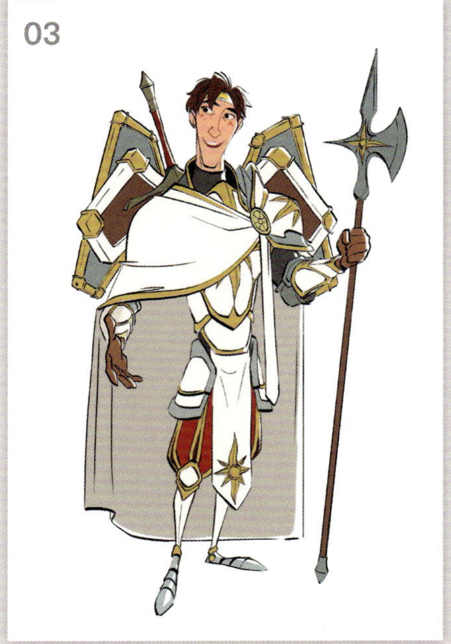

01. This character is a redesign of a paladin that I first drew in 2020. I wanted to simplify the design and make him appear more expressive.

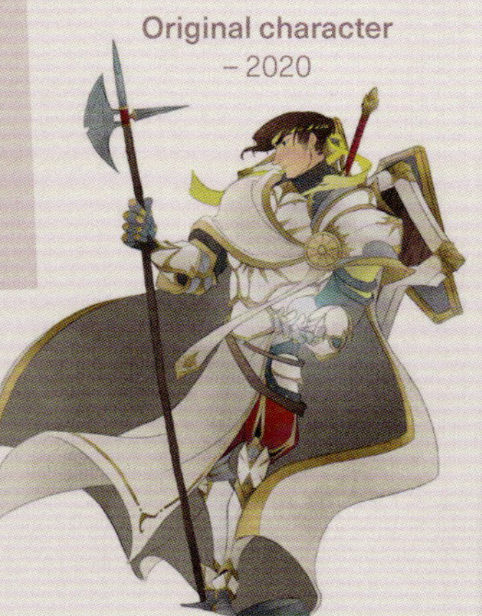

Original character – 2020

02. Once the rough was complete, I added line work to clarify the design.

03. I used the colour of the previous design as a reference for the new version, but I wanted the colours to appear slightly more saturated.

04. The final touch was to add some shadows and some lighting effects to give more life to the drawing.

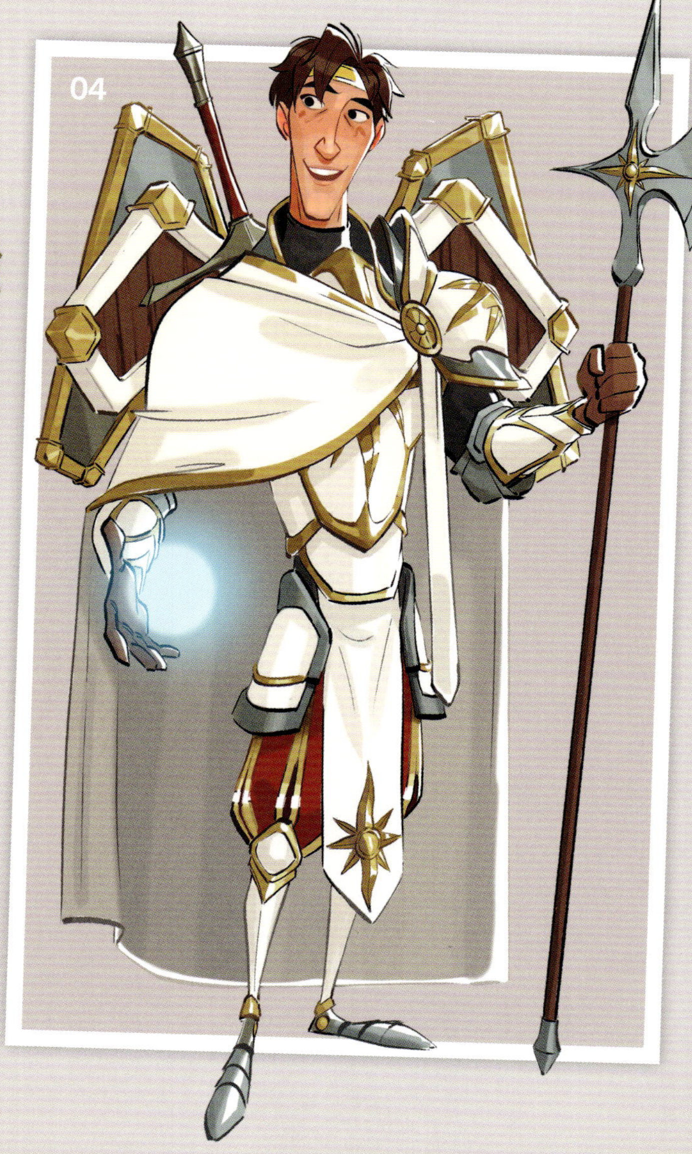

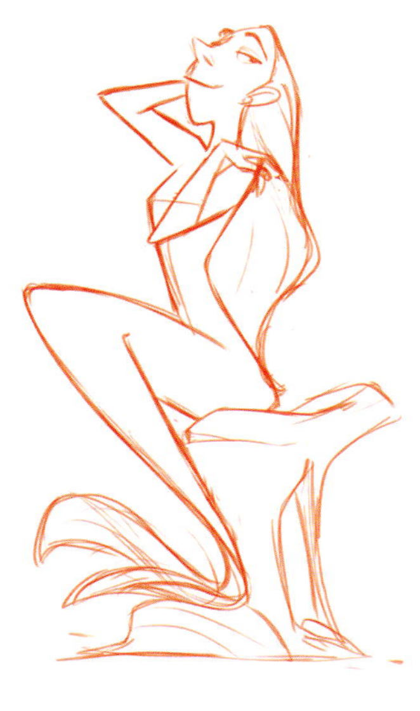

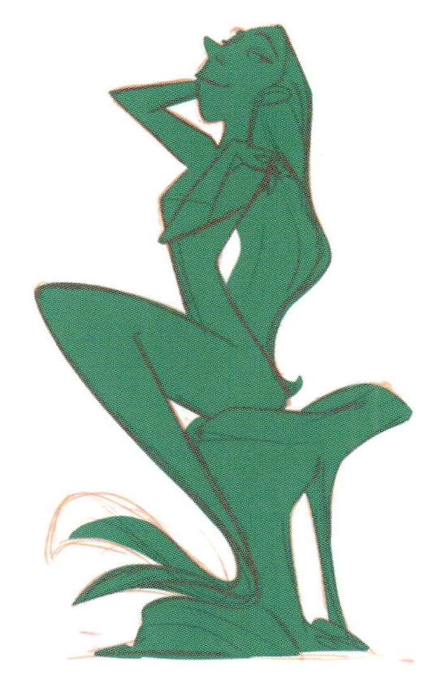

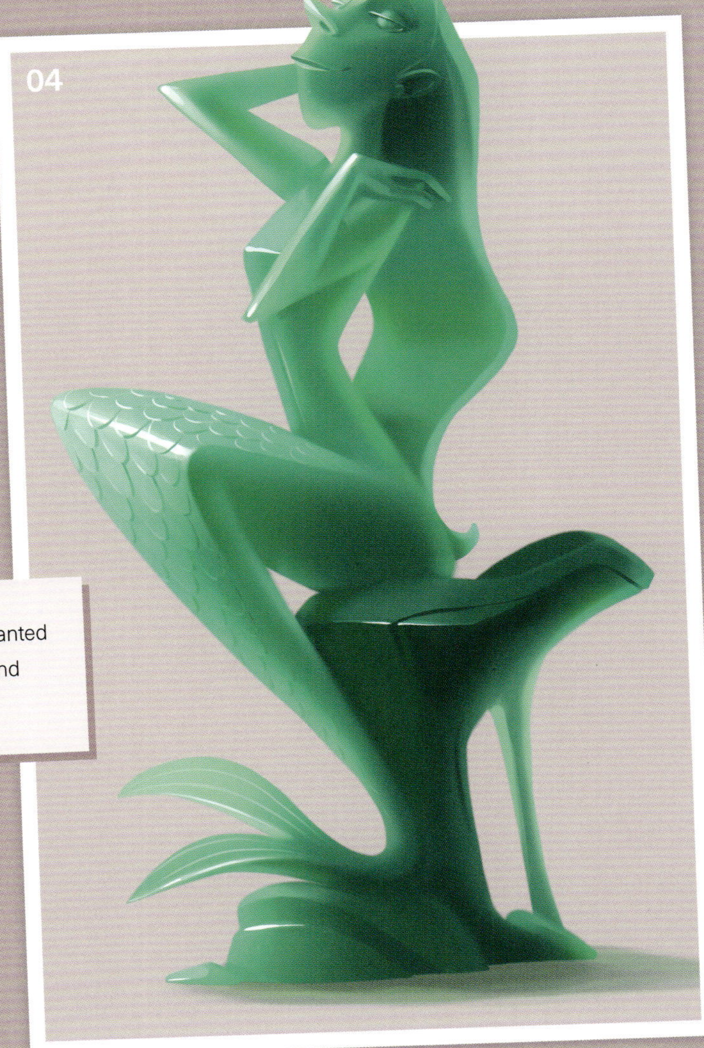

01. This is a drawing I made for MerMay in 2024, with the prompt 'Jade'. I knew right away I wanted to draw a statue. I played with my initial shapes to give her dynamic lines.

02. I didn't want to do line work since I really liked the feeling of the rough, so I directly blocked the shape of the character with a few adjustments.

03. I don't usually create rendered drawings, but I really wanted to for this character. With a soft brush I laid the shadows and lights to sculpt into the mask created by the basic shape.

04. Finally, I added extra details, with some sharp lights and the scales of the tail.

The mighty
mouseket[...]

Sabrina Sentoso

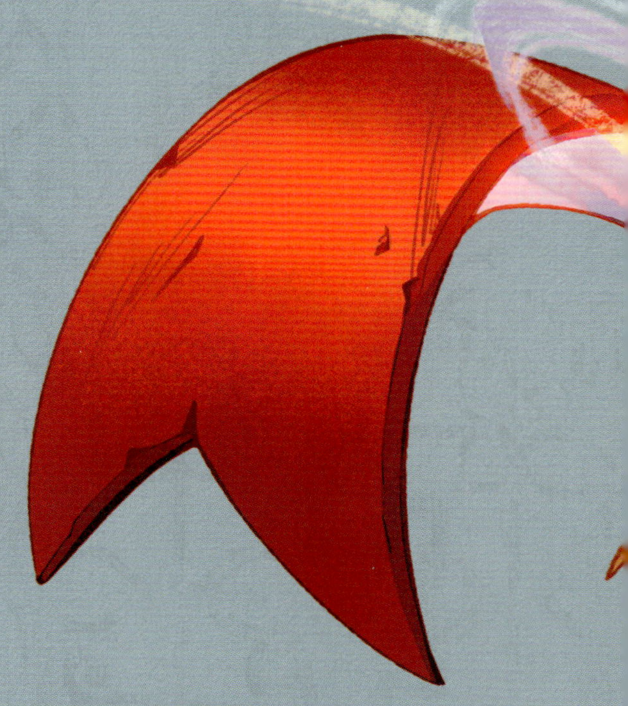

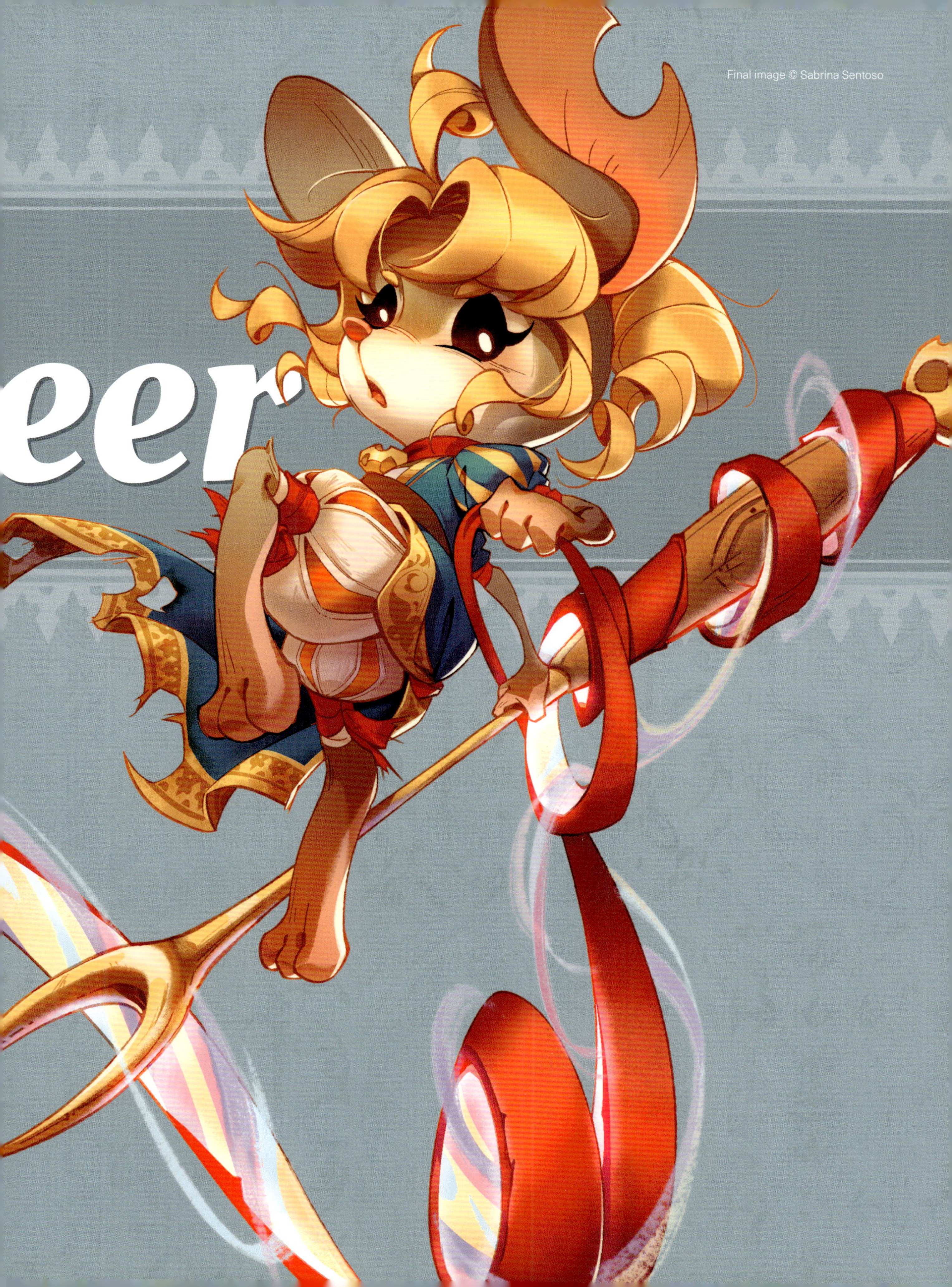

Final image © Sabrina Sentoso

For inspiration, create a mind map of keywords that relate to the prompt

Fondue pick

Guarded by humans

Food

Kitchen

Rapier

French

Musketeer

European

Weapon

Treasure

CHEESE

Cheese knife

MEDIEVAL

Gold

Blue silk

Big ears

Rat Princess

RODENT

ROYALTY

Jerboa

Small body

Dainty

Gown

ELEGANT

Frills

Ballet

Ribbon

Magic

Magical girl

Ribbon dancing

What's the story?

Every new design starts with a prompt or narrative to explore. Who is the character? What are they doing? The possibilities can be overwhelming – creating a mind map makes it easier to break down ideas that relate to the original prompt. For this project, the brief is to design a 'rat princess'. I start by writing down related keywords, such as 'cheese', 'medieval', and 'gown'. From there, I hone in on more specific points of inspiration, like 'ribbon', 'swordfighter', and 'French musketeer'. From this collection of inspirations, I form a short narrative to lead the design process: 'A rat princess is adventuring in search of cheese for her kingdom'.

Explore different styles to figure out a general feeling of the character

Once you've established a base narrative, start to loosely experiment with different styles for the character. There are so many different ways to draw a rat! Some things to consider at this point are the feeling you want the design to convey and what genre and medium you are designing for. In this case, I decide to go for a more whimsical and adventurous feeling, reminiscent of storybooks. Remember to keep it simple and try not to overcomplicate these roughs.

After some head explorations, I move on to creating a base model for our soon-to-be princess. I'm inspired by the jerboa, a species of rodent with big ears and long legs, and try to infuse these elements into my design.

As you continue to sketch, you'll start to notice patterns in overall shapes and proportions. These patterns tend to mean those repeated aspects are working well and so you want to keep them. In this case, I notice that I gravitate towards drawing my mouse princess with rounded features and a larger head to smaller body proportion, as I want her to have a softer, more youthful appearance. This step will help you to establish a strong base to add costuming, detail, and personality later on.

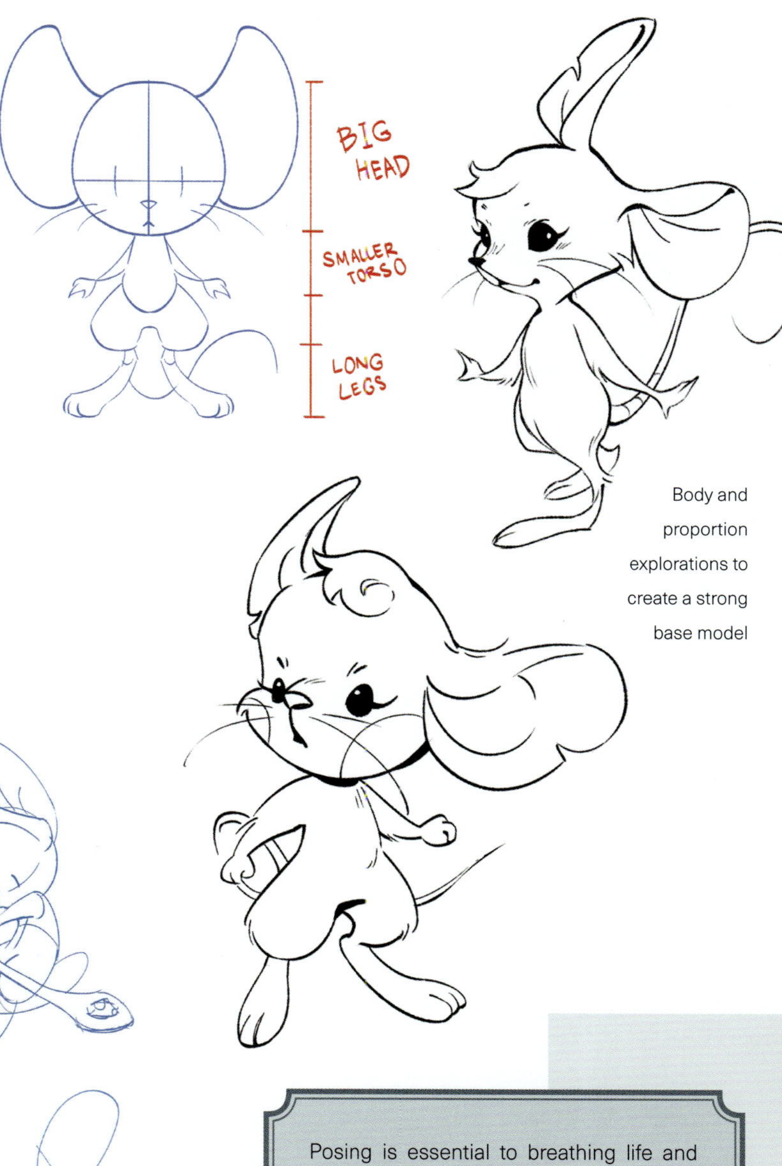

Body and proportion explorations to create a strong base model

Fast and rough pose sketches to get a feel for the essence of the character

Posing is essential to breathing life and personality into any character. How a character is posed shows emotion, intent, and can even hint towards their background and habits. As you sketch poses, don't worry too much about details or proportion, as you want to prioritize keeping them loose and dynamic with a strong line of action. I focus on creating flowing, nimble poses that have a sense of elegance befitting a princess while still being an action pose.

Let's break off into a slightly different – but equally important – part of the process: designing and creating motifs for the character. Motifs can help you to build and showcase a character's narrative and backstory in a subtle way. In this case, since my mouse's design will be inspired by historical French fashion, I design motifs that can be used as crests, emblems, clothing trims, and patterning. Cheese is of utmost importance to our character and her kingdom, so I design patterns based on cheese imagery, combined with inspirations from baroque-era French textiles, to create hypothetical kingdom emblems and logos for her to wear.

Designing
a narrative
and backstory
through motifs

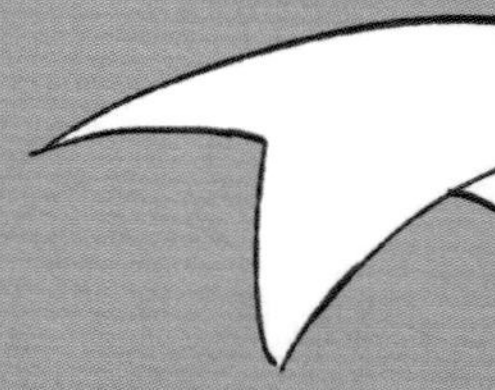
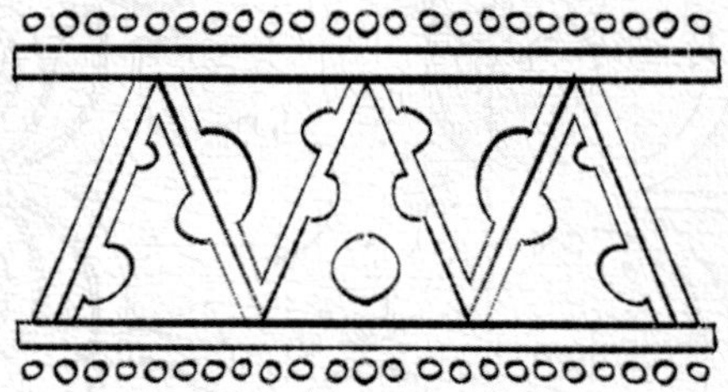

Thumbnails drawn over the chosen pose sketches

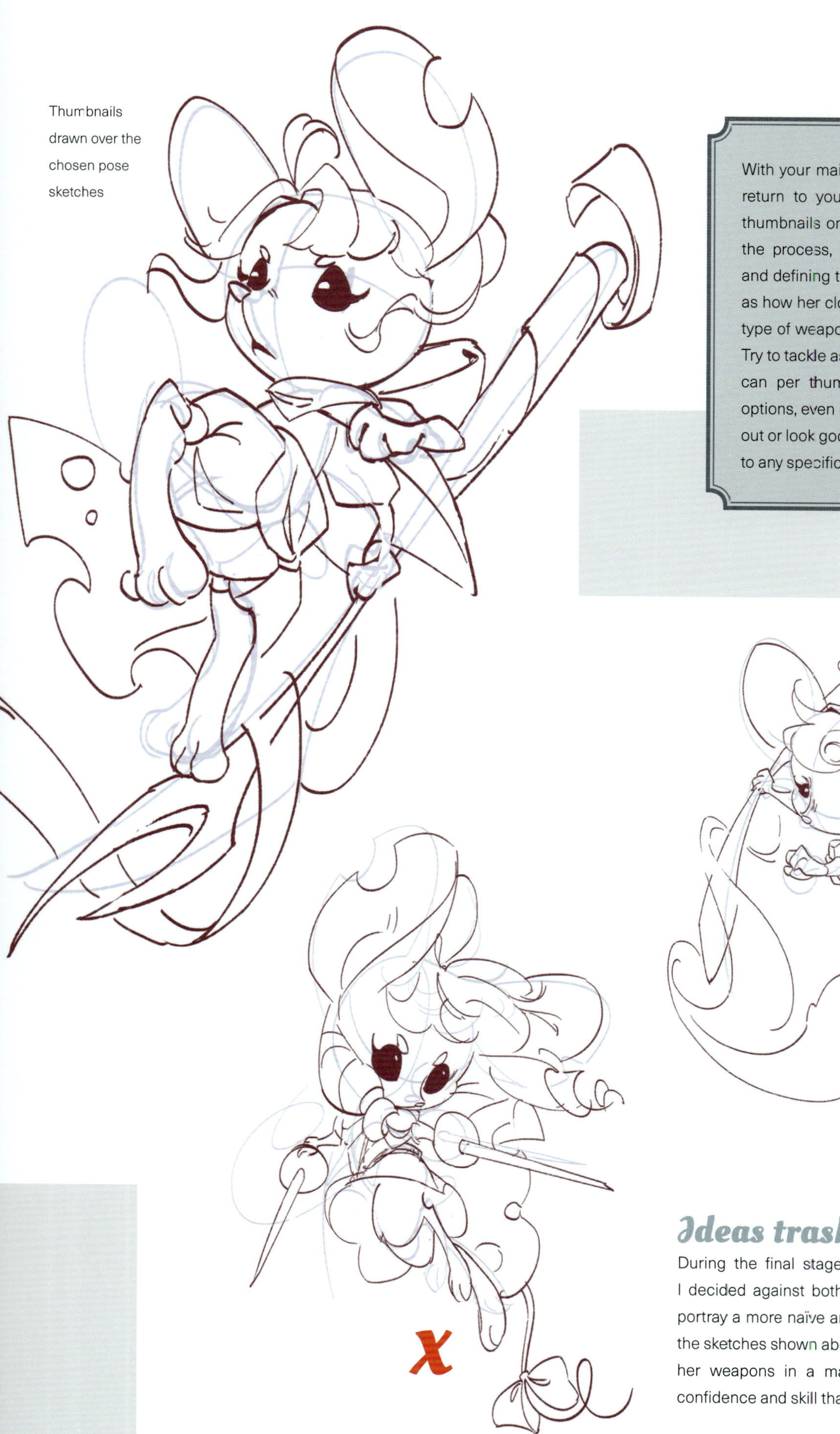

With your main design motifs established, return to your poses and start creating thumbnails on top of them. At this step of the process, you want to start exploring and defining the main design details, such as how her clothing will look, her hairstyle, type of weapon, possible tools, and so on. Try to tackle as many different ideas as you can per thumbnail and try out different options, even if you are not sure it will work out or look good. Try to avoid being too tied to any specific sketches at this stage.

Ideas trash can

During the final stages of the thumbnailing process, I decided against both of these ideas, as I wanted to portray a more naïve and inexperienced fighter. Both of the sketches shown above picture the princess wielding her weapons in a manner that implies much more confidence and skill than I intended.

With the base proportions and model you created back in step three, it is now time to design the mouse's costume. While you could follow this process on the action thumbnails you just made, it might be difficult to figure out her clothing if it gets obscured by the angle and perspective of the pose. This step of the process is where our motifs will start to come into play, as they can be infused into her costume. I added the cheese patterns into the trims of her dress and the cheese emblems as brooches and pins. I also thought about how she would wear her dress – a long gown would get in the way of her movement, so I decide to give her ribbons and bows that tie her sleeves and dress up and away from her arms and legs.

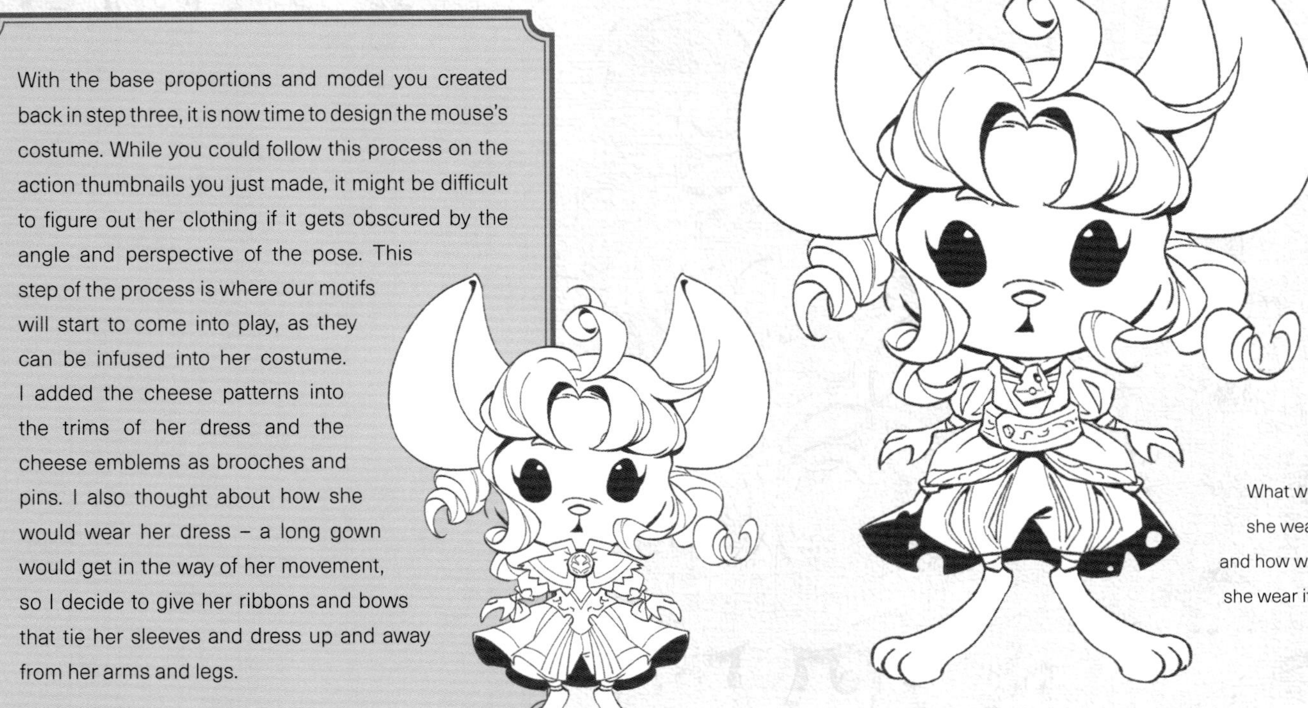

What will she wear and how will she wear it?

Create a weapon that will aid your character on their journey and always keep utility in mind

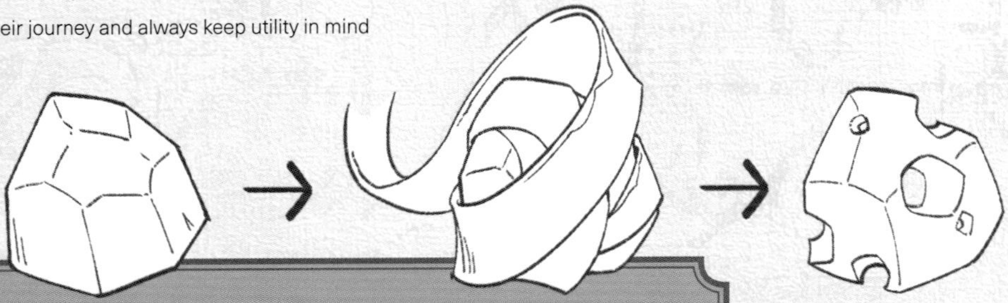

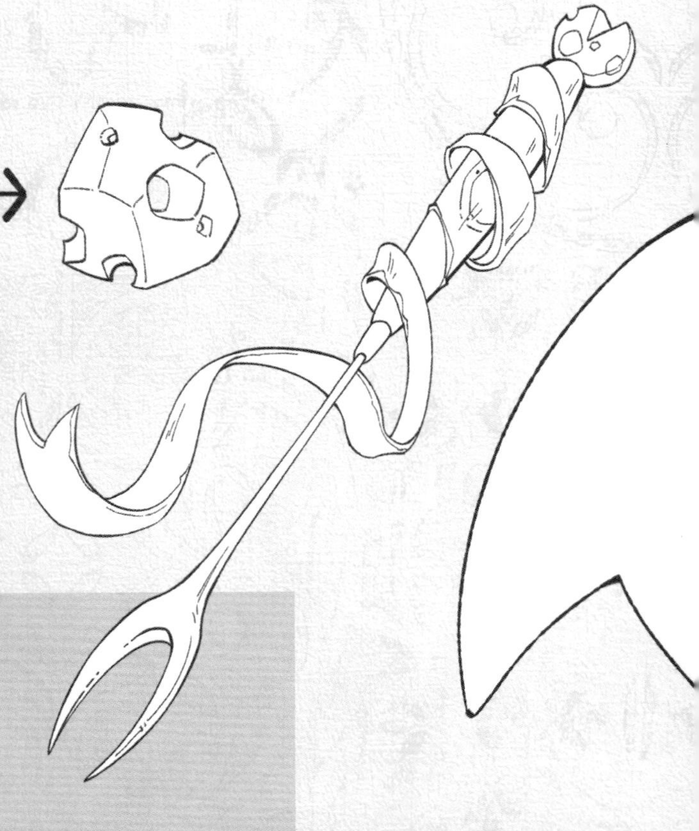

Every good warrior needs a weapon, so let's design her one. In the rough thumbnails I drafted earlier, I wanted her weapon to be reminiscent of tools typically used to handle cheese, such as cheese knives and fondue picks. When designing a weapon, you want to think of utility – how is this weapon used by the character and what makes it unique? To make the design more 'magical girl' inspired, I want to add a ribbon-like design to it and reference ribbon dancing and rope lassos. To push the 'magical' concept further, I give her ribbon the power to transform objects into cheese! Always try to trace the utility of the weapon back to the narrative.

Feedback is your friend

Feedback and critique play a big part in any design process – having someone with a fresh set of eyes look at your work and give you helpful ideas and possible areas of improvement is always helpful. Don't be afraid to share your progress with others, as geting used to having your work critiqued goes a long way, for both personal and professional development.

Design in hand, you can now finally go back to your chosen thumbnail and create a final line drawing. Start drawing in the different details you've meticulously designed while taking note of how they warp and contort according to the pose and perspective of the shot. As you draw, watch out for any awkward tangents and try to keep the character's silhouette readable while keeping the essence of the original base pose.

Keep clothing folds and perspective in mind when laying costuming details on

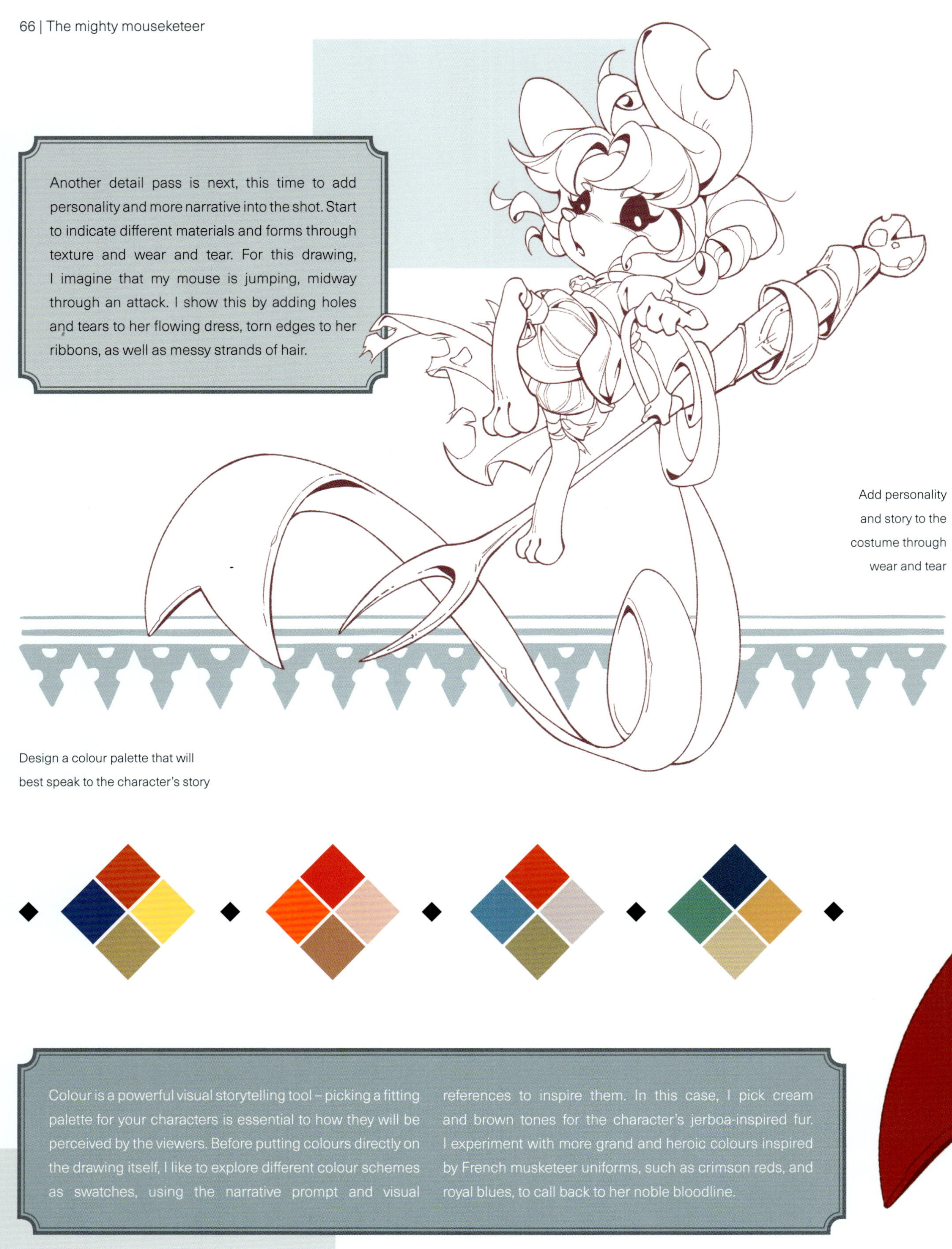

Another detail pass is next, this time to add personality and more narrative into the shot. Start to indicate different materials and forms through texture and wear and tear. For this drawing, I imagine that my mouse is jumping, midway through an attack. I show this by adding holes and tears to her flowing dress, torn edges to her ribbons, as well as messy strands of hair.

Add personality and story to the costume through wear and tear

Design a colour palette that will best speak to the character's story

Colour is a powerful visual storytelling tool – picking a fitting palette for your characters is essential to how they will be perceived by the viewers. Before putting colours directly on the drawing itself, I like to explore different colour schemes as swatches, using the narrative prompt and visual references to inspire them. In this case, I pick cream and brown tones for the character's jerboa-inspired fur. I experiment with more grand and heroic colours inspired by French musketeer uniforms, such as crimson reds, and royal blues, to call back to her noble bloodline.

Once you've selected a colour scheme that you're happy with, you can start to block the base colours for the drawing. Block out different elements and organize them into separate colour layers so they are easier to work on when you begin to render later on. This will also make it easier to perform any colour adjustments. Try to keep your layers neat and labelled as this process tends to lead to a stack full of them!

Colouring your lines

To make the line art less jarring and help it blend in to the illustration more, try colouring it in. Choose colours that are a few shades darker than the colour base you have and set the line art layer to Multiply, adjusting the layer opacity if it appears too dark. This extra step will also help make your colours feel more vibrant and pop more.

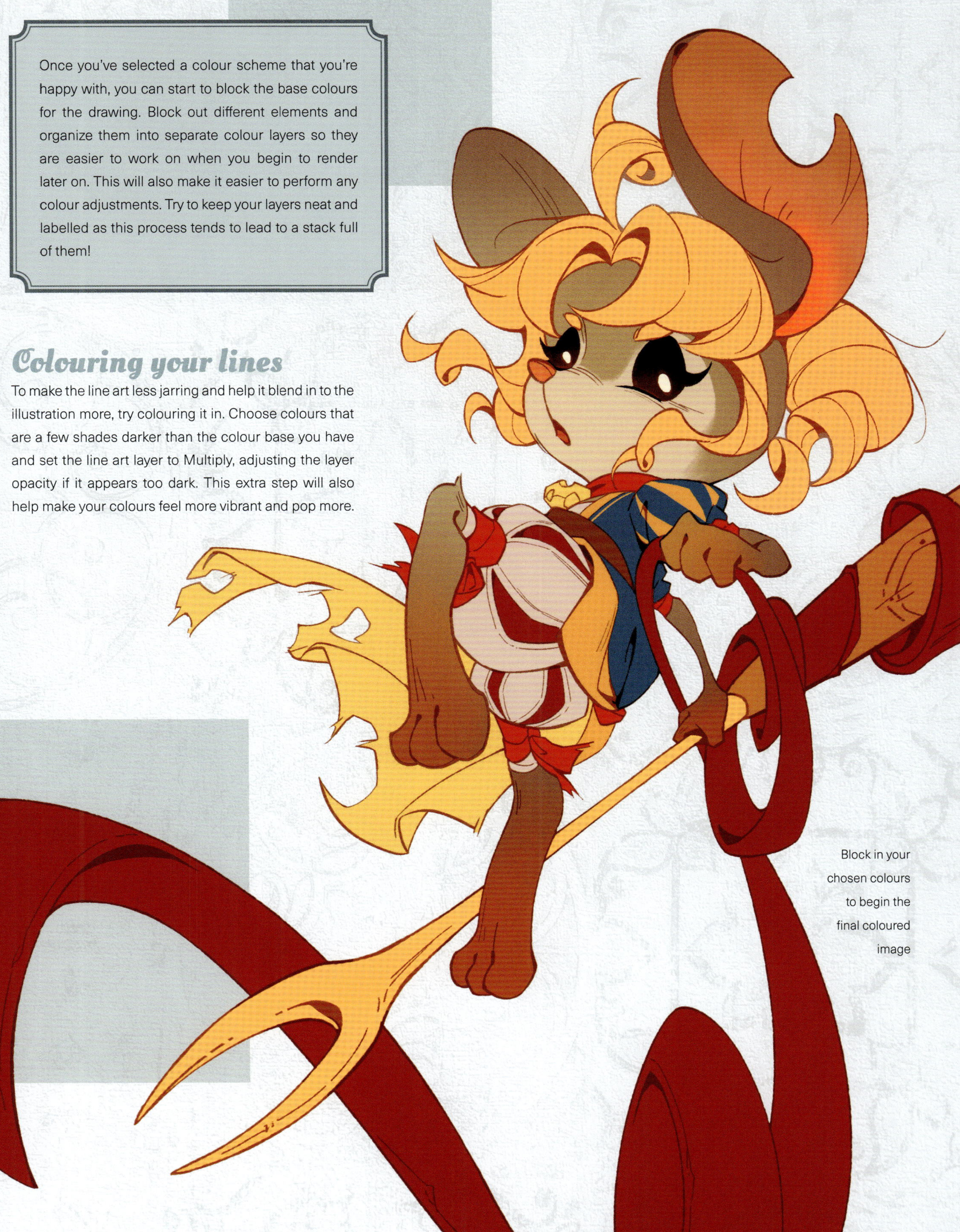

Block in your chosen colours to begin the final coloured image

After blocking in the base local colours add some nuance and appeal through colour variation. I like to add texture to areas of wear and tear, such as the torn-up cape, as well as different tone variations by using a brush with the Colour Jitter setting turned on, or applying gradients. I bring back the cheese-inspired patterns from before and add them to the trim of her dress on a Multiply layer, so that the pattern retains the colour variation and texture of its base. I want the ribbon on her weapon to feel more magical and hint at its power, so I add bright pastels on its inner side to contrast with the darker red outer side.

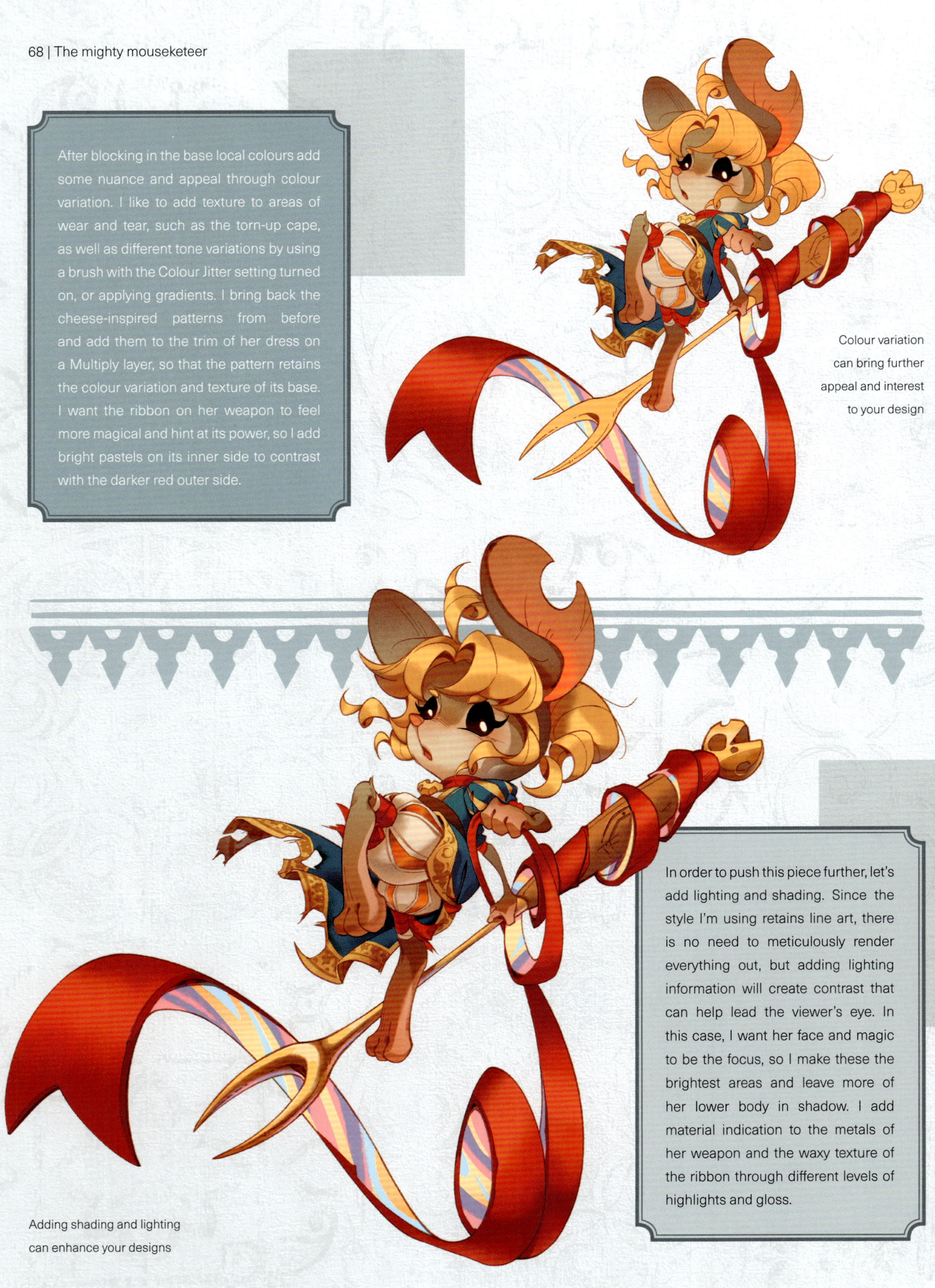

Colour variation can bring further appeal and interest to your design

In order to push this piece further, let's add lighting and shading. Since the style I'm using retains line art, there is no need to meticulously render everything out, but adding lighting information will create contrast that can help lead the viewer's eye. In this case, I want her face and magic to be the focus, so I make these the brightest areas and leave more of her lower body in shadow. I add material indication to the metals of her weapon and the waxy texture of the ribbon through different levels of highlights and gloss.

Adding shading and lighting can enhance your designs

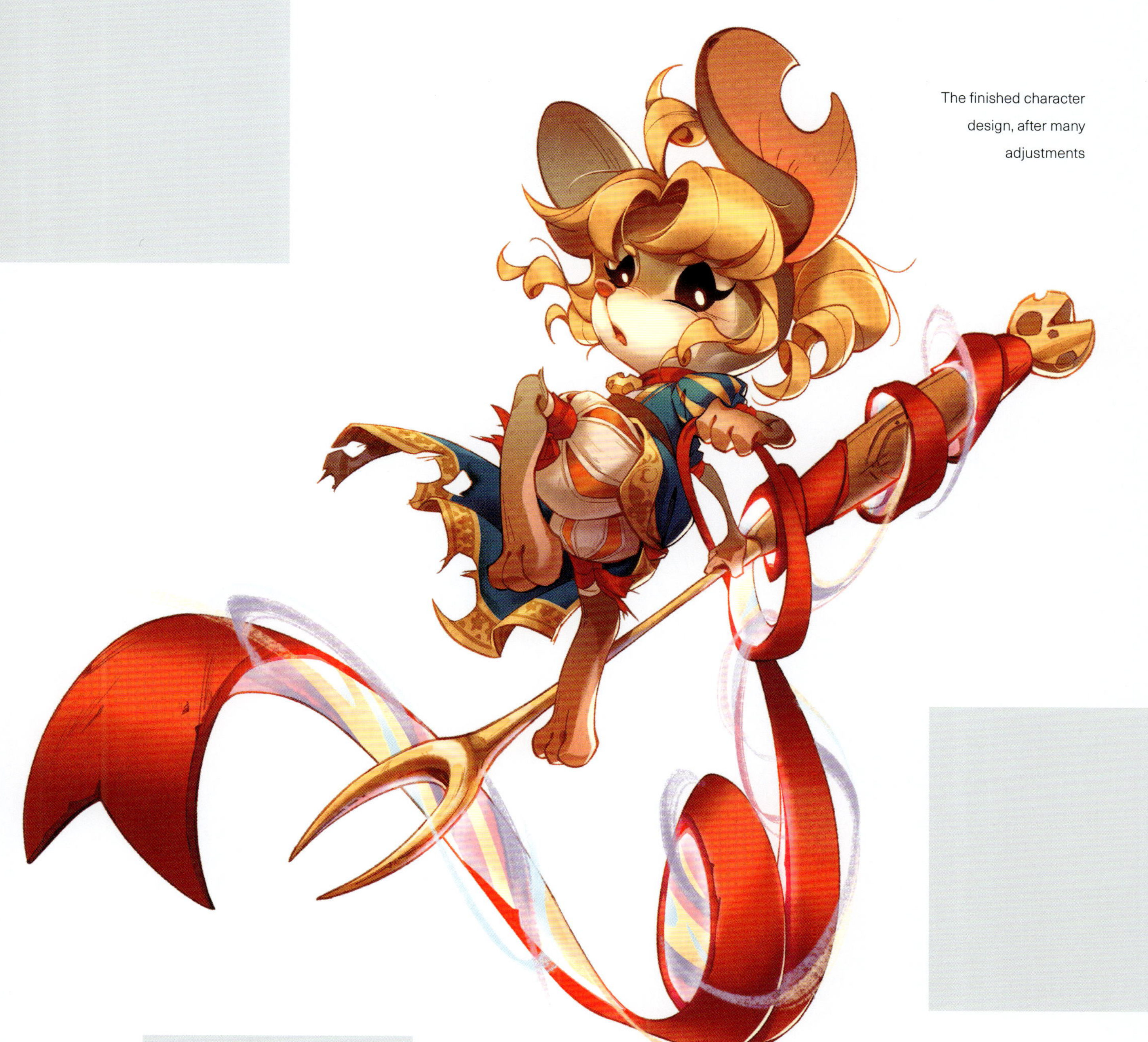

The finished character design, after many adjustments

Finish off the piece by adding more subtle details and fixing elements and lighting to pull it all together. This is where special layer effects shine, such as Overlay and Multiply layers. They are very useful in adjusting the piece for more uniform colour tones and pushing the grouping of light and shadow to add depth. You want to really zoom in at this stage to etch in all those textures, effects, and even minute things like loose hair strands. Staring at the piece for too long can make adjustments hard to judge at times, so I recommend taking breaks and stepping away from the screen to think about these final edits with a fresh eye. Once you're satisfied with the piece, congratulations – you're done!

Final image © Sabrina Sentoso

All images © Derek Laufman

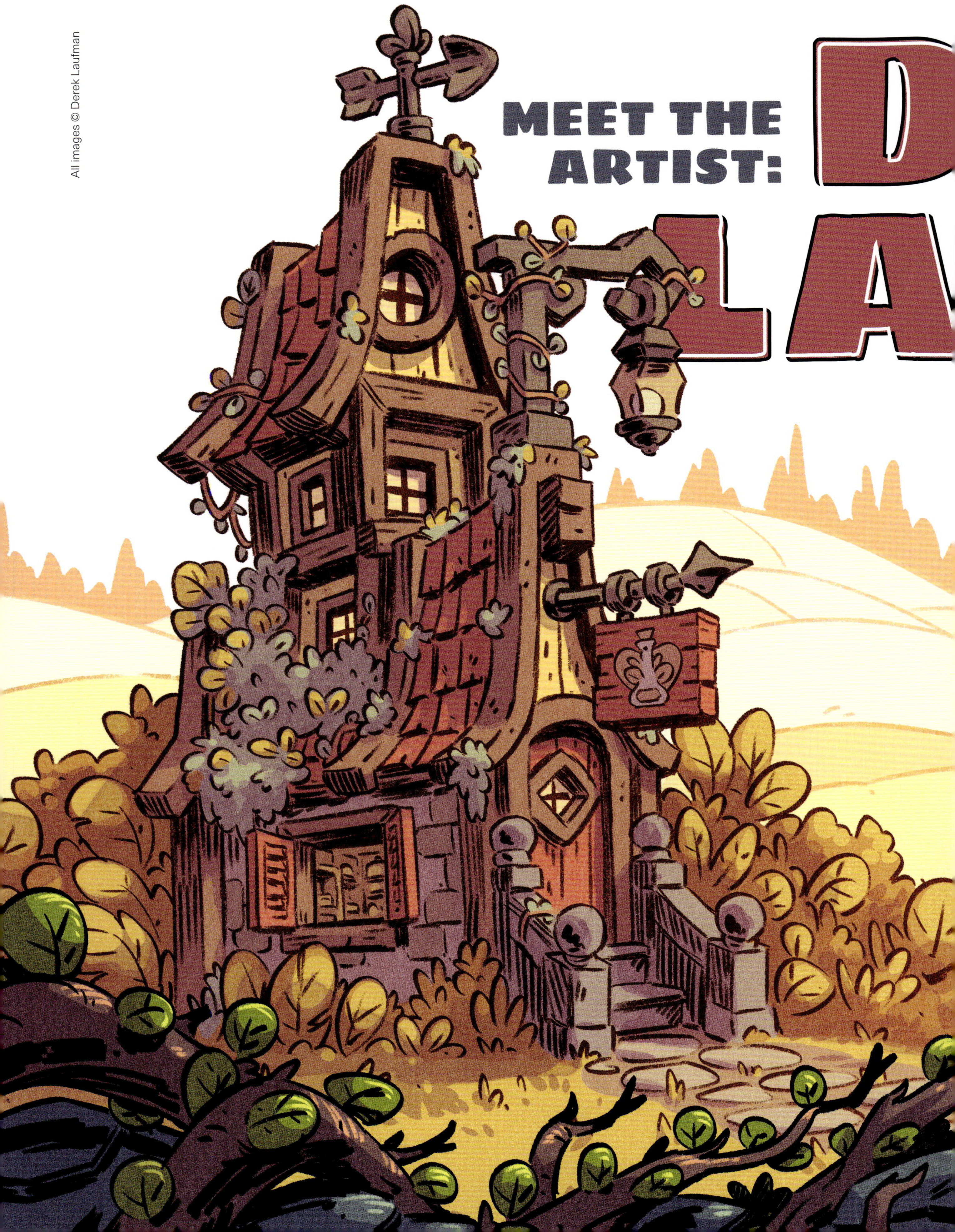

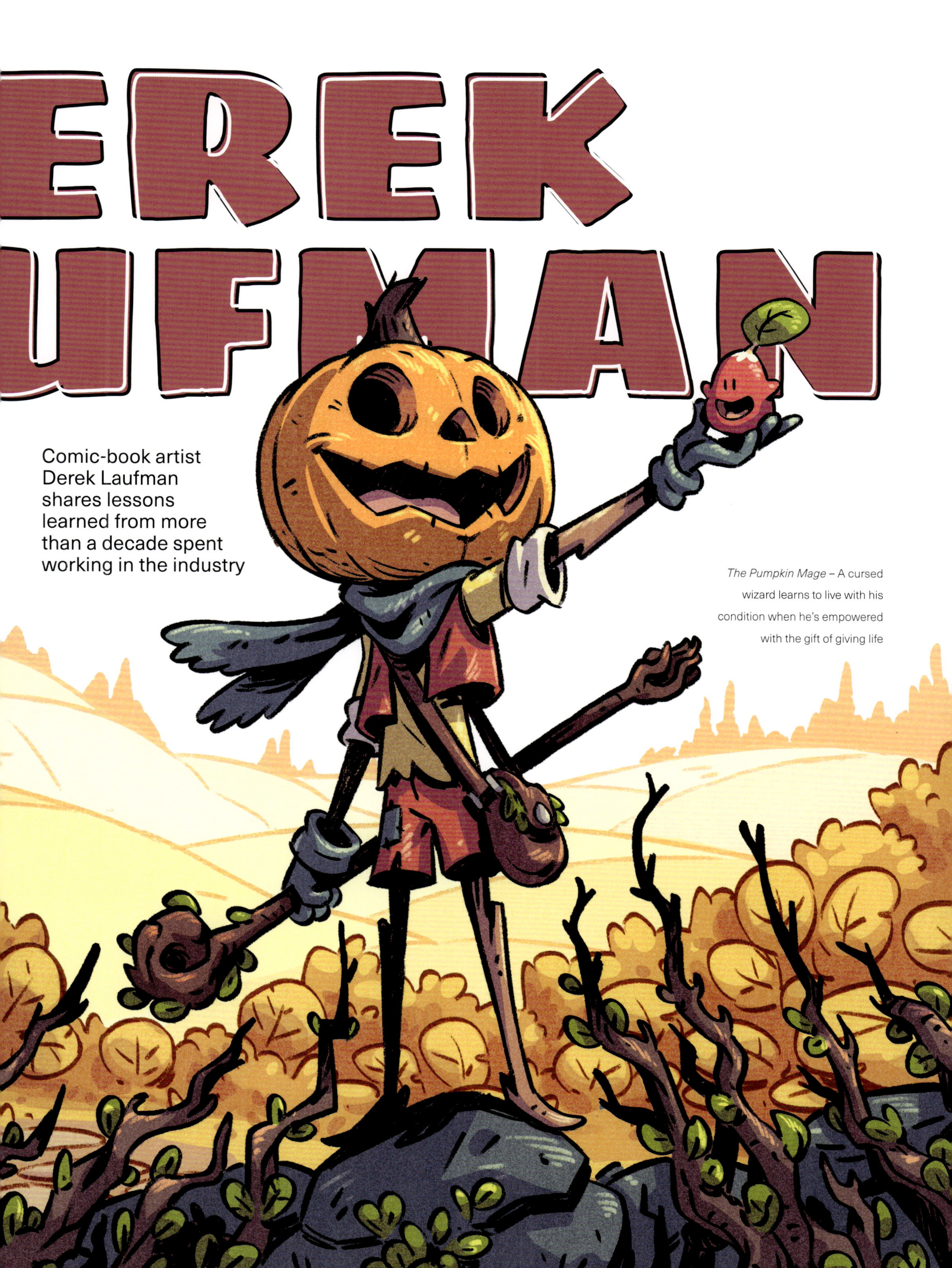

EREK
UFMAN

Comic-book artist Derek Laufman shares lessons learned from more than a decade spent working in the industry

The Pumpkin Mage – A cursed wizard learns to live with his condition when he's empowered with the gift of giving life

Hi Derek, welcome to *CDQ*! Can you start by telling our readers a little about yourself and your career so far?

Thank you for having me! I've been an admirer of *CDQ* for many years and it has been a valuable source of inspiration – I'm honoured to get a chance to connect with you and your readers. My twenty-five year journey as an artist has been a bit of a winding road. I grew up a few hours outside of Toronto and from a young age I loved to draw and was a big fan of comic art. By the time I was thirteen, I was dead set on a career as a comic artist – what could go wrong? I went on to study classical animation at Sheridan College in my early twenties, while at the same time freelancing for a few indie comic studios. Sheridan had a well-known animation program and it was close enough to where I lived that I could take a train each day to campus. Although it wasn't comic-book training, I knew they taught layout and storyboarding so it felt like the skills could be easily applied to making comics. With 3D animation taking over the animation scene the 2D animation industry was hit hard by layoffs. By the time I had finished my first year the prospect of landing a job in the field seemed pretty slim for me and my peers. But I wasn't worried, as I was going to be working in comics – or so I thought.

After I graduated I worked with one particular indie comic studio for a few years and one of our projects was going to be picked up and published by Image Comics. This studio flew me out to San Diego Comic Con to promote the project. All my dreams were coming to fruition right before my eyes – I was going to 'make it'! But tragedy struck when the publisher I was working for cut me from the project and used a different artist. I was confused – my work had landed us the project, so why was I being cut out? It was a rough time and I never got a straight answer why. That experience tainted the comics industry for me and I walked away. I was now out of college and jobless with my hopes and dreams dashed.

I spent the next few years working as a graphic designer and then I found an opportunity in London, Ontario, working for game developer Big Blue Bubble as a 2D artist, just a few hours from where I was living. They were in need of a 2D artist with animation experience so Valerie (my wife) and I packed up and moved to London. I worked at BBB for nearly five years and I had some great opportunities there, learning all aspects of game development and eventually becoming one of their creative directors. We focused mainly on mobile and casual web games. It was fun at times, but the games we were making didn't inspire me so I decided to leave.

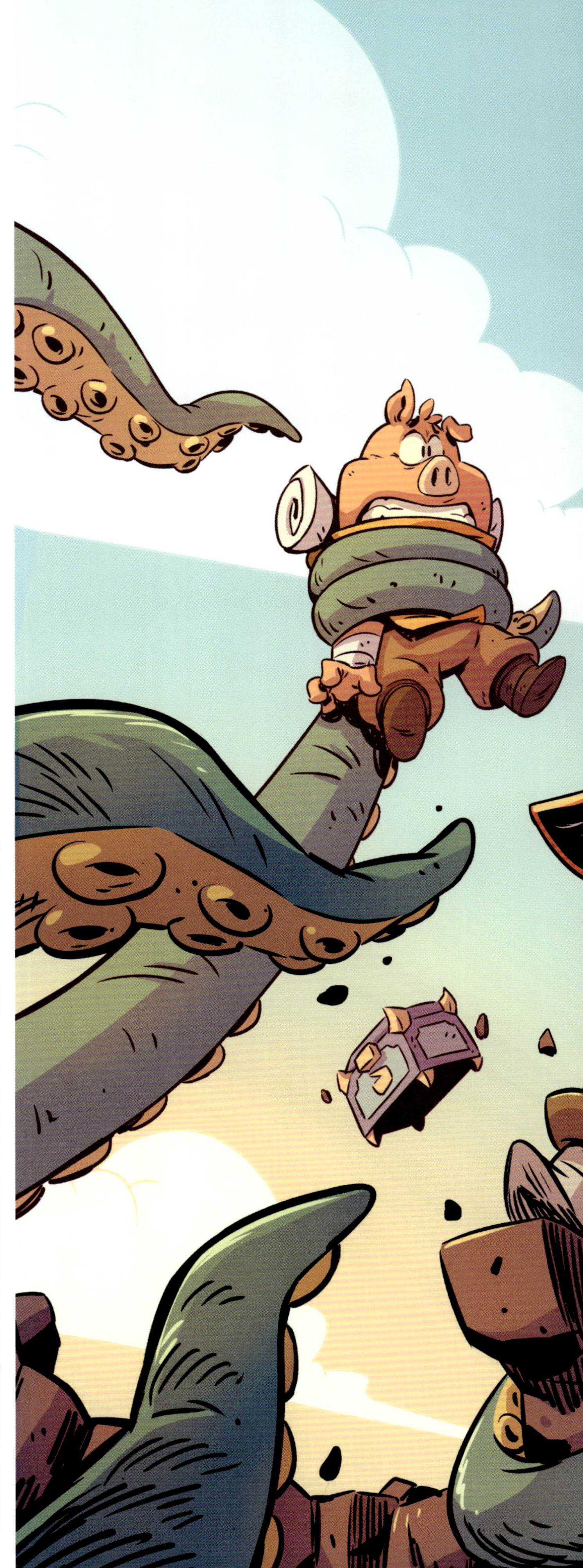

RuinWorld – The first story I ever wrote was about two unlikely companions on a quest for treasure and glory, all while the fate of the world rests on their shoulders

After a short break, I started my own indie studio called Halfbot with a programmer friend of mine. Having complete freedom to make any game we liked was just the creative boost I needed. However, it quickly became apparent how hard it was to make money as an indie game studio and I found myself needing to work long hours doing freelance work for other game studios remotely. After five years of trying to make Halfbot profitable, we decided to close the company.

It was around this time that my good friend Sean Galloway reached out and asked me to help develop a *World of Warcraft* graphic novel. I got the opportunity to storyboard the 120+ page book and it really helped ignite my passion for comics again. Sean gave me a few more opportunities to assist on a *Batman Black and White* story and an *Adventures of Superman* book. Without Sean, I don't think I would have found my way back into comics – I'm forever grateful for that.

Freelancing had now become my full-time job. Social media started to really take off for me around this time. I had been drawing game sprites for so long that I had adopted a 'Chibi' style that began to catch people's eye when I would post fan art on social media. Over the next year I refined that style and quickly became known for that look. The popularity of these drawings kickstarted what would become a very active freelancing career and led to me working with Marvel, developing their toddler-friendly brand *Marvel Super Hero Adventures*. It was a dream come true to be working with Marvel, and I also had the chance to develop toddler branding for DC Comics, as well as multiple design jobs for Hasbro and Mattel.

With my passion for comics reignited, I decided to work on my own books. I was very fortunate that Whitney Leopard, editor at BOOM! Studios at the time, took a chance on my first ever comic pitch, *RuinWorld*. I was able to develop a five-issue mini-series, writing and illustrating each book. I have since gone on to self-publish three more books, *The Witch of Wickerson*, *BOT-9*, and my latest book, *Crimson Fall: Lambs of God*.

Bastion – I will often explore story ideas through character design. Bastion was part of a dungeon crawling adventure I have yet to bring to life

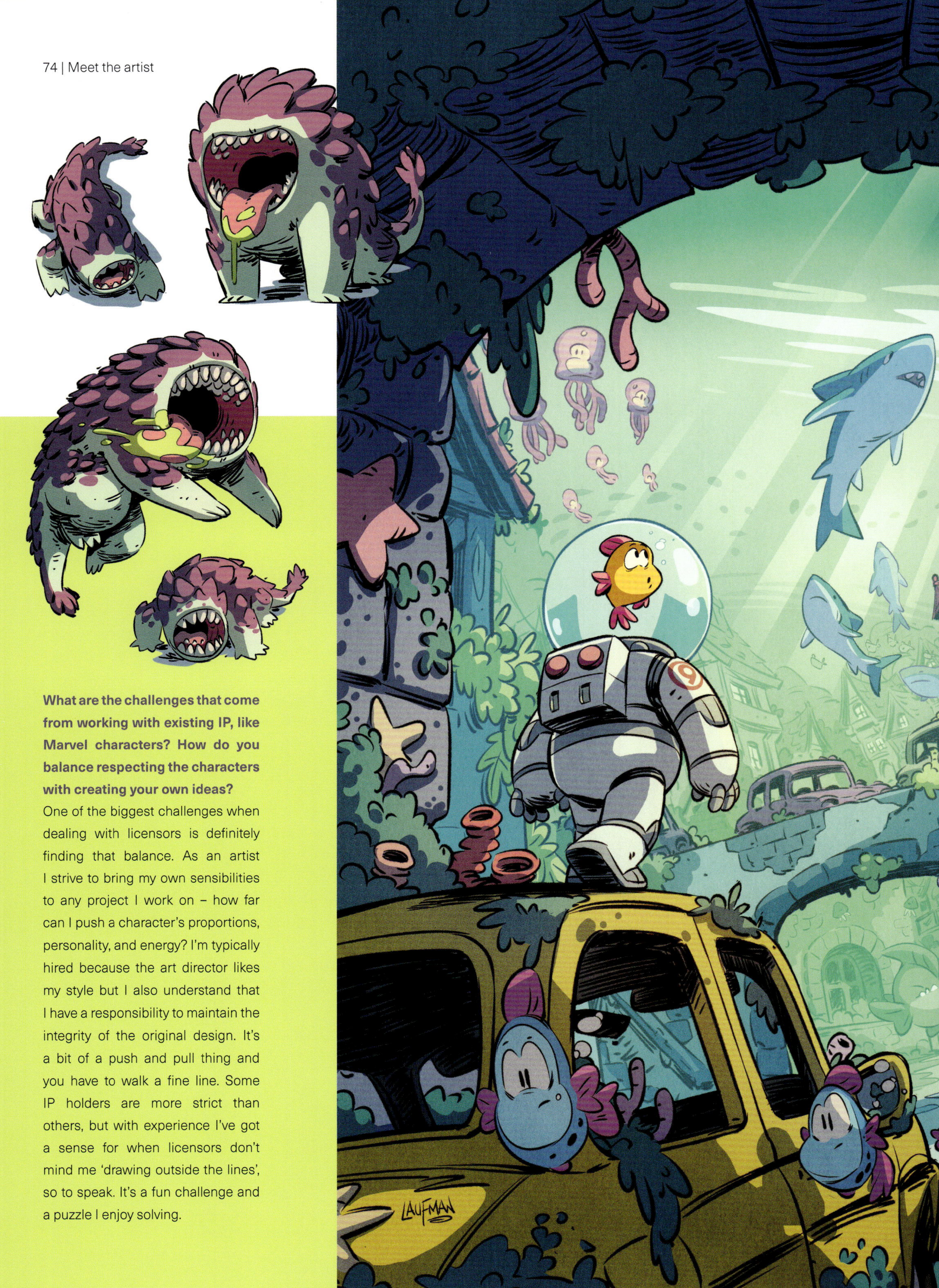

What are the challenges that come from working with existing IP, like Marvel characters? How do you balance respecting the characters with creating your own ideas?

One of the biggest challenges when dealing with licensors is definitely finding that balance. As an artist I strive to bring my own sensibilities to any project I work on – how far can I push a character's proportions, personality, and energy? I'm typically hired because the art director likes my style but I also understand that I have a responsibility to maintain the integrity of the original design. It's a bit of a push and pull thing and you have to walk a fine line. Some IP holders are more strict than others, but with experience I've got a sense for when licensors don't mind me 'drawing outside the lines', so to speak. It's a fun challenge and a puzzle I enjoy solving.

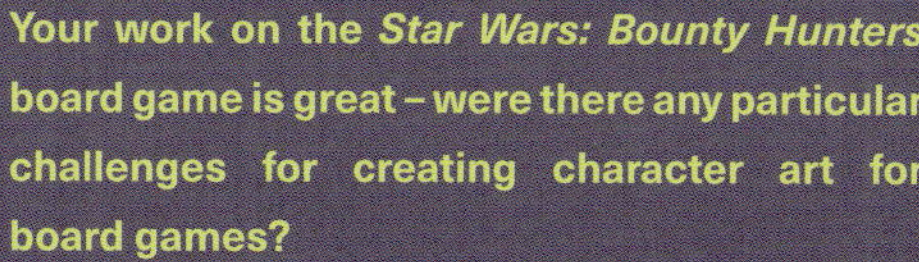

Your work on the *Star Wars: Bounty Hunters* board game is great – were there any particular challenges for creating character art for board games?

I have to be 100% honest here – out of every licence I've worked on throughout my career, working in the *Star Wars* universe has the most restrictive guidelines and approval process, hands down. I've had so many illustrations rejected over the years and many revisions submitted. I love *Star Wars* and I love drawing content from that world but it certainly comes with its frustrations. For *Star Wars: Bounty Hunters* it was more of the same – I must have drawn Grogu ten times before it was finally approved. I get it, though – they want to protect their brand. I do wish they would allow a little more creative freedom at some point as I think it would be great to see them loosen the reins a little bit. That said, I was so happy with how the art for *Bounty Hunters* turned out and I will always jump at the chance to play in their sandbox.

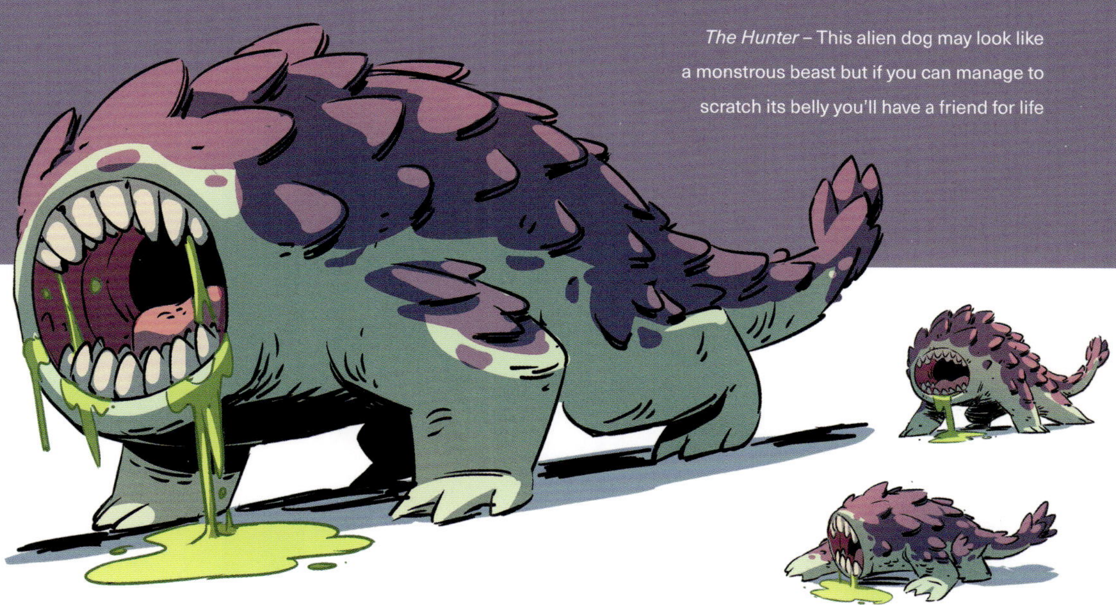

The Hunter – This alien dog may look like a monstrous beast but if you can manage to scratch its belly you'll have a friend for life

Who are the major influences behind your art style and how has your style evolved throughout your career?

Sean Galloway is a master of shape and posing dynamics – when I had a chance to work with him I tried to soak up as much of his super power as I possibly could. I've also been greatly influenced by Fabien Mense who designs some of the most appealing and likeable characters I've ever laid eyes on. Finally, and probably the most influential, has been Mike Mignola. Shape and silhouette are so masterfully used in his characters, pages, and layouts. I hold his work in high regard and do my best to emulate those qualities and design sensibilities when drawing anything.

The principles that each of those artists possess are their acute understanding of shape, silhouette, and how to create balanced, eye-catching designs. In my teens I would try and copy the flashy Image Comics art without truly understanding shape and form and as a result developed some really bad habits. I skipped gaining a basic understanding of the human form and jumped straight into trying to make my drawings look 'cool'. My classical animation teachers really helped to hammer into me the importance of understanding shapes and how they fit together to create a cohesive design. Life drawing was an essential tool to help me further develop an understanding of how a body's form comes together. It didn't fully click right away and I would spend the next ten to fifteen years really trying to develop those skills. I'm a slow learner, but I'm persistent!

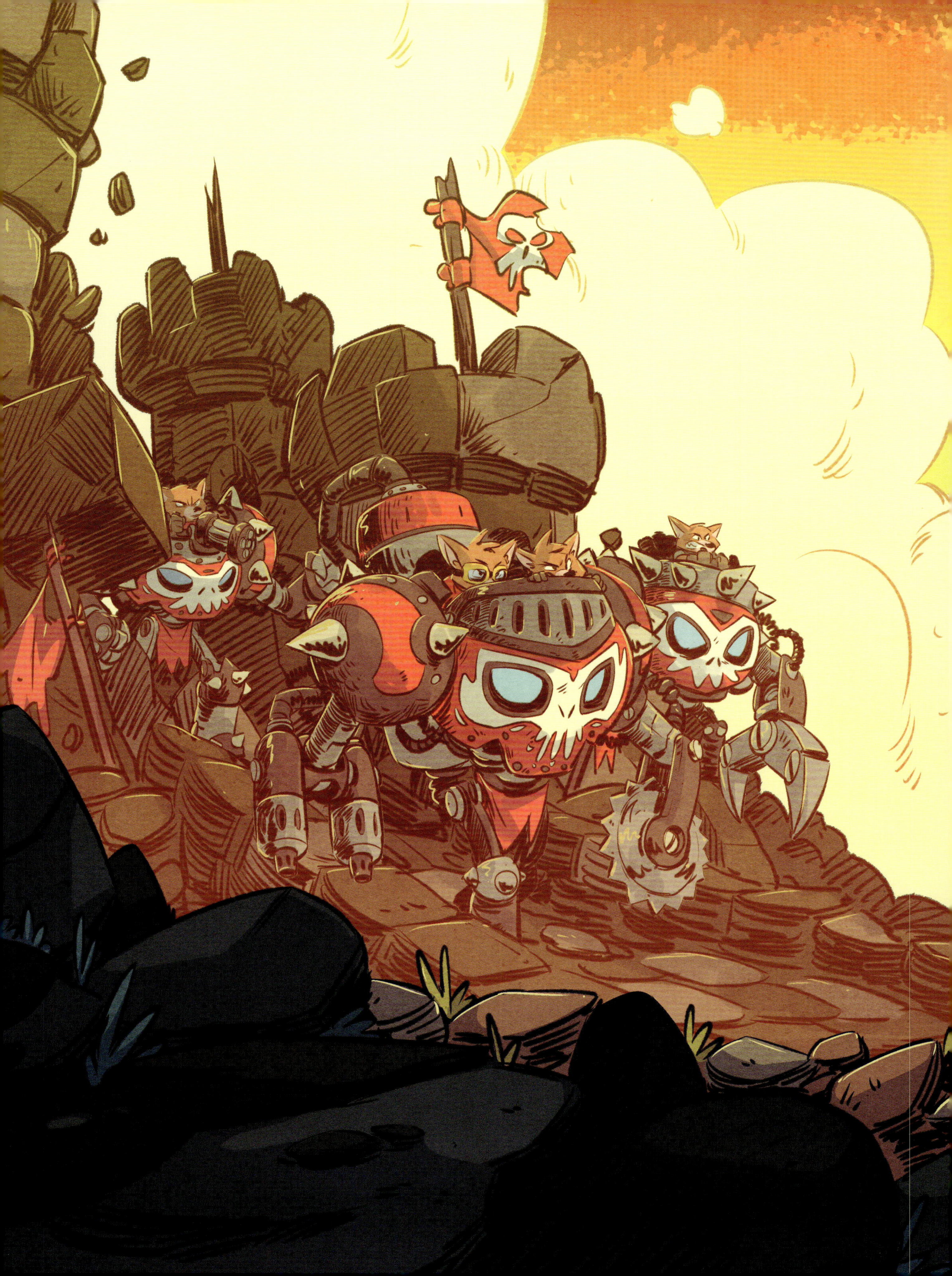

What are the challenges and rewards of working as a freelance artist?

The challenges are many, but so are the benefits. I pick my own hours and so I have almost unlimited flexibility. If a friend asks me out to lunch, I rarely have to say I can't because of work, and I can take as long as I want. I then have the freedom to make up the lost time at any point during that day. It's been an incredible asset while we raised our children, being able to walk them to the bus stop and be there for them when they came home from school. A lot of parents now work from home and can relate, but I've had that luxury for the last fourteen years.

Freelancing certainly does have its share of challenges, though. My wife and I will often sit down and try to plan out our budget for the upcoming months for which I need to have work constantly in the pipeline and payments coming in. I don't have a steady paycheck – my income comes from multiple sources, including clients, my online store sales, conventions, and Patreon. We also try to run a Kickstarter once a year for one of my projects. It's a lot to juggle and the pressure to keep the money coming in can really take its toll on my stress level. That said, I've been very fortunate in that I've been able to carve myself a nice little spot in the art world. I don't take that luxury for granted and I'm always grateful that my clients keep coming back to give me more work. I would never go back to a studio job, I'm far too comfortable living the life of a freelancer.

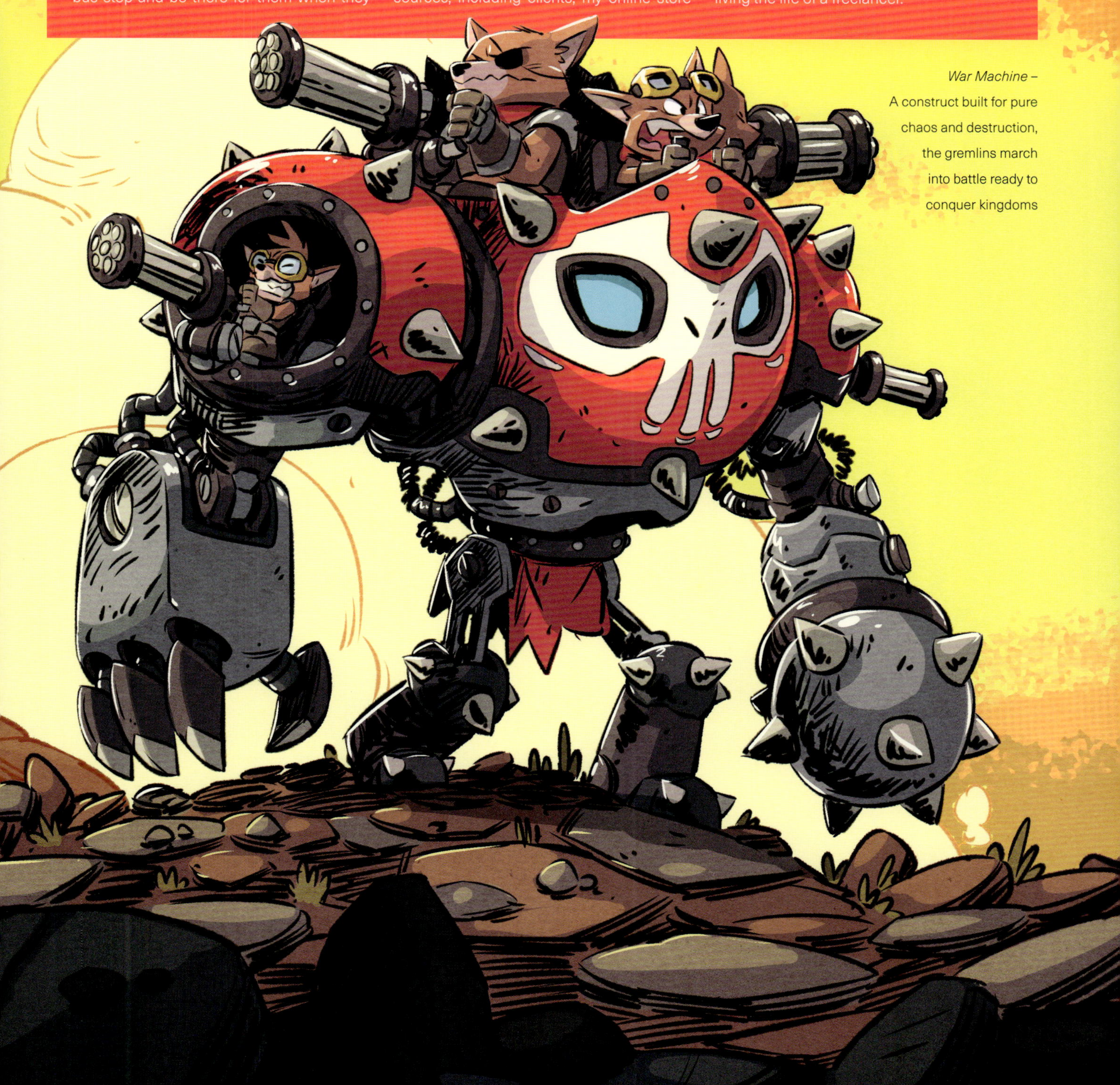

War Machine –
A construct built for pure chaos and destruction, the gremlins march into battle ready to conquer kingdoms

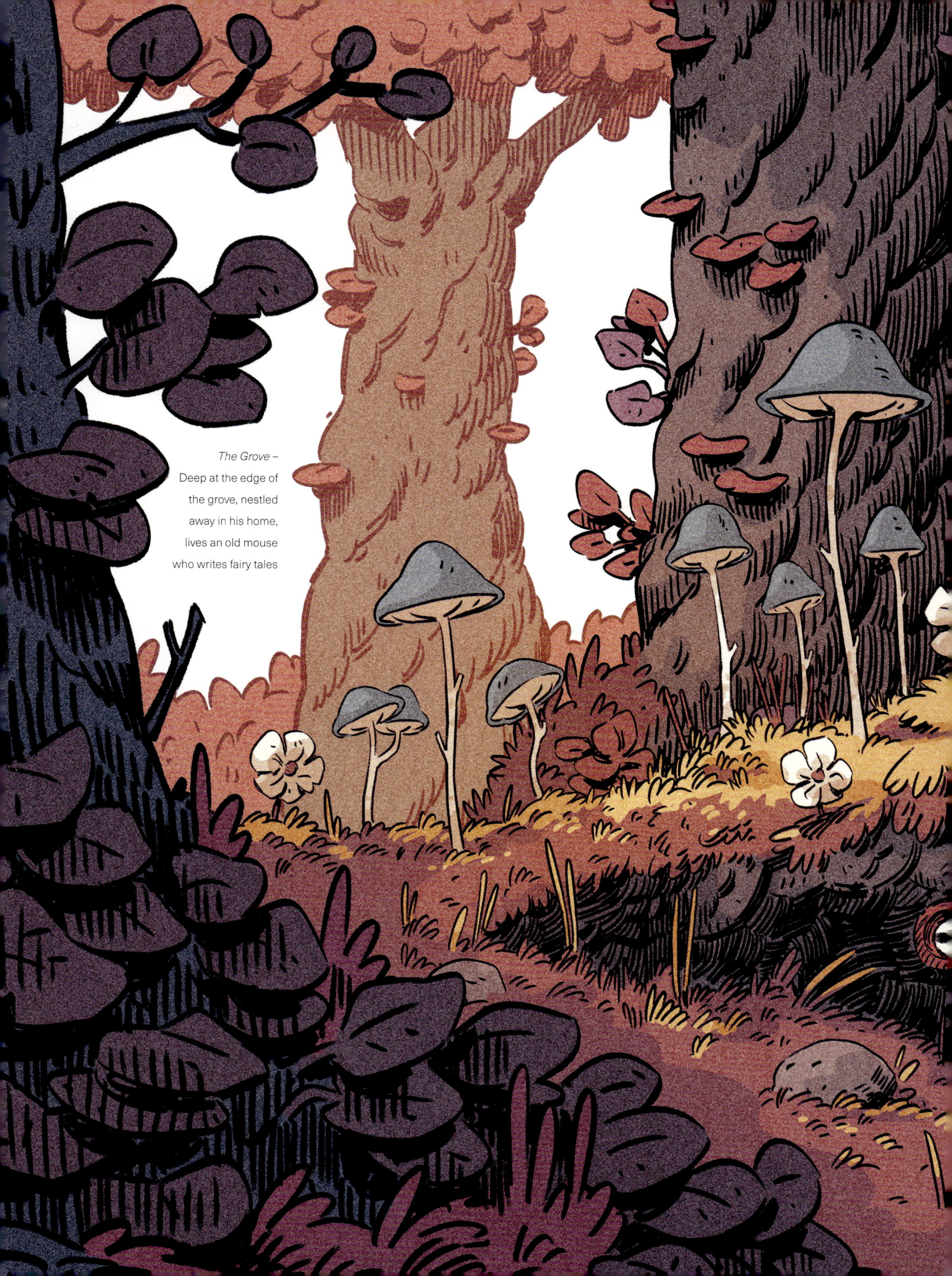

The Grove –
Deep at the edge of
the grove, nestled
away in his home,
lives an old mouse
who writes fairy tales

What would you say are the most important things to remember when designing characters specifically for comics?

The most important thing is their story. It doesn't have to be fully fleshed out, but understanding some very basic aspects of who this character is and what their motivations are helps me get closer to nailing down a design I'm happy with. Once I have a basic story for the character in mind I start with simple shapes and silhouettes, the linchpin of any design and the framework for the character. I will often draw that basic design in multiple rough poses, showing the character in its basic form moving and emoting before locking down the final design. Balancing and refining proportions takes time. Simple decisions like where to place the eyes, how big they are, and how they sit in the skull can mean the difference between a character design that works and one that does not.

Colours are also an important factor when creating an appealing character, finding the right tone and colour balance is crucial. It's an aspect of design I still struggle with. Rarely do I nail colour on my first pass, typically I'll explore many colour combinations to find the right shade of red or blue to balance everything out. It's like unlocking a code, and when you hit the right colour notes, you just know it and the character comes to life. Developing my eye for design has taken many years and it's something I'm always striving to refine.

Can you talk us through the process when creating your own original comics, like *RuinWorld*? Are you writing the script before you start drawing, or is everything coming to life at the same time?

Typically everything starts to come together at the same time. I feel like I have an unorthodox approach to making comics compared to mainstream comics, where a writer will hand a final script off to an artist. The luxury I have when writing and drawing is that I can do both at the same time. I can edit on the fly and sometimes that can be to the benefit of the story but also can slow down the creative process as I often get hung up on deciding the best path for the narrative to take. I will often write a loose story outline in bullet points, perhaps a paragraph here and there better explaining key moments in the story. At this stage, the dialogue is rough because I don't always fully know and understand the characters yet. Character design usually starts about this time and I will do my best to lock down the main characters before I start storyboarding anything. Once I have my characters and a basic outline I will try and thumbnail out the entire book in rough page layouts. Then I take those roughs and start to write the text bubbles over the top of them in Clip Studio Paint – 90% of my dialogue is written right on the page. I find it easier to write when I have a drawing to reference with the scene. Almost magically the story starts to play out like a movie – that's when the characters and story start to come to life for me.

The Great Owl – The giant winged beast challenges Sir Galant, Ironwood's legendary knight, to a battle to the death

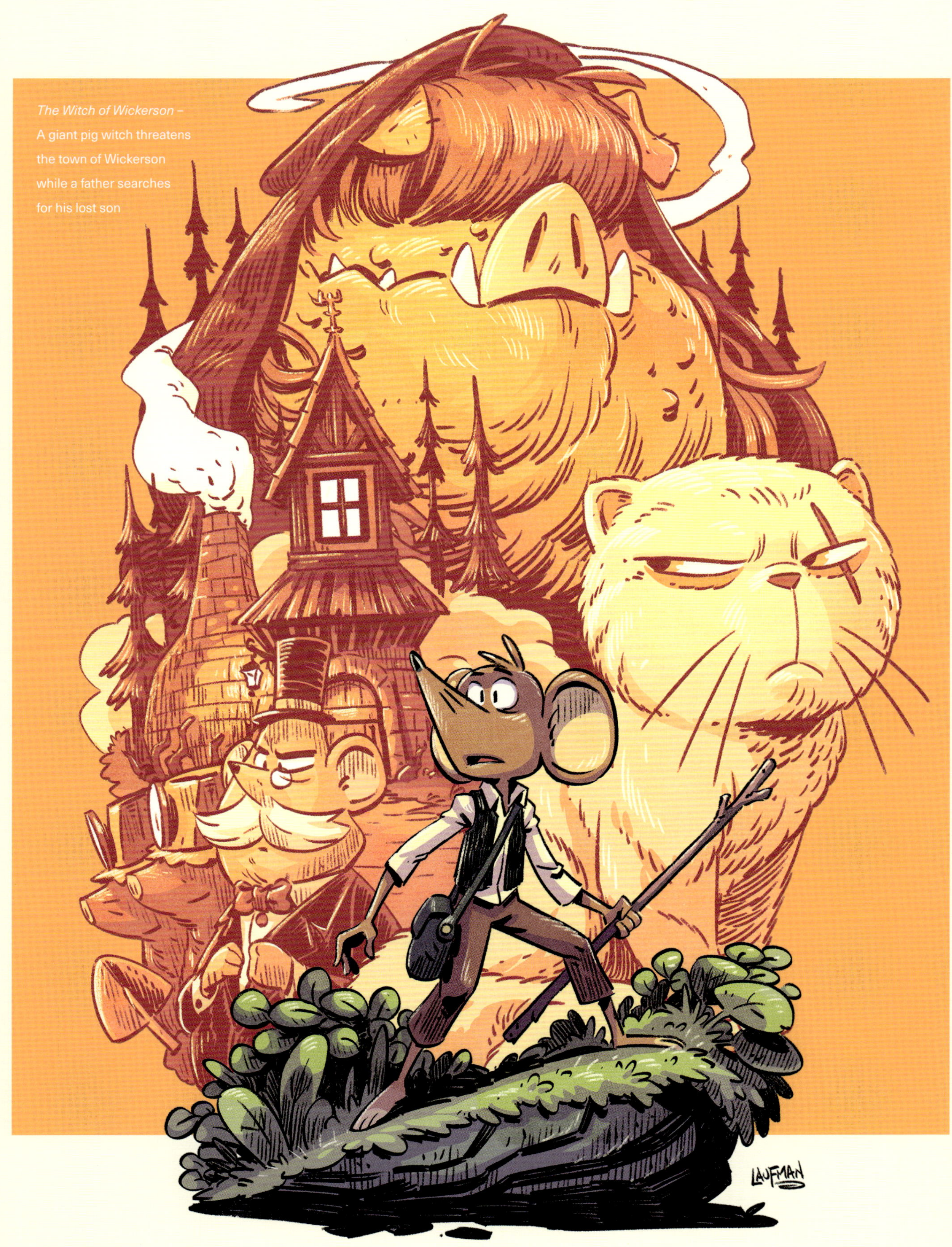

The Witch of Wickerson –
A giant pig witch threatens the town of Wickerson while a father searches for his lost son

What has been your favourite project to work on, and is there a dream project you'd still like to be involved with?

My favourite project so far has probably been *The Witch of Wickerson*. I had challenged myself to do a comic for Inktober: thirty-one pages in thirty-one days. I gave myself two weeks of pre-production to design and write the story and then I was off to the races. It was an intense month, to say the least! I was drawing the pencils digitally and then printing them out and inking them traditionally with a brush pen. I would then scan the pages back into Clip Studio Paint, where I would colour and letter the page to be posted the next day. It was a daunting task but the fact that it came together the way it did will always surprise me. I had created this rich world and story in less than two months and by the end I had a book to share with the world. I'm not sure I could pull off something like that again but I'd love to try sometime, if my body allows it. As for dream projects, I don't know if I have one. I have a lot of story ideas, some of which I'm currently working on and some that I've put into the storage locker of my brain to haul out down the road. Hayao Miyazaki has been a big influence on my comic career in that he's created all these beautiful movies, each one its own special thing that will live on forever. I find that really appealing, so I guess my dream is to have a body of work to leave behind that people can enjoy long after I'm gone.

Foley – A big beefy warrior whose appetite for adventure is almost as big as his appetite for food

Dragon Fighter – Grogun is an ancient dragon who's fallen on hard times. He yearns for the day when dragons weren't seen as the enemy of the people

Are there any upcoming projects we should be looking out for?

I'm currently working on a new *Crimson Fall* story titled *The Shore Tower*. In this latest story I bring back Sir Duncross and Father McKellen as they hunt down a fearsome monster on a deserted island. I've really enjoyed expanding on the world of *Crimson Fall* and I hope my readers enjoy this next story in the series. I have also been slowly working on a much larger follow up to *The Witch of Wickerson* called *The Rats of Ironwood*. This next story explores the town of Wickerson following the death of the pig witch, whose path of destruction has left the town in a state of turmoil. I'm hoping to expand on this world and explore all the wonderful characters and adventures that have been knocking around in my head for the past few years.

All images © Dan Gartman

HOW I
STYLIZE

Dan Gartman shares the secrets behind his geometric character designs

The geometry of shapes is the basis of my approach to stylization. It's a balance between creating strict and organic forms and trying to maintain dynamism without going headlong into cubism. I like a particular kind of humour: the head is a square, the arm is a cone, the chest looks like a ball. This helps to make my characters unique and highlights their special features. If a big-nosed old man with a trapezoidal head is a handsome character in your opinion, then you're welcome!

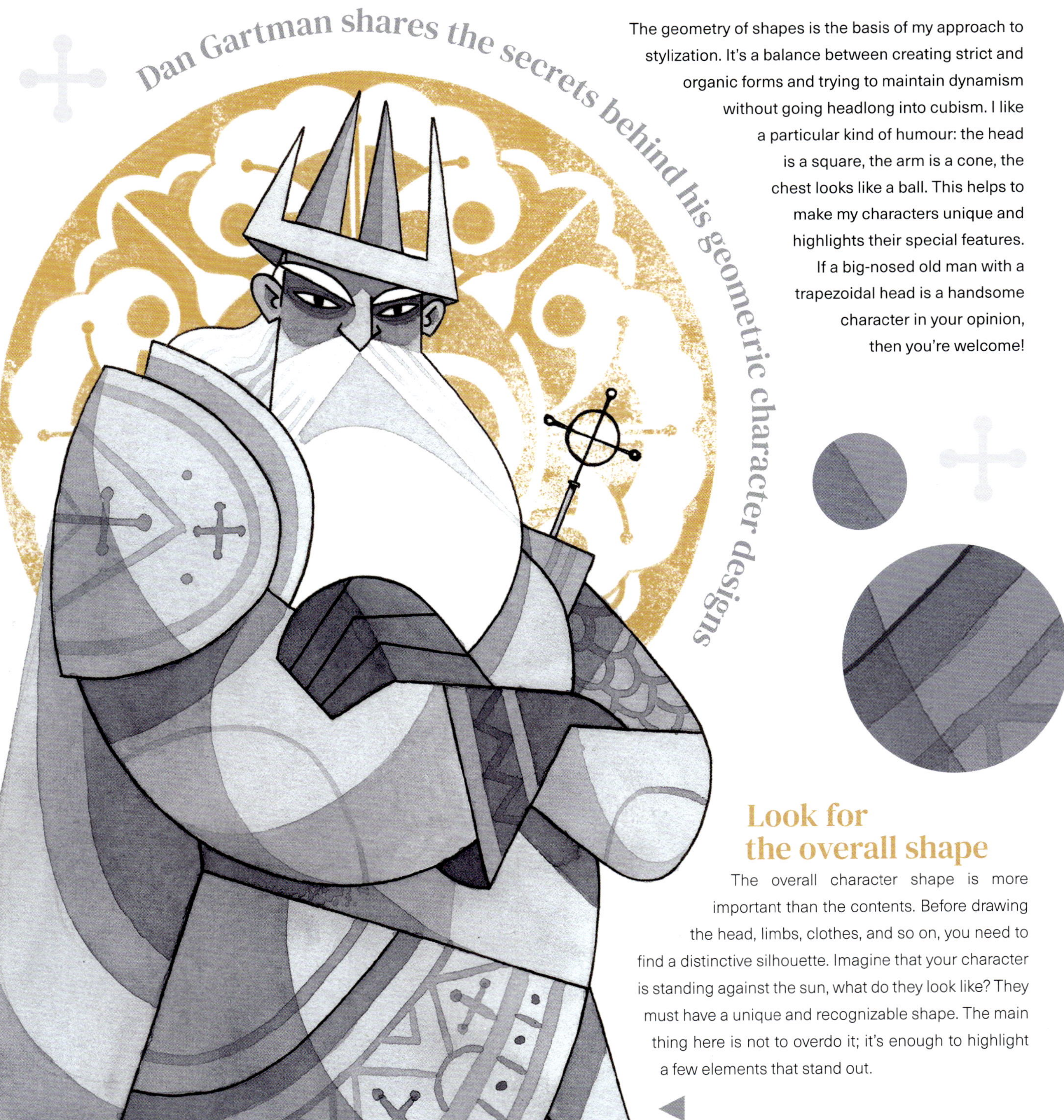

Look for the overall shape

The overall character shape is more important than the contents. Before drawing the head, limbs, clothes, and so on, you need to find a distinctive silhouette. Imagine that your character is standing against the sun, what do they look like? They must have a unique and recognizable shape. The main thing here is not to overdo it; it's enough to highlight a few elements that stand out.

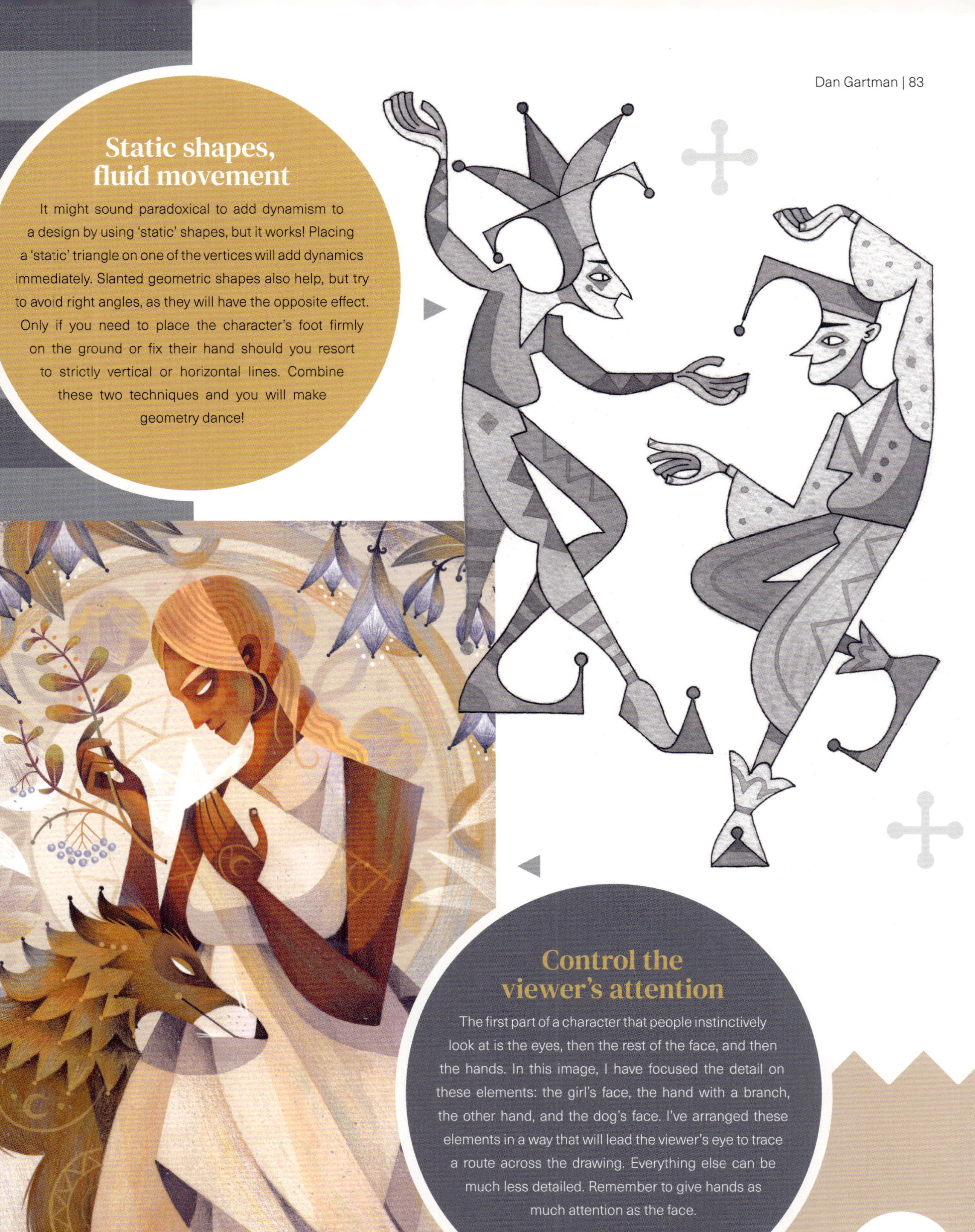

Static shapes, fluid movement

It might sound paradoxical to add dynamism to a design by using 'static' shapes, but it works! Placing a 'static' triangle on one of the vertices will add dynamics immediately. Slanted geometric shapes also help, but try to avoid right angles, as they will have the opposite effect. Only if you need to place the character's foot firmly on the ground or fix their hand should you resort to strictly vertical or horizontal lines. Combine these two techniques and you will make geometry dance!

Control the viewer's attention

The first part of a character that people instinctively look at is the eyes, then the rest of the face, and then the hands. In this image, I have focused the detail on these elements: the girl's face, the hand with a branch, the other hand, and the dog's face. I've arranged these elements in a way that will lead the viewer's eye to trace a route across the drawing. Everything else can be much less detailed. Remember to give hands as much attention as the face.

Simplify and break proportions

Take a look at any part of your body: its shape consists of curves, bends, and bulges – when creating a character, you can simplify each of these elements. You need to replace biological shapes with straight geometric lines while preserving their essence and position. Only the outer lines should change. To highlight the features of a character's figure you can radically change their proportions. For example, deliberately enlarge the hands in relation to the forearm, or significantly alter the head to be markedly larger or smaller than the body.

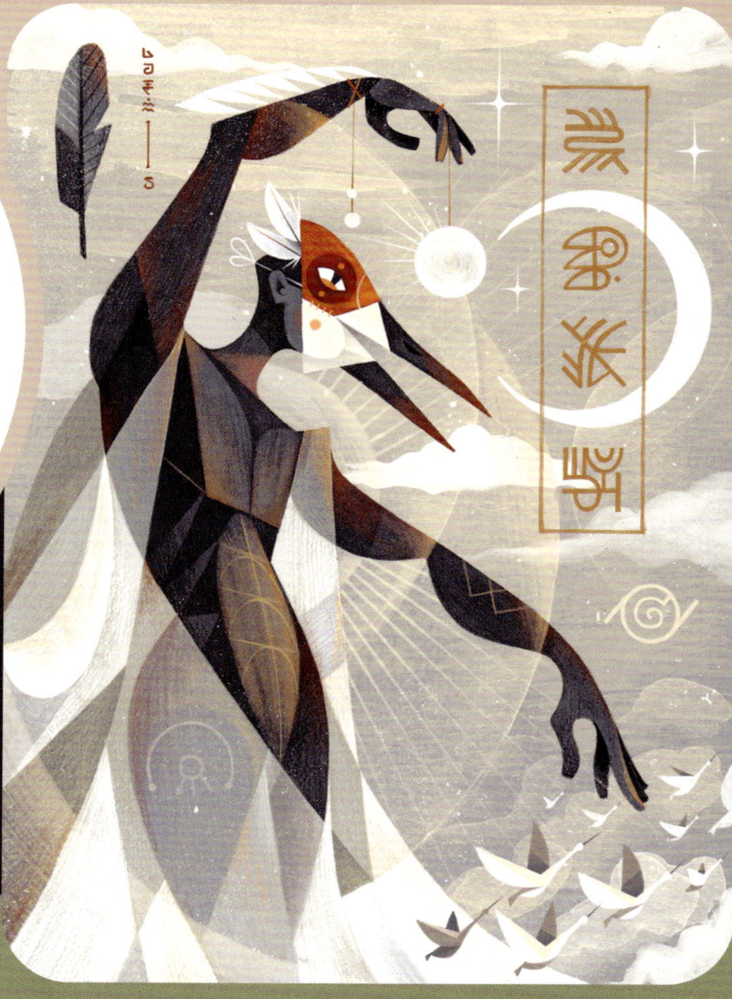

The more things change...

The more characters are different from each other, the better. You can achieve this by varying shape sizes, proportions, and clothing. However, at the same time it's important to maintain an overall coherent style. To do this, you need to decide how you will draw generic details, such as eyes, fingers, and other parts of the body, and use the same method for each character. They may differ in size, colour, and volume, but the principles behind their construction should remain the same.

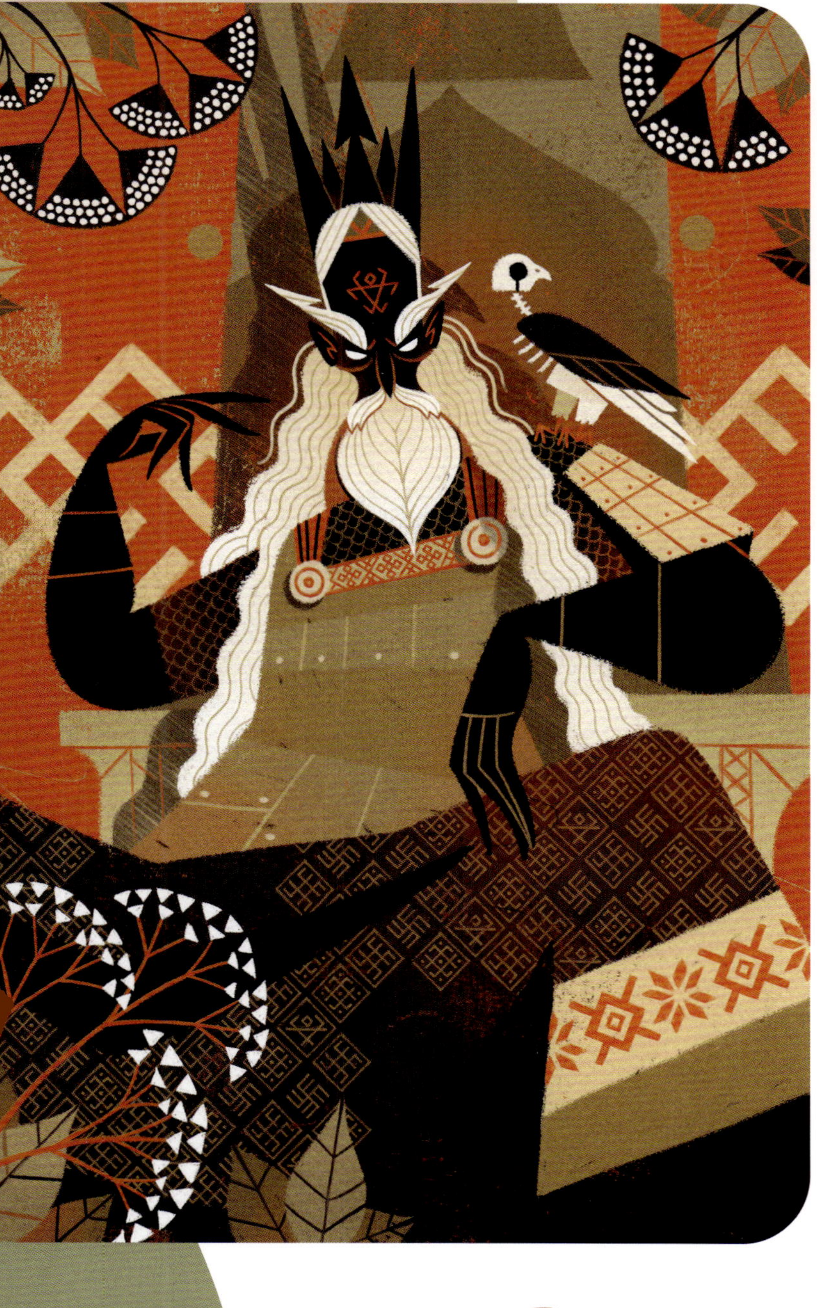

Story through surroundings

Props, patterns, and ornamental features can help explain a lot about the origin of a character, the culture they belong to, or the type of activity they do. For example, complex, elaborate, detailed designs are associated with wealth, power, and status, whereas a simple polka dot pattern would suggest simplicity and fun. Showing the material used can also suggest the status of the character.

Be ridiculous

Don't be afraid to add something unusual or goofy to your designs, like a fish wearing trousers, or a frog who's a priest. Anachronistic elements will help make your character memorable and stay in the viewer's mind. Mix different parts of creatures, give them human characteristics – put your smartphone aside and free your imagination!

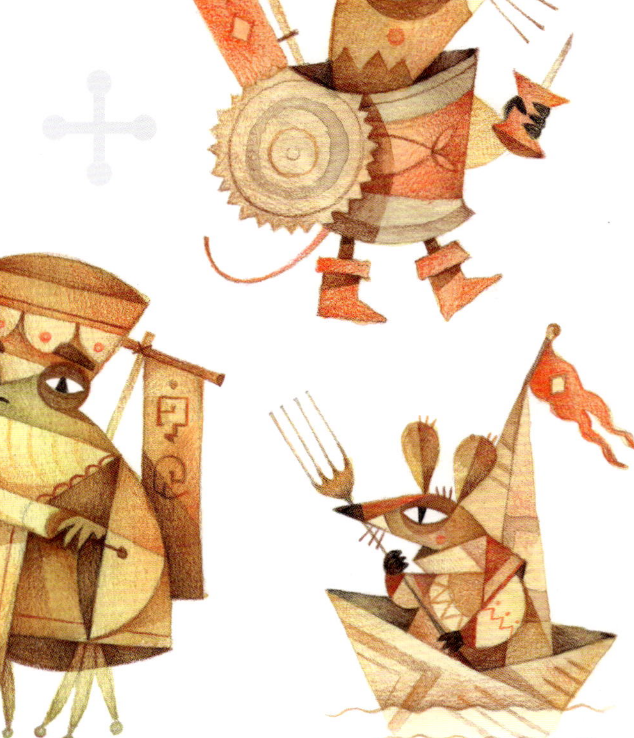

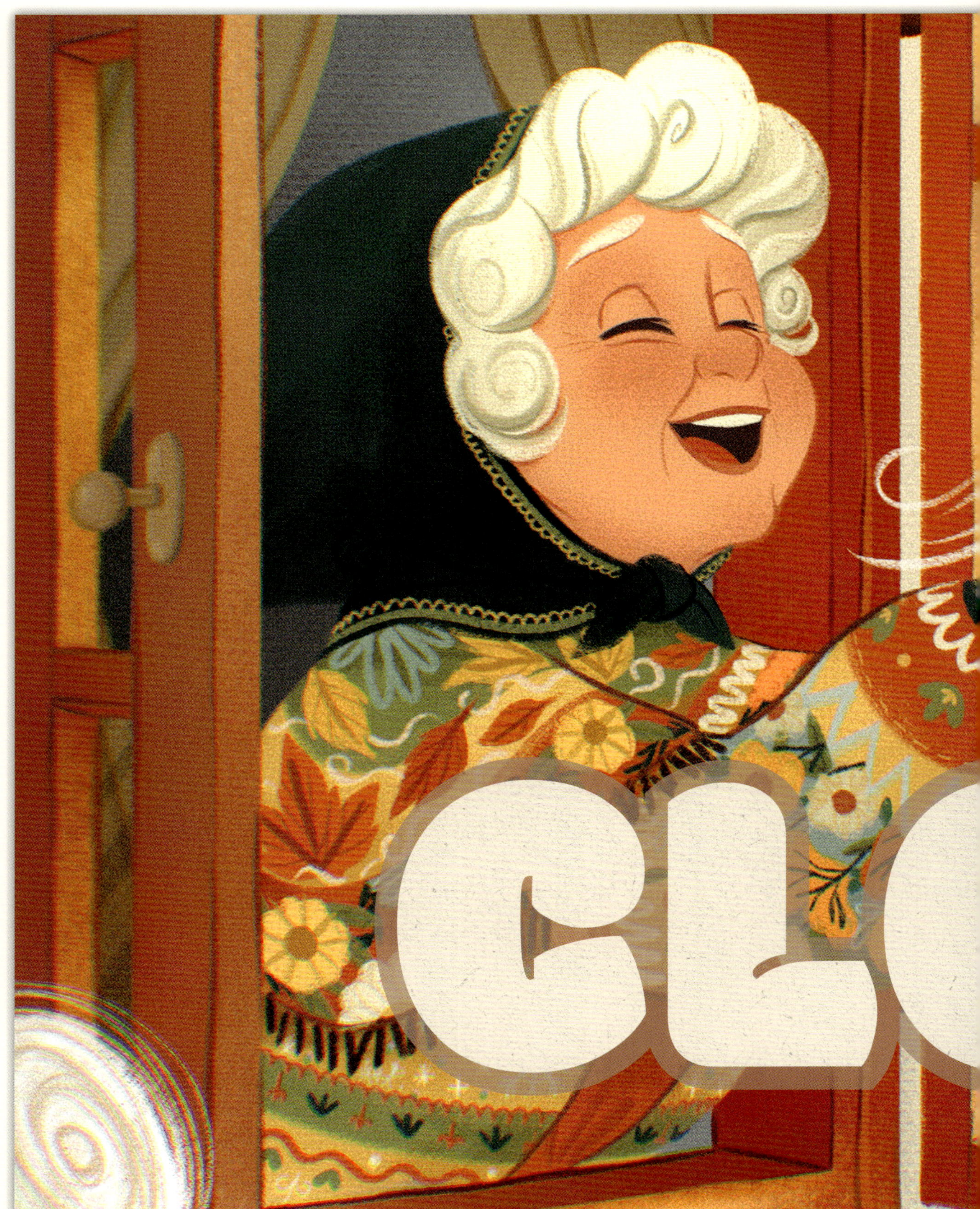

Final image © Meike Schneider

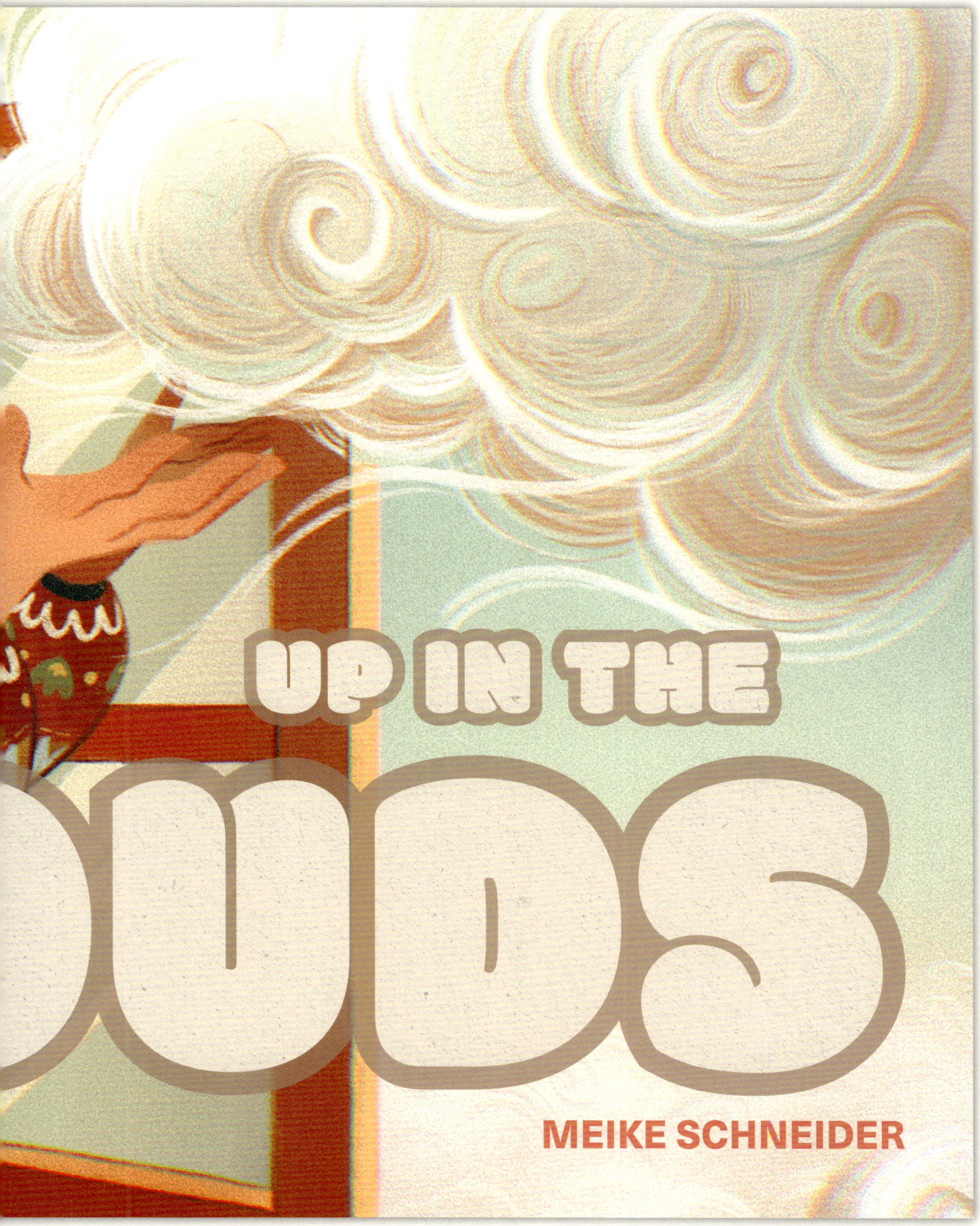

UP IN THE
CLOUDS
MEIKE SCHNEIDER

In this tutorial, I will be reimagining the Germanic fairy-tale character, Mother Hulda. The first step in designing a character is to create a mood board to gather inspirations and set the tone for the project. I start by collecting a variety of reference images, focusing on art styles, patterns, and colour palettes that align with the character's concept. The mood board has both warm and cool colour schemes, allowing for the exploration of a range of different aesthetics.

I conduct market research to analyse existing designs and trends. This helps ensure that the character remains unique and doesn't inadvertently replicate existing work. By understanding what's already out there, I can refine the design to stand out while staying true to the intended vision. This combination of creative inspiration and strategic research forms the foundation for a compelling and original character design.

WARM UP

One of my favourite warm up methods is the shape challenge. It's simple: use a bold brush and create a few different shapes. After that, go ahead and fill the shapes with characters. I always try to limit myself to one or two minutes per shape and I keep the sketch very simple. This exercise helps me to think less and experiment more. It also forces me to draw things I usually wouldn't draw.

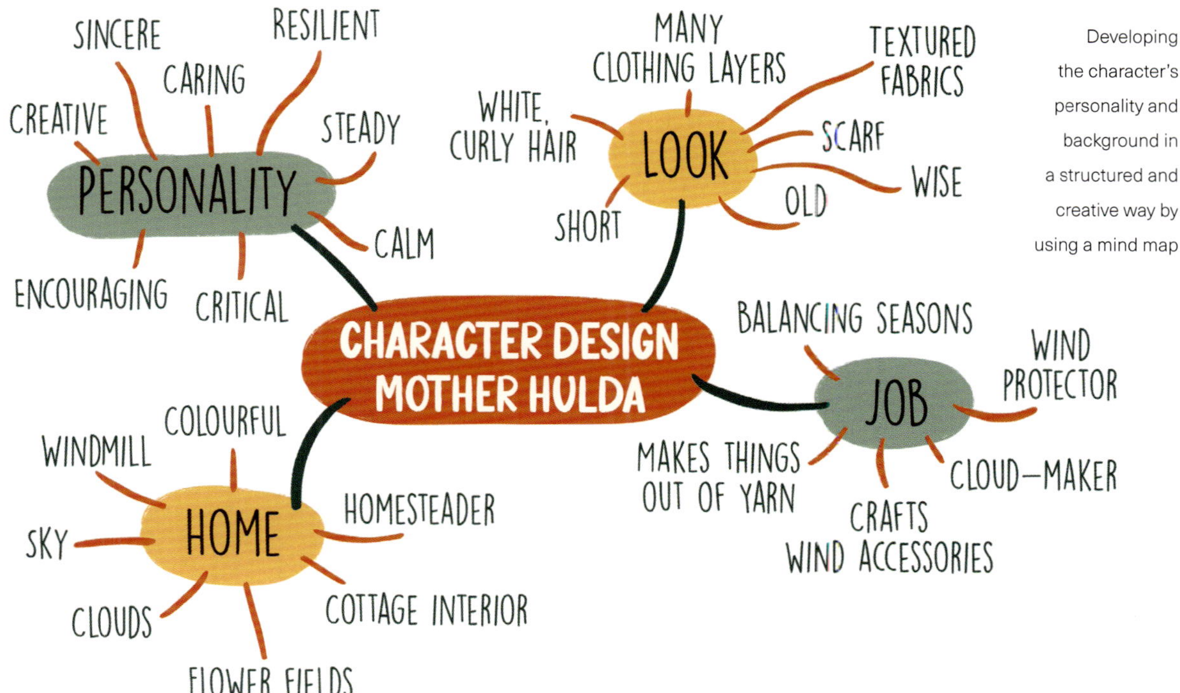

Developing the character's personality and background in a structured and creative way by using a mind map

With a clear visual direction established, the next step is to delve into the character's personality and backstory. I create a mind map to help explore and organize various aspects of their identity. This part of the process involves brainstorming ideas for the character's hobbies, personality traits, and background. Additionally, at this point I consider the location where the story unfolds and key story elements that could influence the character's development. The mind map allows for a holistic view of the character, ensuring their personality is well-rounded and cohesive. By connecting these elements, I can shape a character who is not only visually distinct but also rich in depth and relatability within the story's context.

STORY STRUCTURE

A visual story structure helps map out key plot points for the character development and emotional beats for a cohesive and engaging story

To develop my story around Mother Hulda, I begin by researching her historical interpretations and significance. This informs my retelling, allowing me to challenge outdated stereotypes and gender roles. My goal is to create a relatable, original character, while maintaining the essence of Mother Hulda.

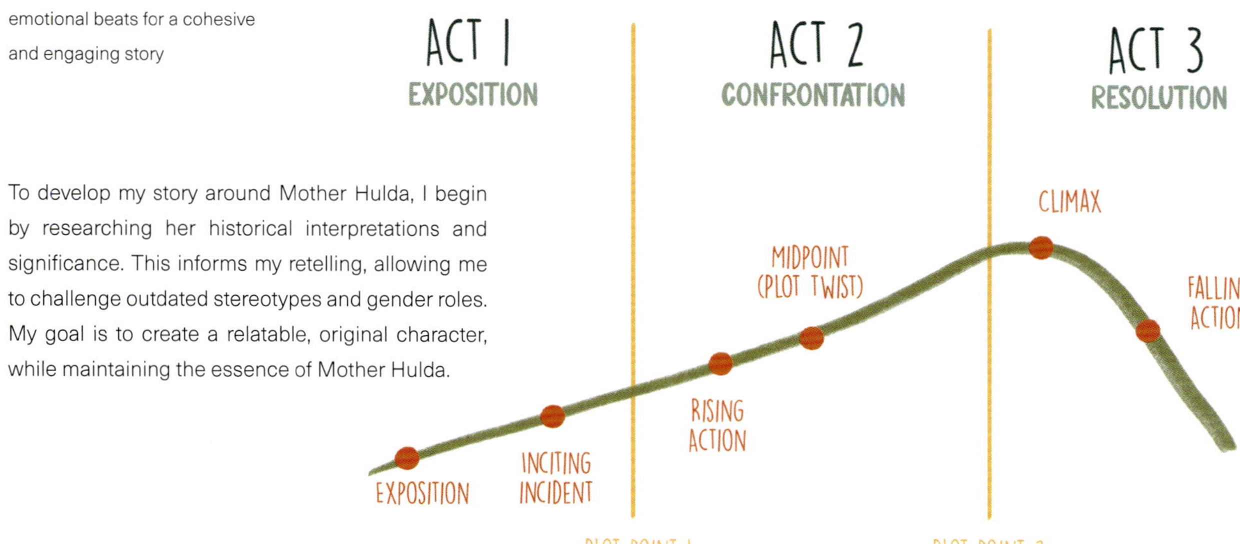

MY STORY CONCEPT

A young girl felt lonely and misunderstood after a fight with her parents. Seeking peace, she discovered a mysterious well from which enchanting sounds drifted. A gust of wind snatched her cap, sending it into the well. Climbing down to retrieve it, she found herself entering a magical realm.

There, she met Hulda, a wise cloud weaver living in a majestic windmill. Captivated, the girl watched as Hulda crafted clouds from shimmering threads, reflecting nature's moods: gentle rain, fierce storms, and brilliant sunshine. The girl learned that each cloud had its unique purpose, and it was futile to label anything as simply 'good' or 'bad'. In this world, she found the true gifts of diversity and acceptance.

In this stage, I focus on creating very rough and preliminary sketches of Mother Hulda. This exploration allows me to experiment with a wide range of ideas, particularly those that may not come to mind initially. I believe this step is crucial, as artists often become attached to their first few concepts and may overlook the potential of alternative approaches. By pushing beyond my comfort zone, I can uncover unique characteristics and design elements that elevate the character. Each sketch serves as a stepping stone, allowing for organic development and the opportunity to blend traditional elements with fresh interpretations. Ultimately, this process fosters creativity and will open the door to crafting a truly distinctive and memorable portrayal.

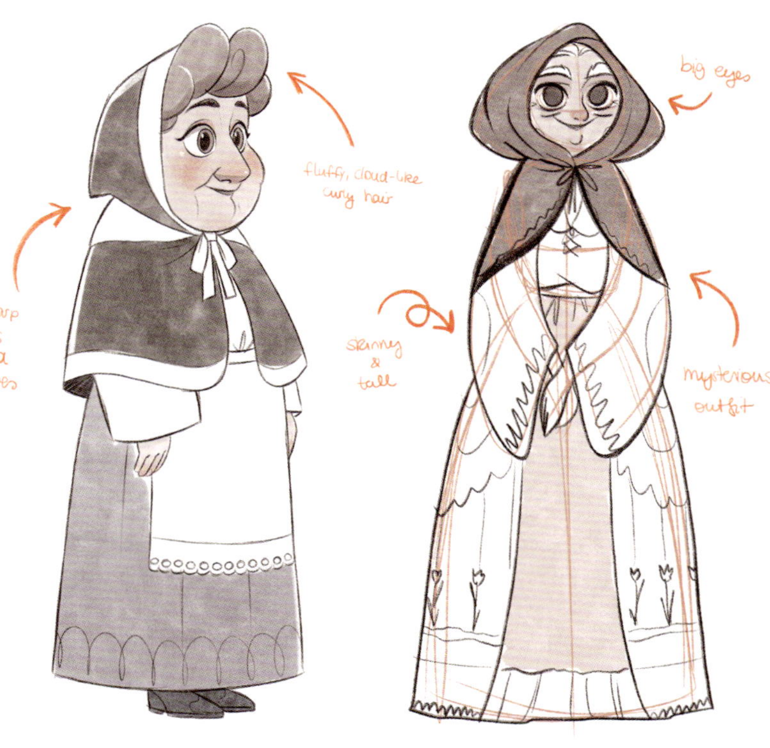

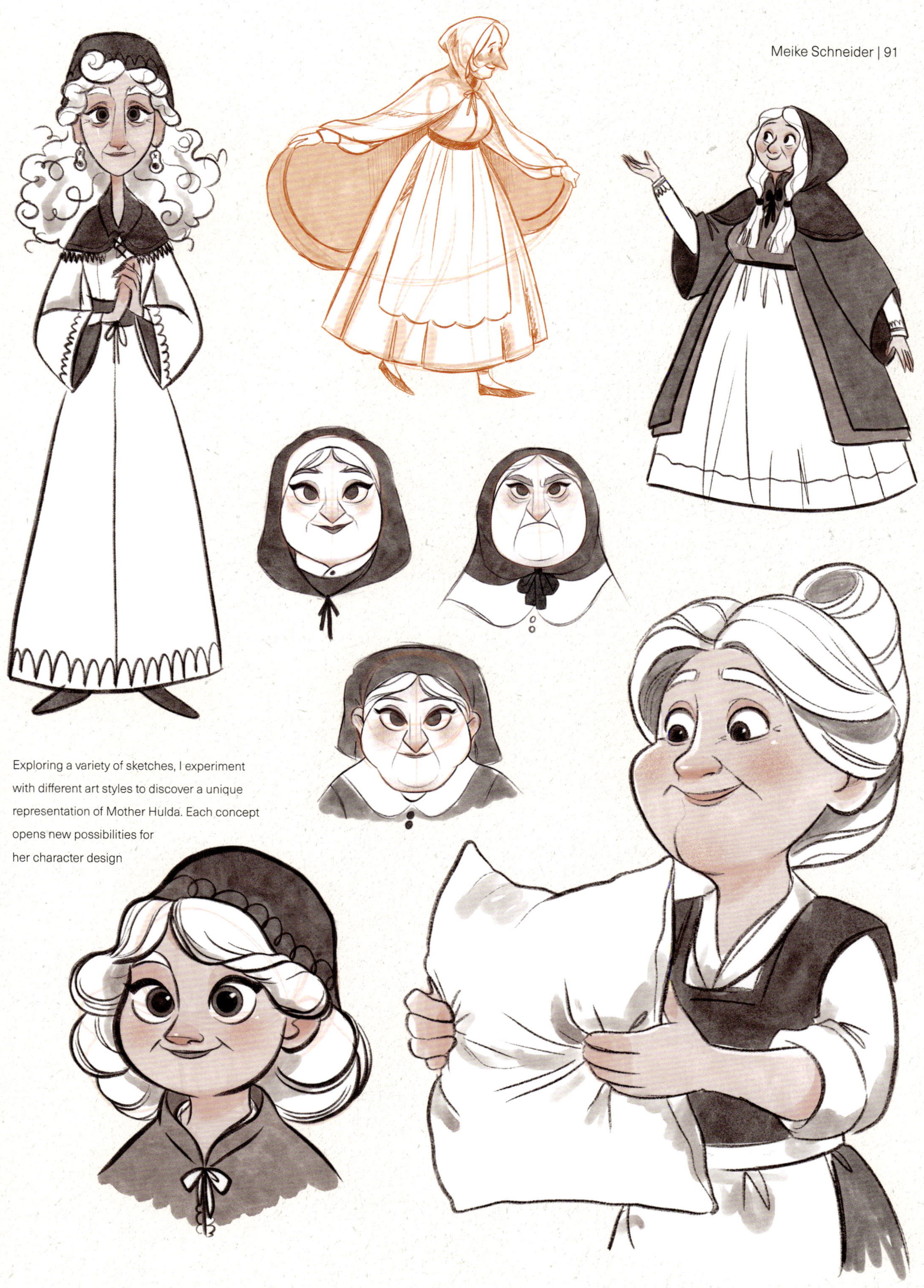

Exploring a variety of sketches, I experiment with different art styles to discover a unique representation of Mother Hulda. Each concept opens new possibilities for her character design

In this step, I delve into the concept of shape language to refine the proportions. I experiment with various shapes to explore her age, size, and overall body proportions. Shape language is a powerful tool in character design; it can convey emotions and traits effectively. To embody Mother Hulda's calm, creative, and light nature, I focus on using soft, round shapes that evoke a sense of harmony, allowing her to feel at home in the sky. Her hair, fluffy like clouds, enhances this ethereal quality. Additionally, I incorporate some square forms to instil feelings of trust and stability, creating a balanced design that reflects her nurturing essence. This careful consideration of shapes helps to visually communicate her character traits and enrich her overall portrayal.

A strong silhouette ensures instant recognition and helps convey character traits effectively

USE SHAPES TO ADD PERSONALITY

Shape language is a powerful tool in character design – basic shapes like circles, squares, and triangles can be used to convey personality. Circles often evoke friendliness, warmth, and softness, making them ideal for gentle, approachable characters. Squares suggest stability, strength, and reliability, giving a character a grounded, dependable feel. Triangles can imply energy, danger, or sharpness, adding a sense of dynamism or edginess to a design. By starting with one of these shapes as a base, a designer can then effectively communicate a character's core traits and bring their personality to life visually.

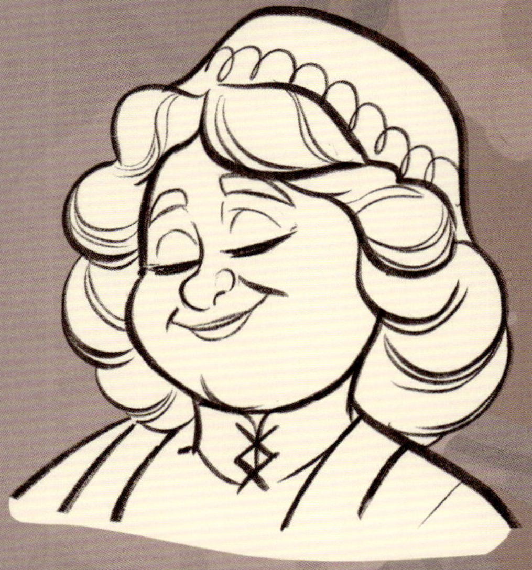

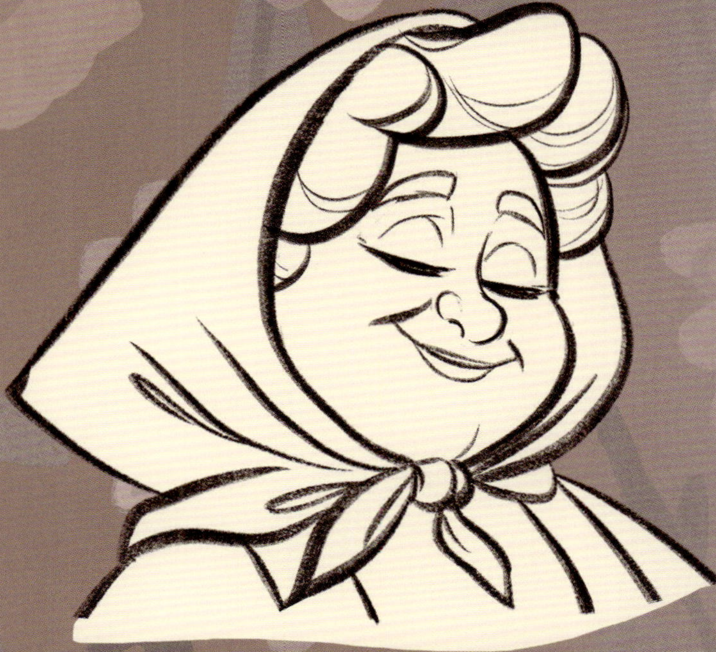

In this stage, I explore various hairstyles and hats to complement Mother Hulda's character. Her hair should embody her personality while being practical for her many household tasks. I envision an updo that reflects her busy nature, opting for curly, fluffy locks that resemble soft clouds. It's important that her hairstyle feels relaxed and inviting, avoiding a tight or stiff appearance. Alongside the hair, I experiment with different hat styles to enhance her overall look, aiming for a balance between functionality and charm. This exploration allows me to find a hairstyle that not only suits her character but also adds depth to her design.

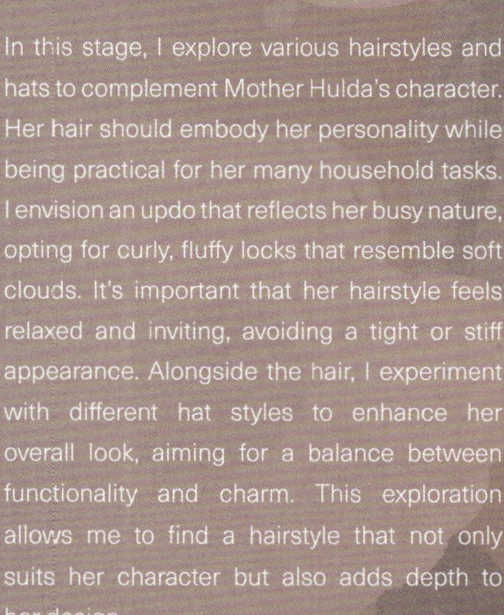

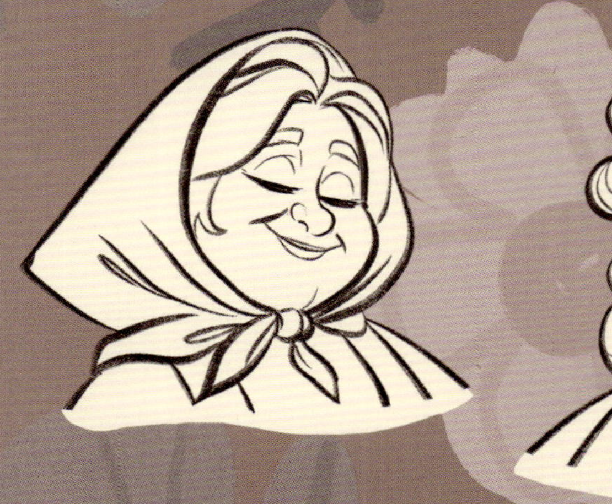

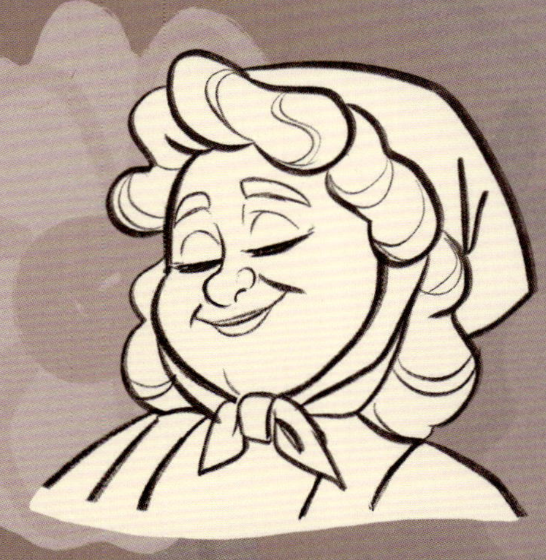

A character's design should be strong enough to be recognizable even without the hair, ensuring that other aspects, like shape and silhouette, contribute to their distinct identity

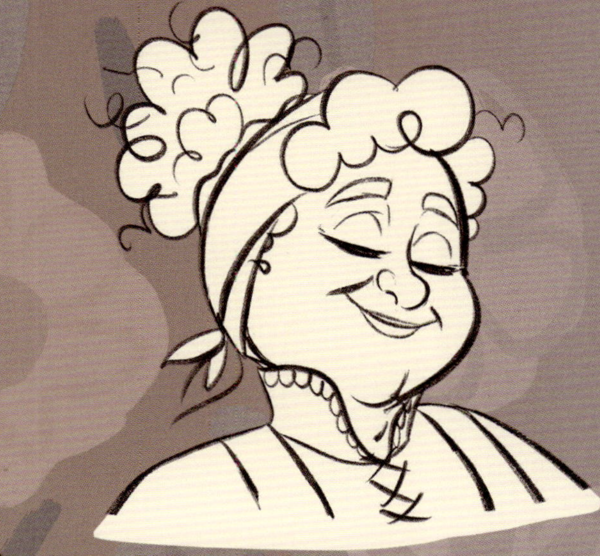

Costume design is vital in establishing a character's connection to their story and setting. For Mother Hulda, whose tale originates in Hessen, Germany, it's important that her clothing reflects the historical period and cultural context of the region. As she spends her days engaged in household tasks and weaving clouds, her outfit needs to be practical and functional, allowing her to move freely and comfortably. However, it should also stay true to the era she lives in, incorporating traditional elements from the attire of that time.

Mother Hulda represents the seasons, the weather, and the earth, so I'm integrating these elements as patterns into her clothes. In some designs, she wears floral patterns or a coat adorned with motifs representing all four seasons. By balancing functionality with symbolic design, her costume not only enhances her character's identity, but also deepens her connection to the natural world, making her a more relatable and authentic figure within the narrative.

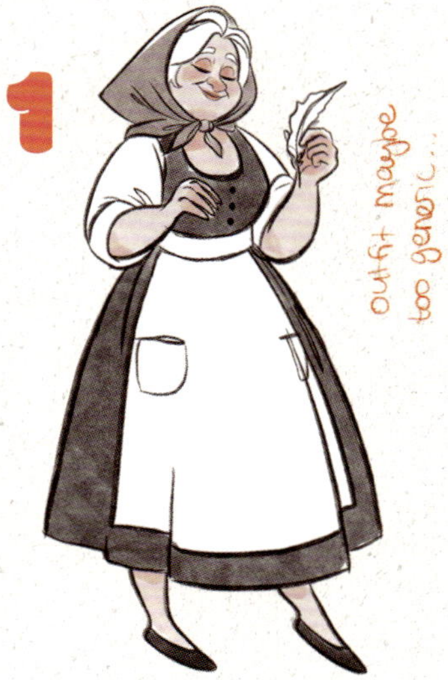

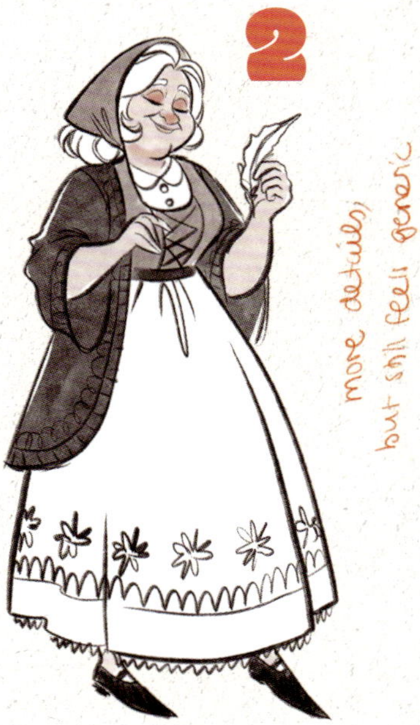

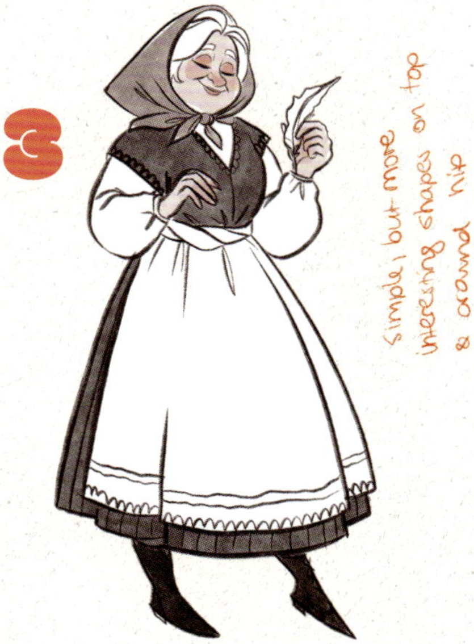

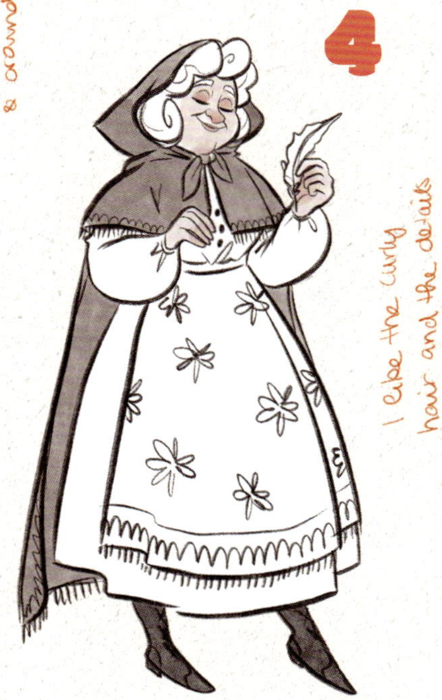

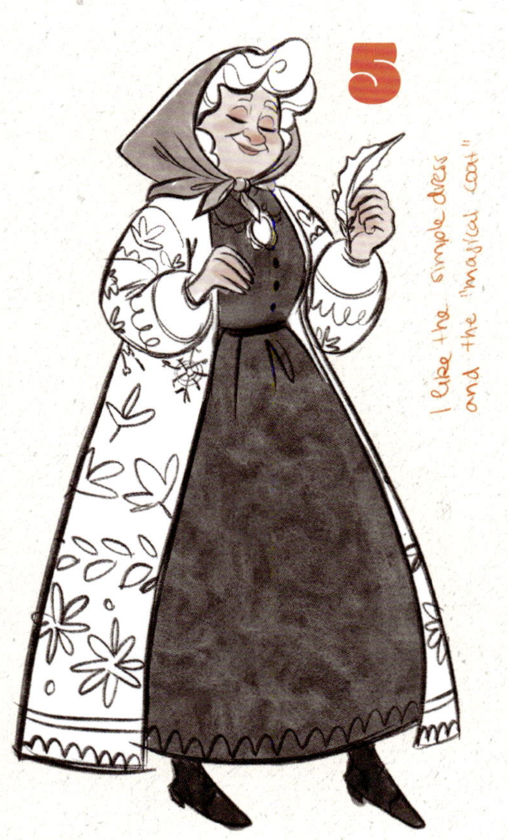

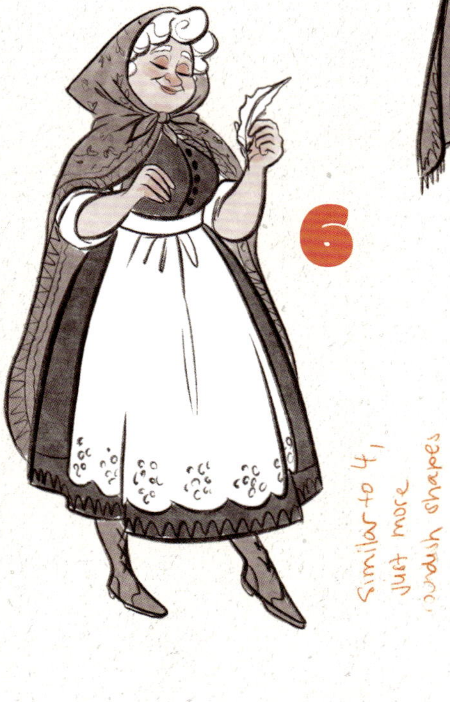

By carefully selecting fabrics, patterns, and accessories that align with historical influences, the costume becomes a bridge between the character and her environment, reinforcing her role within the story and making her more relatable and believable to the audience

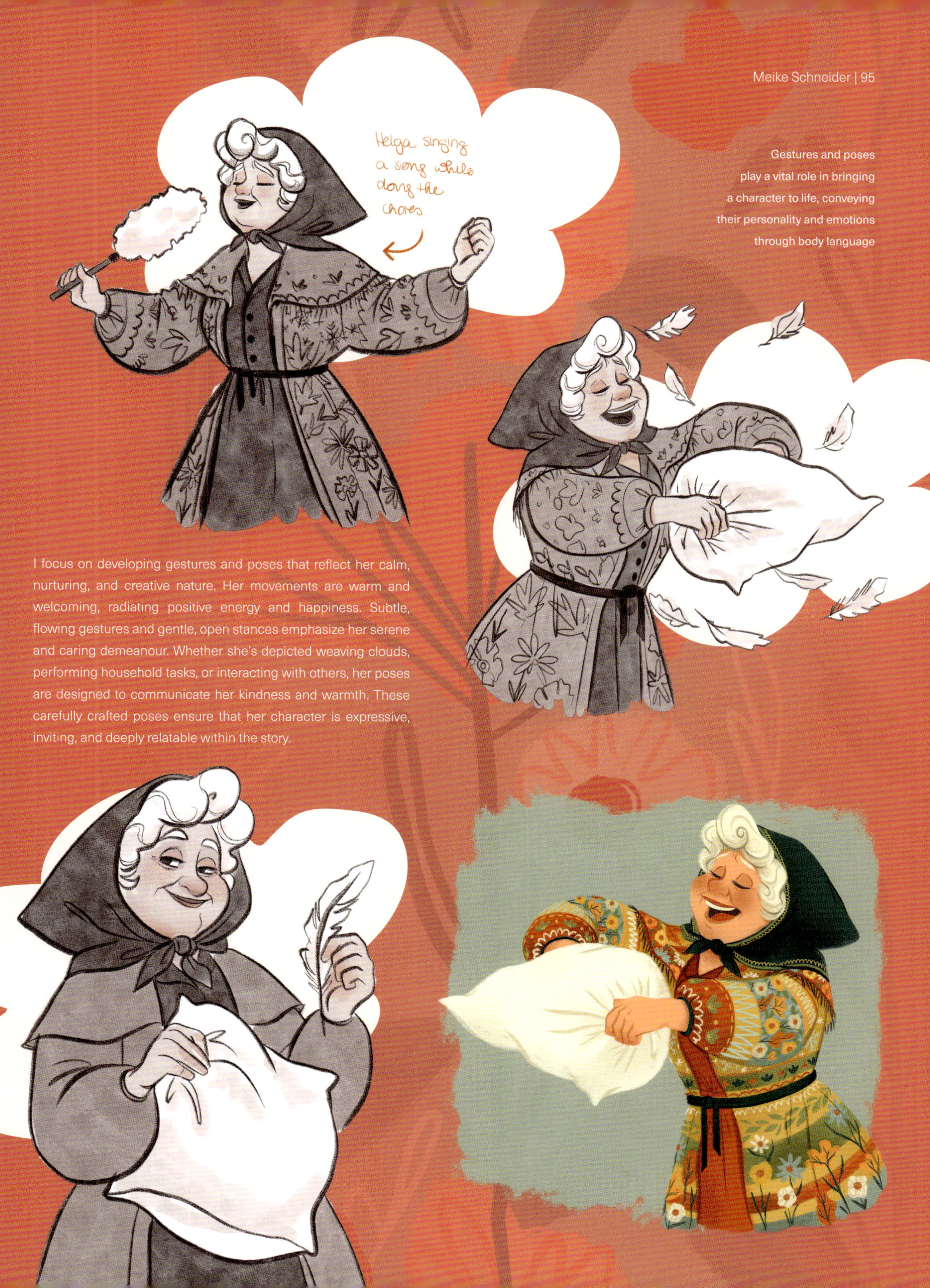

Gestures and poses
play a vital role in bringing
a character to life, conveying
their personality and emotions
through body language

I focus on developing gestures and poses that reflect her calm, nurturing, and creative nature. Her movements are warm and welcoming, radiating positive energy and happiness. Subtle, flowing gestures and gentle, open stances emphasize her serene and caring demeanour. Whether she's depicted weaving clouds, performing household tasks, or interacting with others, her poses are designed to communicate her kindness and warmth. These carefully crafted poses ensure that her character is expressive, inviting, and deeply relatable within the story.

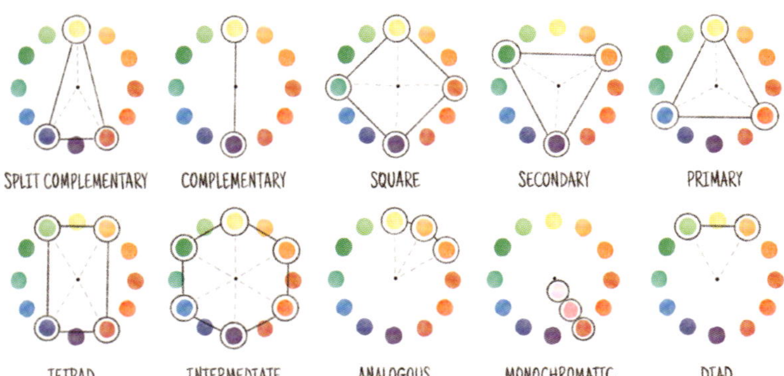

Selecting the right colour palette is essential in setting the tone and atmosphere of the story

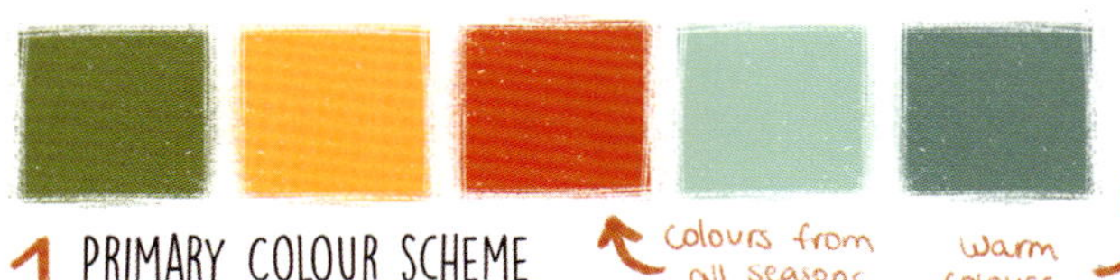

The palette needs to harmonize with both the characters and backgrounds, seamlessly transitioning through different times of day. I start by exploring various colour schemes that reflect the story's vibe, testing a range of tones to find the perfect balance. In my initial drafts, I experimented with palettes that evoke autumn or winter vibes, offering a distinctly seasonal feel.

However, since Mother Hulda represents all seasons, I decide to integrate colours from each season into her design, while keeping the overall look easy on the eye. I settle on faded, desaturated blues, greens, and more dominant reds and yellows. This 'square' colour scheme combination effectively captures the essence of all four seasons, complements the environment, and ensures that Mother Hulda stands out, maintaining focus on her character while allowing her to blend naturally with the surrounding world.

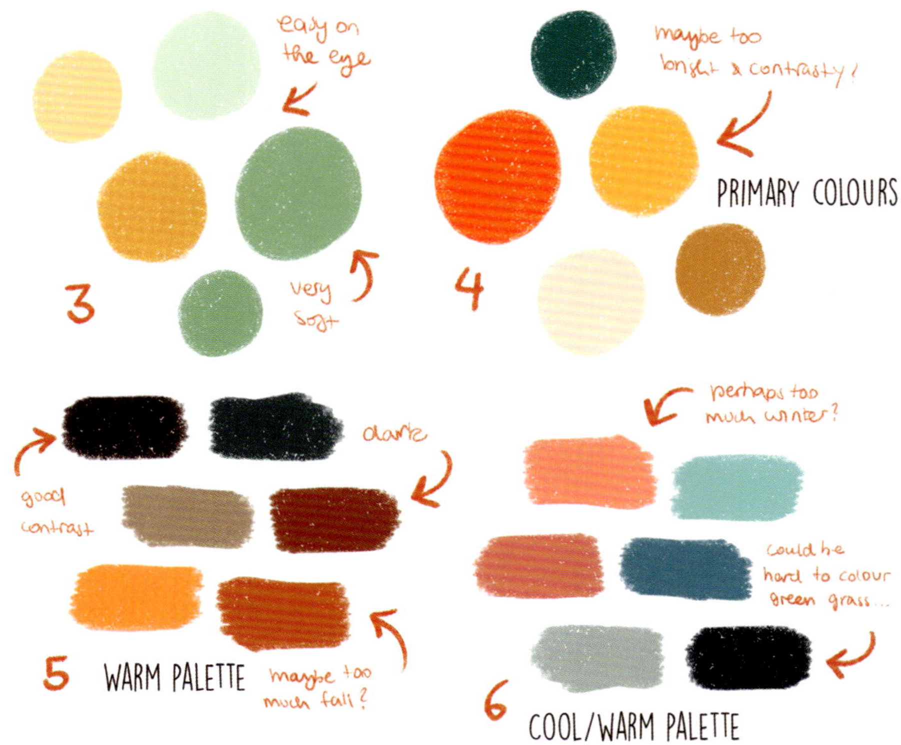

EFFECTIVE COLOUR PALETTE DESIGN

When creating colour palettes, limit your selection to three main colours and two complementary side colours. Incorporate a range of saturation and brightness to create contrast and visual interest. This approach ensures that different elements of your design remain distinct and easy to read. Additionally, choose colours that psychologically align with your character's personality, reinforcing their traits and enhancing their overall presence in the design.

Colour distribution plays a crucial role in defining the mood, look, and meaning of a character design. The amount of space each colour occupies can dramatically influence the overall visual impact. Dominant colours set the tone and convey primary emotions, while accent colours add contrast and highlight key features. To determine the best colour balance, I use rough thumbnails, which help me experiment with how much space each colour should take. This approach allows me to see how different distributions affect the character's mood and overall design, ensuring a balanced and harmonious look that aligns with Mother Hulda's personality and the story's atmosphere.

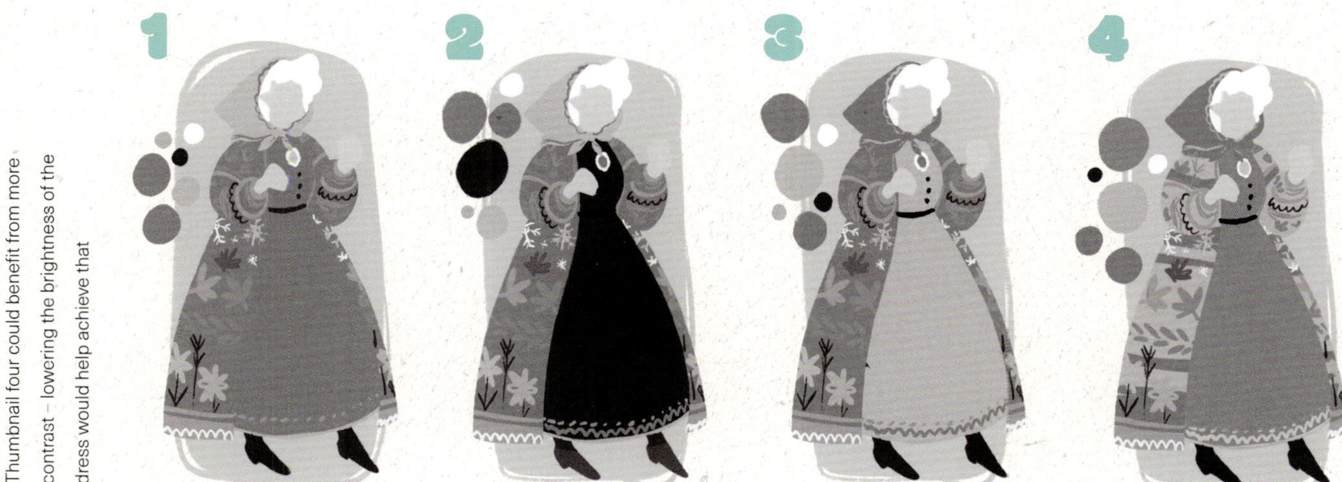

I applied the same colour palette to all four thumbnails, only varying the colour distribution – notice how each thumbnail evokes a distinct vibe

Thumbnail four could benefit from more contrast – lowering the brightness of the dress would help achieve that

Values, or the range of light and dark in a design, are essential for creating depth, focus, and clarity. Effective use of contrast ensures that key elements stand out and the design remains visually engaging. For Mother Hulda, I carefully consider how different values interact, using contrast to guide the viewer's eye to important details, such as her facial expressions or the flow of her clothing. Strong contrasts can create a sense of drama or highlight certain features, while subtler contrasts can evoke a softer, more serene atmosphere. By balancing values thoughtfully, I can enhance the overall readability of the design and reinforce the character's personality within the story.

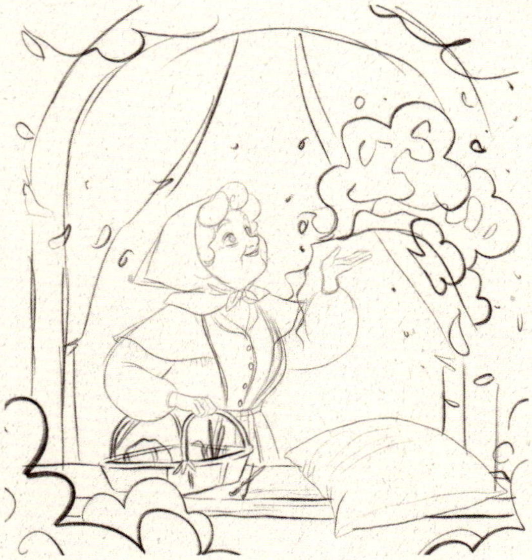

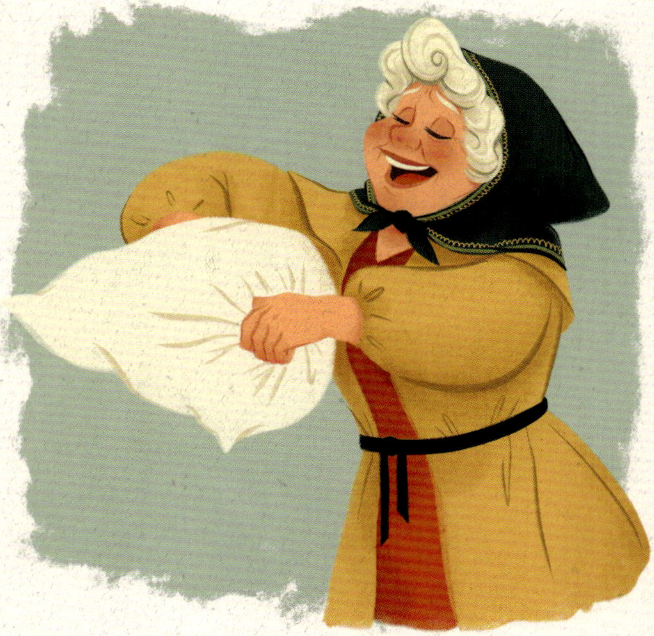

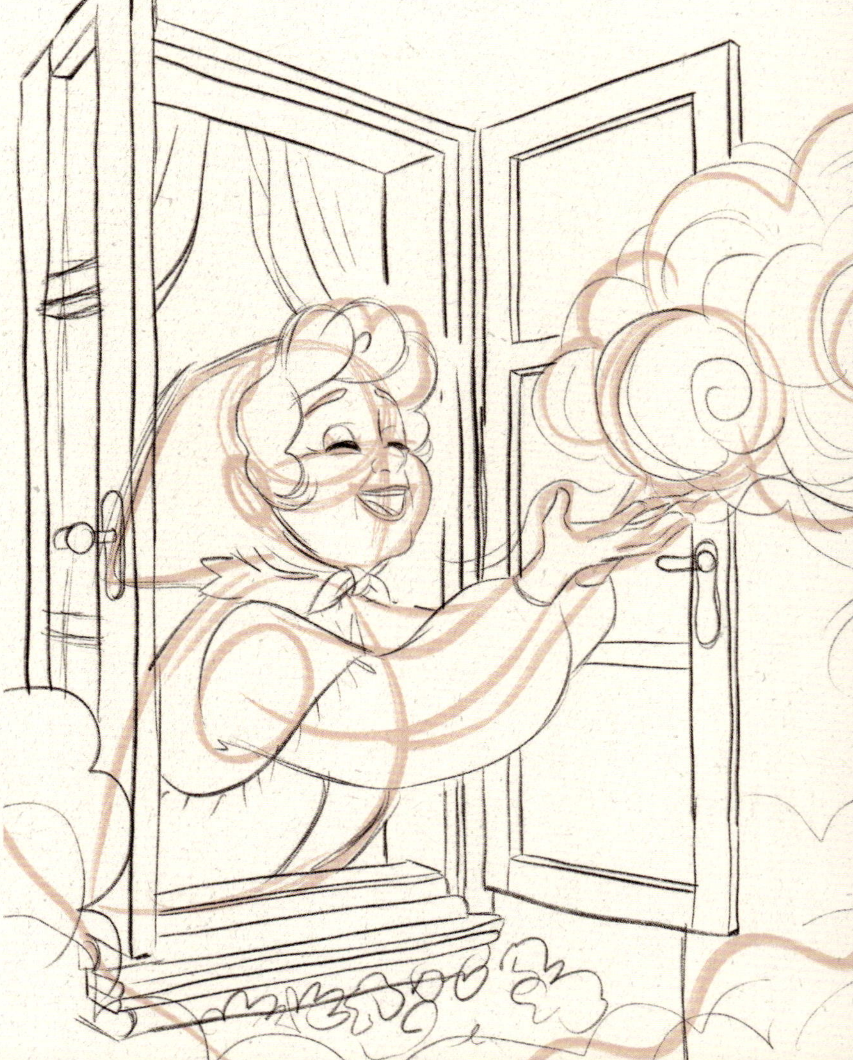

In this step, I gather all the elements I've created and review the entire character design. This is the time to make any last tweaks, ensuring that every detail aligns with the character's personality and the story's tone. I carefully examine the design to see if anything feels incomplete or if adjustments are needed to enhance the overall look. Whether it's fine-tuning the colours, refining shapes, or adjusting proportions, these final touches are crucial to perfecting the character and ensuring that Mother Hulda is both visually striking and true to her essence.

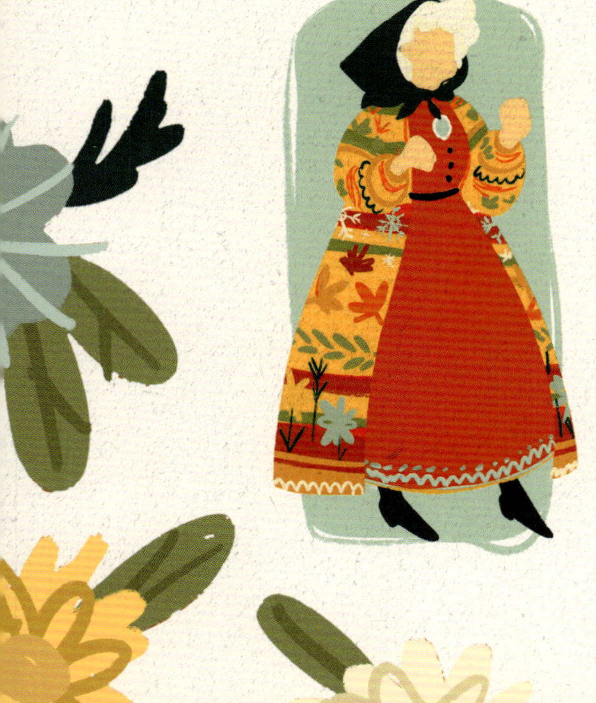

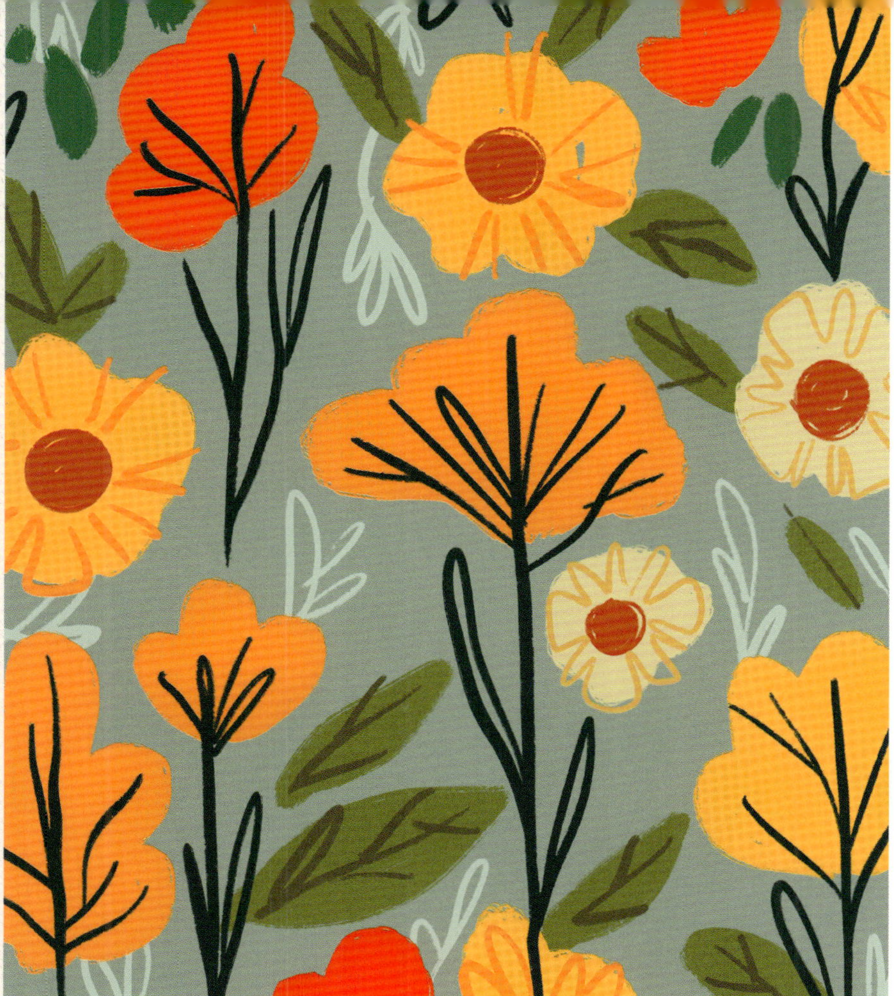

'The coat is designed to represent all four seasons, with each floral motif symbolizing a different time of year'

In this step, I focus on creating patterns for Mother Hulda's clothing. Drawing inspiration from historical patterns of the time, I integrate floral designs into her coat to reflect her connection to nature. The coat is designed to represent all four seasons, with each floral motif symbolizing a different time of year. This approach not only ties her wardrobe to the natural world but also enriches her character, making her a true embodiment of the changing seasons.

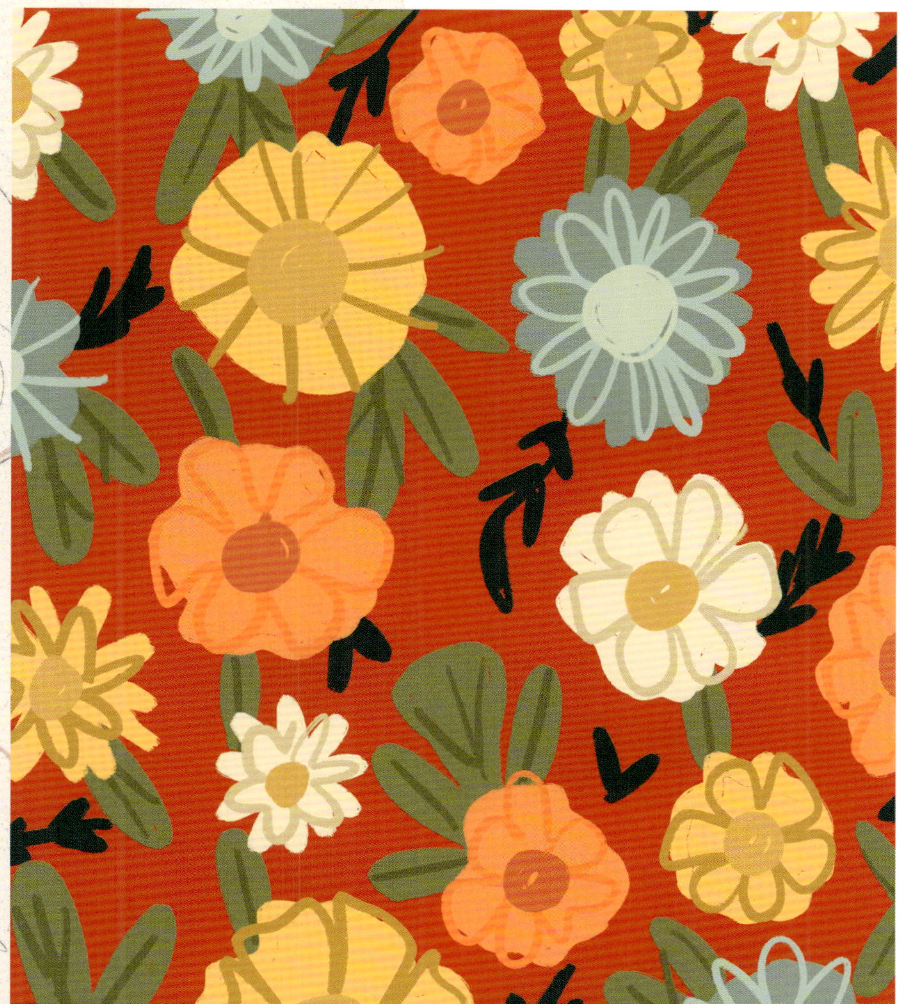

Floral patterns adorn
Mother Hulda's coat

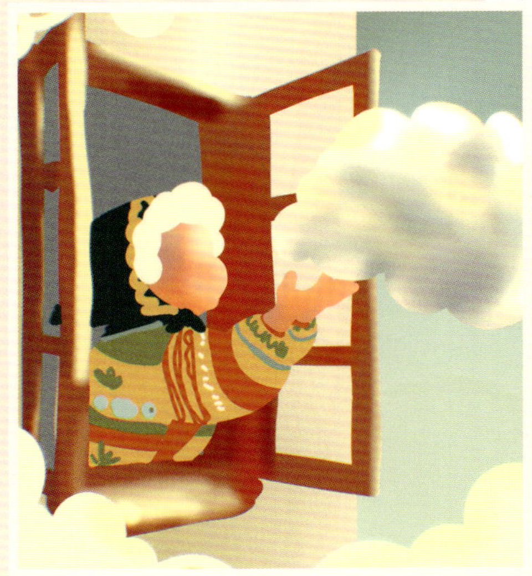

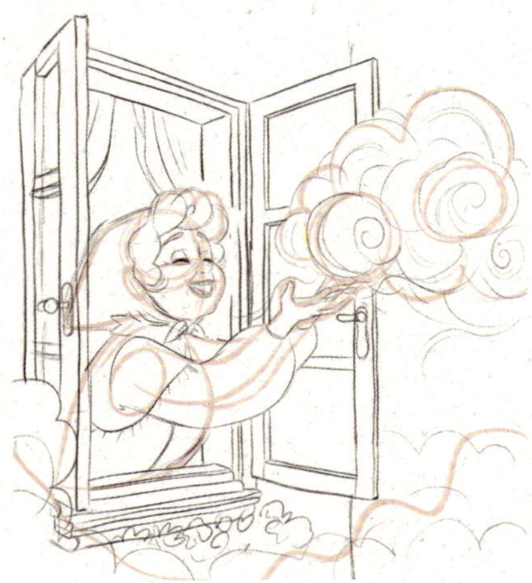

In the last step, I bring Mother Hulda's design to life through a fully rendered image. I begin by blocking in solid colours and shapes, establishing the foundation of the design. Once the base is set, I add depth by carefully applying shadows and highlights, which enhance the character's three-dimensionality, and brings out the details in her clothing and features. To fully integrate her into a scene, I focus on creating a lighting setup that adds atmosphere and complements her character. The lighting not only sets the mood but also ensures that the colour palette shines, reinforcing the thematic elements of her design. Throughout this process, I continually refine the composition to make sure every element – colour, light, and form – work together harmoniously, resulting in a final image that captures the essence of the character and her story.

The final rendering brings the design
to life, adding depth, atmosphere,
and rich, cohesive detail

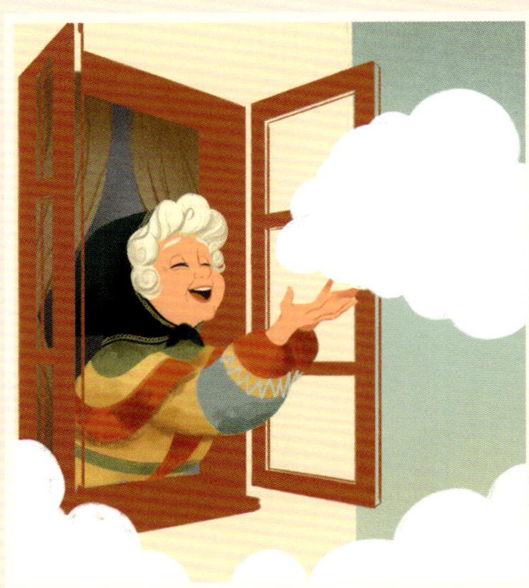

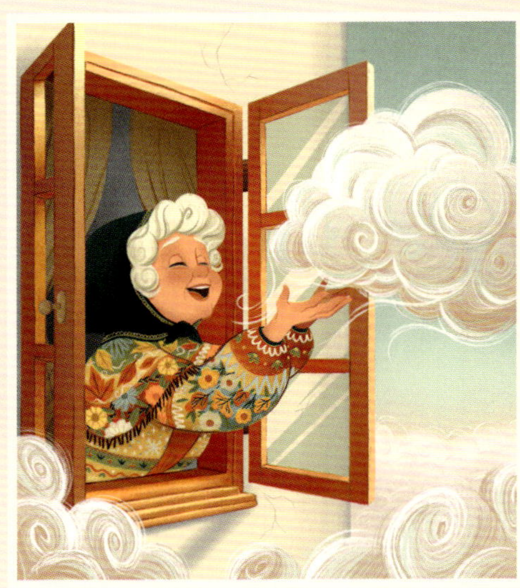

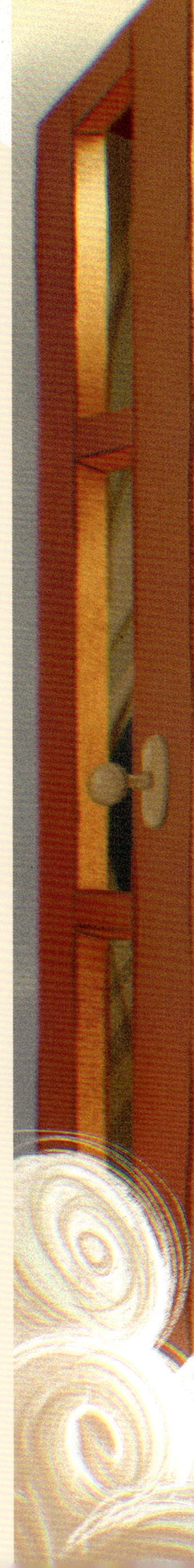

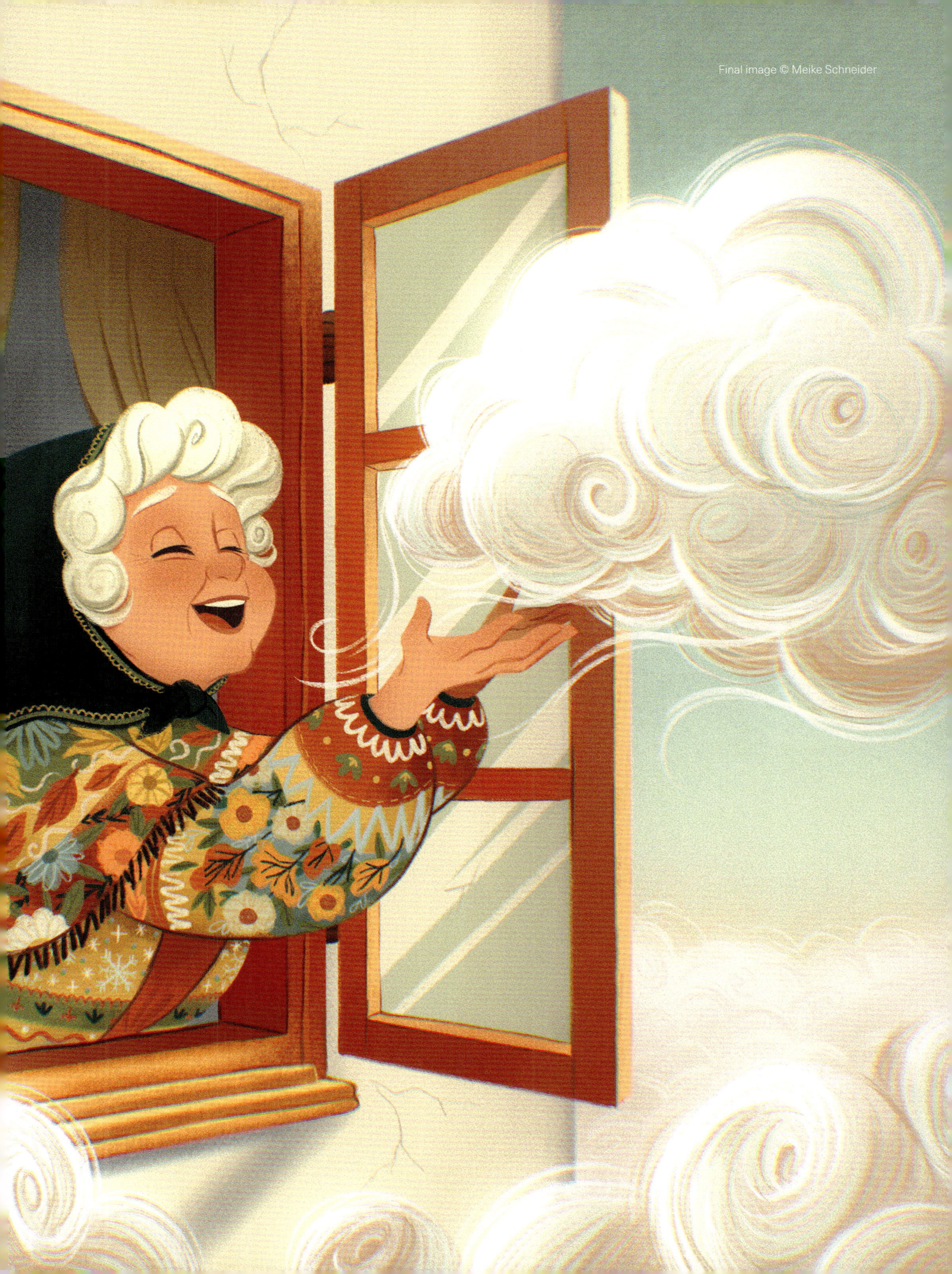
Final image © Meike Schneider

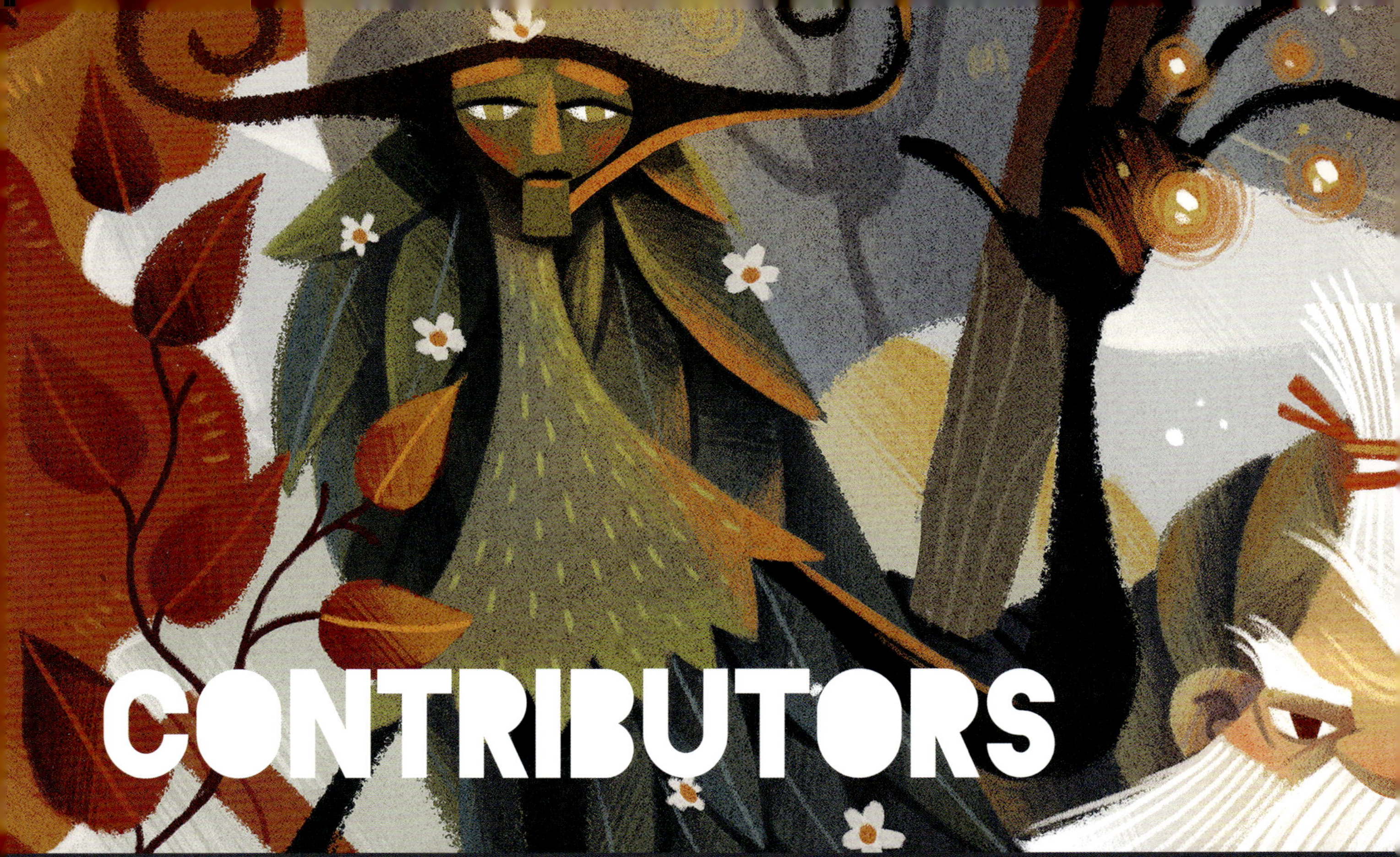

CONTRIBUTORS

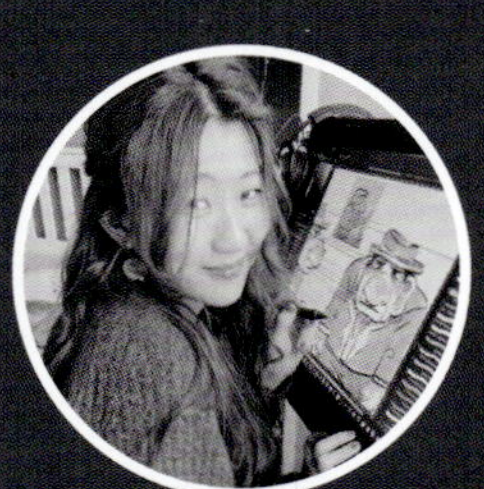

LULU CHEN
Freelance illustrator & Concept Artist
instagram.com/salululuart
Lulu is a graduate of Sheridan College who created the award-winning film *The Market* and also worked on *Spider-Man: Across the Spider-Verse*

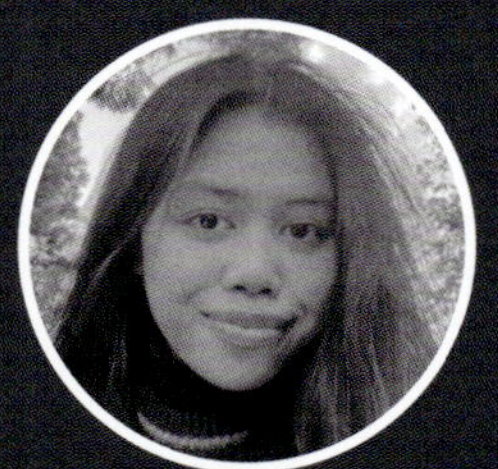

ATHENA DELA VICTORIA
Freelance Character Designer
instagram.com/myrthena
Athena derives inspiration from both Western and Japanese animated films, with a particular interest in works from the 1990s and early 2000s.

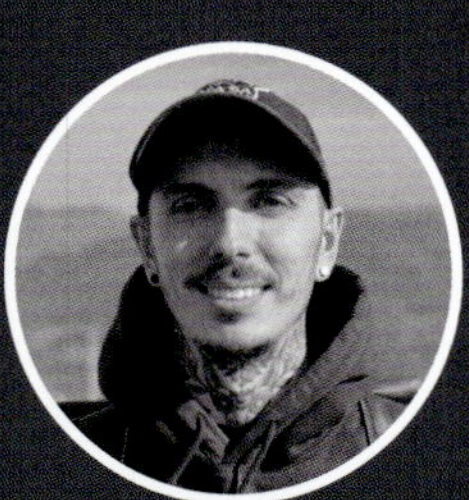

DAN GARTMAN
Freelance Illustrator & Artist
dangartman.com
Dan has over thirteen years of experience in many fields, including game development, animation, and illustration. He combines digital and traditional techniques.

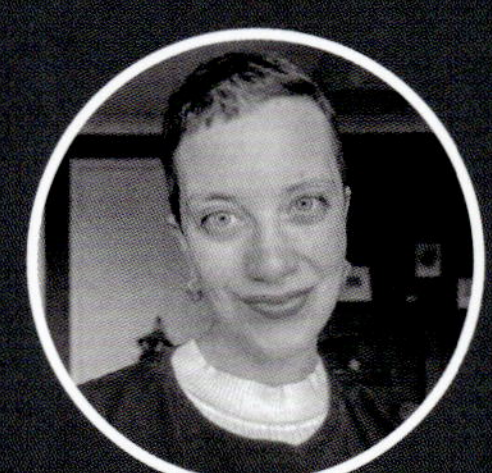

VALENTINA GRAZIUSO
Freelance Character Designer
instagram.com/letsbevale
Valentina Graziuso is a self-taught 2D artist who specializes in character-focused illustrations. She has most recently worked on *Disney Lorcana*.

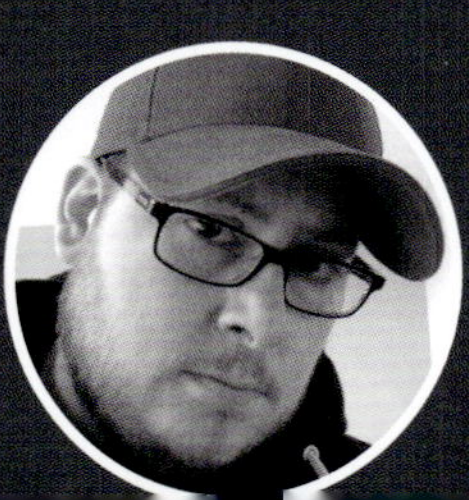

DEREK LAUFMAN
Comic Artist & Cartoonist
dereklaufman.com
Derek is a Canadian artist with 25 years of experience in comics, video games, and animation. He has worked with Marvel, Disney Warner Bros, and more.

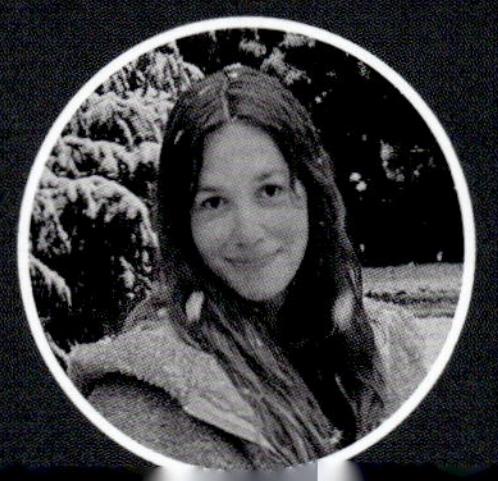

GRETEL LUSKY
Illustrator & Comic Artist
gretlusky.com
Gretel is an Argentinian illustrator with several years of experience in comics and character design for animation. She has worked f   C, Netflix, Disney, and more.

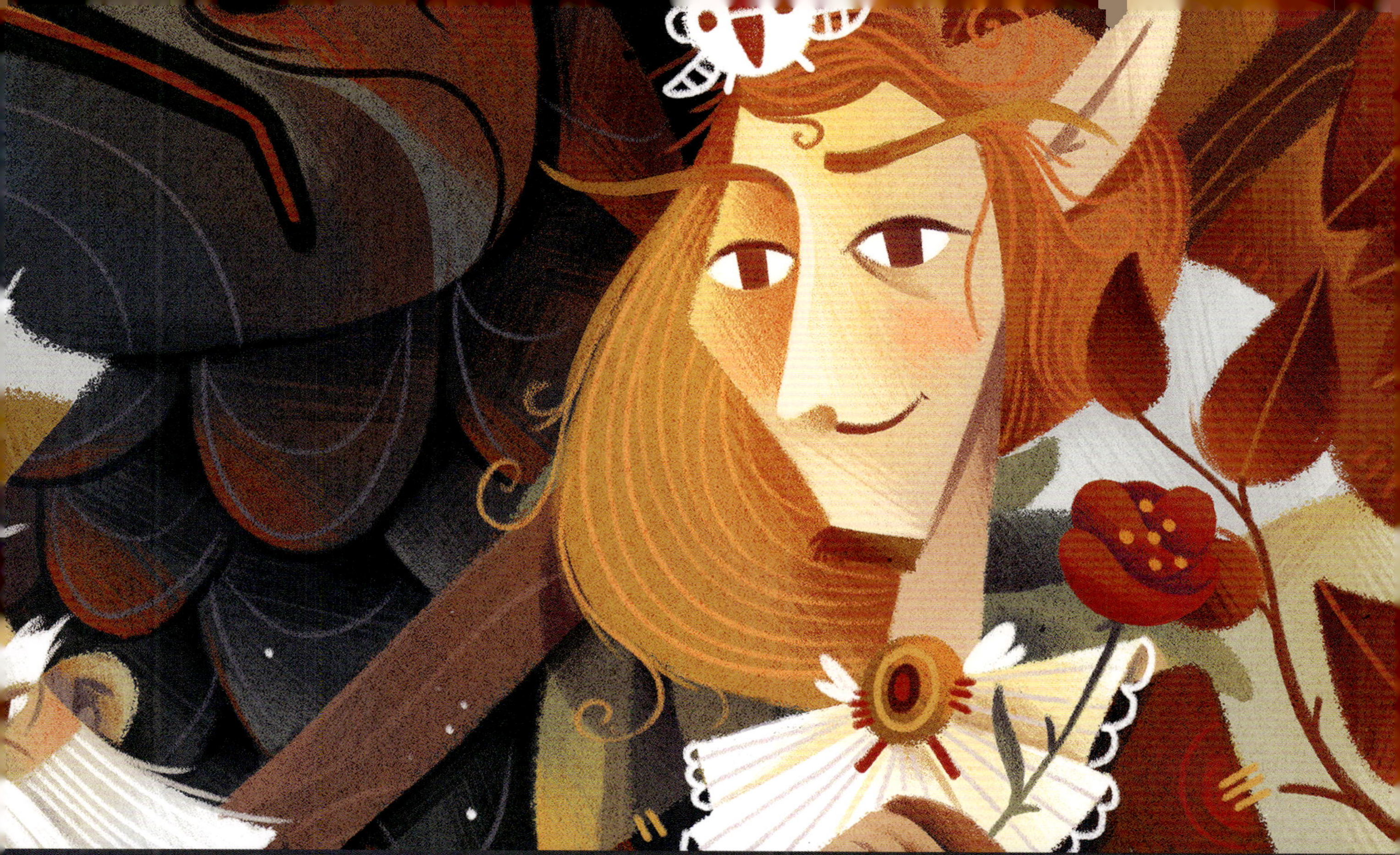

Image © Dan Gartman

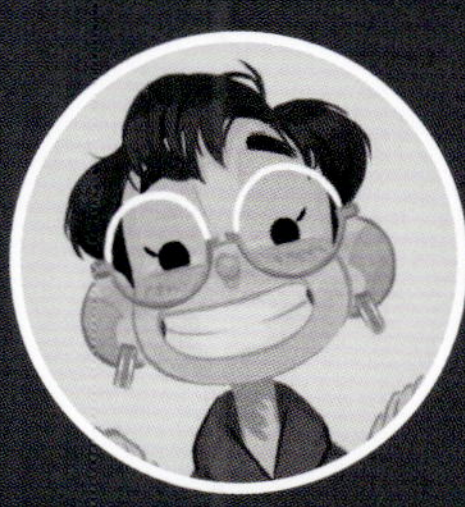

AGATHE MOLIN
Character Designer
agathemlmolin.wixsite.com/monsite
Agathe is a character designer based in Versailles. She created the short film *Guardian* and her clients include Cube Creative Company and Ellipse Animation.

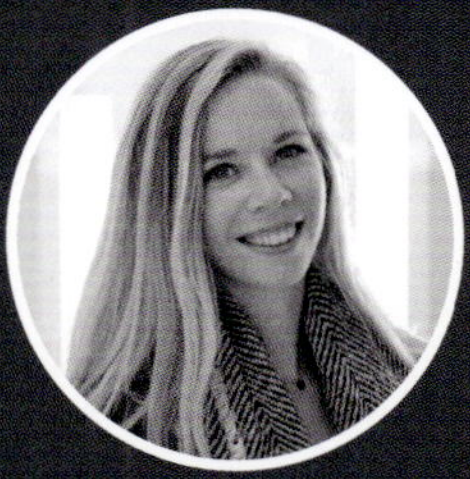

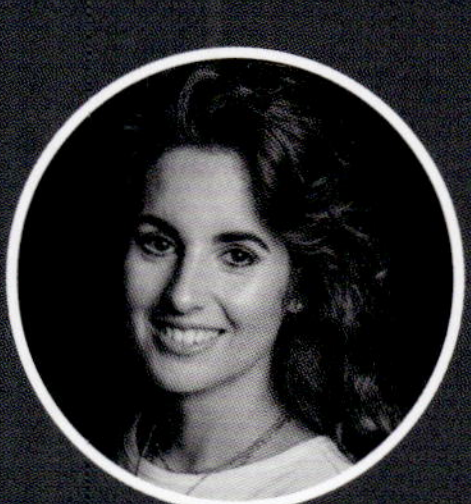

MEIKE SCHNEIDER
Freelance Character Designer
meikearts.com
Meike is a freelance artist from Cologne, with a lifelong passion for drawing. She has worked on projects for children's books, film, television, and much more.

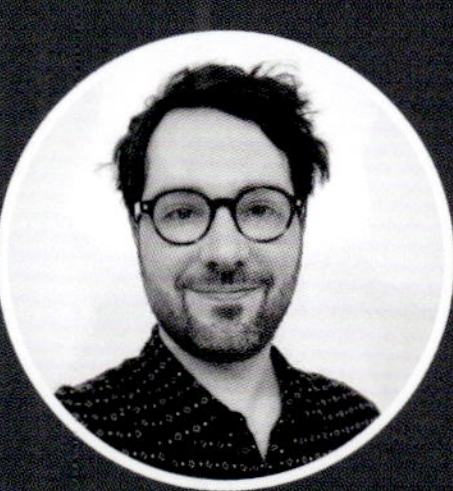

BRIAN WEISZ
Character Designer
brianweisz.com
Brian Weisz is a character designer from Southern California who has worked in games, film, and beyond, with clients includiing Framestore and Disney TVA.

TESSA NELISSEN
Illustrator
instagram.com/jessali_tn
Tessa is a Dutch illustrator residing in Norway. She mostly uses digial media to draw cute and colourful characters and scenery, often containing cats.

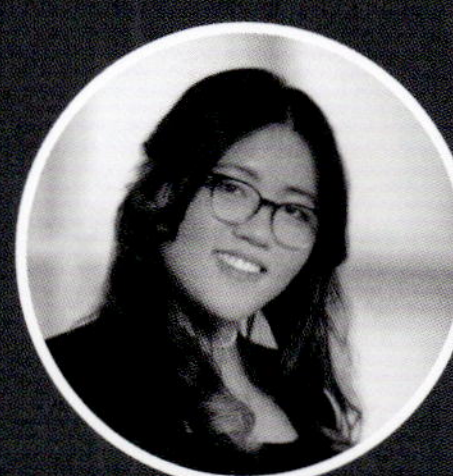

SABRINA SENTOSO
Illustrator & Freelance Concept Artist
sabrinasentoso.com
Sabrina is currently an illustrator at Blue Mammoth Games. She has previously worked for Blizzard Entertainment, Elodie Games, and on *Disney Lorcana*.

50%
of net profits donated
TO CHARITY

In 2022, 3dtotal Publishing became successful enough to make a pledge to donate **50% of its net profits to charity**. This continues to be possible due to the incredible support from all our customers, employees, and partners. At the time of printing, we have donated over $1.62 million (USD) to charity.

We focus our giving on three charitable areas: **environmental, humanitarian, and animal welfare**. We use organizations such as Effective Altruism and Founders Pledge to guide who we help within these causes. Some ways of doing good are over 100 times more effective than others, so donating this way hugely increases the impact of our contributions.

**See 3dtotal.com/charity
for full details.**

3dtotal Publishing